Towards a Philosophy of Education
in Modern English

Volume 6 of Charlotte Mason's Series

paraphrased by Leslie Noelani Laurio

Towards a Philosophy of Education by Charlotte Mason
paraphrased by Leslie N Laurio

Table of Contents

Forms and Corresponding Grade Levels:
   Form I   (roughly grades 1-3)
   Form II   (roughly grades 4-6)
   Form III and IV   (roughly grades 7-9)
   Form V and VI (roughly grades 10-12)

A Note About Schools in England: Public schools were the prestigious boarding schools in CM's day, and they weren't free, like public schools in the US are. They were open to the paying public, as opposed to religious schools that were limited to those of their doctrine. Private schools, also called independant schools, were more like Prep schools. They weren't under government regulation and often achieved higher academic standards; private primary schools were supposed to increase a child's chances of getting into a better Public Middle school, like Eton, Winchester College, and Charterhouse. Public schools were very successful—many Prime Ministers and Chancellors came from either Eton or Winchester. Private schools were more elite than public schools. They were usually, but not always, boarding schools. The very rich sometimes had the most private education of all—a tutor. ;-)
Poor people went to State Schools, also called secondary modern, grammar, comprehensive or technical schools.

The grade/age breakdown:
Primary: Years 1-6 (ages 5-11)
Secondary: Year 7-9 (Forms 1-3, middle school, or high school, ages 11-14)
          Year 10-11 (Form 4-5, Upper School, ages 14-16)
          Year 12-13 (Sixth Form College, ages 16-18)

Charlotte Mason in Modern English

Charlotte Mason's ideas are too important not to be understood and implemented in the 21st century, but her Victorian style of writing sometimes prevents parents from attempting to read her books. This is an imperfect attempt to make Charlotte's words accessible to modern parents. ~L. N. Laurio

A Philosophy of Education, Volume 6 of the Charlotte Mason Series
[pg xxv]

Author's Preface

It doesn't seem like the story of *Undine* has much to do with a varied, generous education, but there is a connection. Love awakened the water sprite Undine's soul to life. And I have a story about how knowledge awakened the souls of people. Eight years ago [*in 1914*], the souls of some children in a poor mining village awakened with the magic touch of knowledge—and are still awake. We know that Christianity can awaken souls. We know that love can reform a person. A calling and a purpose can do that, too. In the Renaissance, the collective soul of an entire society awoke to knowledge. But we don't hear of this kind of awakening in our time. Sure, schools pride themselves on their pleasant lessons and their emphasis on good grades. But I believe that the thirst for knowledge in the children of the mining village is a marvel that indicates new possibilities. Thousands of British children had already experienced this kind of intellectual conversion, but those were the privileged children of the educated classes. Finding out that even children of poor mining parents were just as responsive seemed to spark new hope for the world. Perhaps *all* children are waiting for the call of knowledge to awaken them to a life of delight.

Mrs. Francis Steinthal, who started the educational awakening in Council Schools, wrote, 'Think what this means for children—disciplined lives, no rebellious labor strikes, justice, an end to struggles between classes, developed minds, and [pg xxvi] no demand for trashy, corrupt books! We shall, or, rather, they shall, live in a redeemed world.' She wrote this in a spontaneous burst of excitement when she heard that Council Schools had made a decision to use her plan for that pioneer school. Our enthusiasm makes us tend to see future prospects brighter than usual, but, really, this new education is bound to have excellent results. It hasn't even been nine years since Council Schools reformed their method, and already thousands of its students have found that lessons are enjoyable.

Certainly children could be content and get a sufficient education from their lessons the way things were, and Council Schools was doing just fine before the reformed plan. Yet both teachers and students find a huge difference between the kind of casual interest in learning that comes from good grades, pleasant lectures and other school methods, and the kind of passionate thirst for knowledge that comes with an awakened soul. The students have even convinced the school inspectors. One inspector listened to the long, detailed, animated narrations of one class and was astonished. Over the last thirty years, my co-workers and I have taught thousands of children in our schools, in homes and other places. As we've worked, we've kept the Dean of St. Paul's School, Mr. Colet's prayer in mind: 'Pray that all children will thrive on good life and good literature.' Probably all children who are taught this way grow up with the kinds of principles and interests that make their lives happy and useful.

I don't have any bones to pick against education. Our interest is only what's good for the society. The methods we propose will work in any school. I offer this book to the public to convince everyone involved with education of a few significant principles that have been either forgotten or were never known, and a few methods that are so simple that, like bathing in the Jordan river, [pg xxvii] they seem too humble to create a stir. Yet these principles and methods make education completely effective.

I'd like to add that nothing I've said in this book is mere opinion. Every point has been proven in thousands of cases, and the method can be observed at work in many schools, both large and small, both elementary and secondary.

My apologies to anyone who is asked to consider my method from various angles. I can't explain any better than by quoting old Fuller. 'Good reader, I suspect I've written some things twice. Although not word for word, the meaning is the same. I beg you to skip over anything that's redundant. You can imagine how challenging and tedious it was in such a long book to find all the repetitions! Besides being a challenging task, searching them out would take more time than I can afford. Even now, my life is growing short and I can't afford to spend even one minute in something as trivial as nit-picking for straws. But, since advice must be given line upon line, and precept upon precept, I'll repeat the words of St. Paul—'It doesn't bother me to write the same things to you that I have written before. In fact, it is for your own good.' [*Phil 3:1, CEV*]'

I'd like to close what is probably the last preface I will ever write again by gratefully acknowledging those friends who are working with me in what we believe is a great cause. The Parents' National Educational Union has accomplished the mission that is stated in its first proposal, and it has done so nobly and generously. 'The PNEU exists to help parents and teachers of *all* classes in society.' For the last eight years, the PNEU has taken on the work and cost of an ambitious conviction to help elementary schools. There are [pg xxviii] now about 150 such schools using the Parents' Union School programmes. In this past year, an encouraging development has taken place, thanks to the Honorable Mrs. Franklin. She made a suggestion to the Head of a London County Council School about forming an association of parents. It would require some minor dues to cover expenses, but would offer them certain advantages. At their first meeting, one of the fathers who was there got up and said that he was very disappointed. He had expected to see three hundred parents and there were only about sixty there! But those who promoted the meeting were encouraged to see sixty. Most of those sixty became members of the Parents' Association, and their work goes on enthusiastically.

We have many fellow workers to thank, but even the very courteous Paul who wrote a letter to the Romans wouldn't be able to sufficiently acknowledge all of the people who are responsible for the success of this movement, which I'll attempt to explain thoroughly in the pages of this book.

CHARLOTTE M. MASON
HOUSE OF EDUCATION
AMBLESIDE, 1922

[pg xxix]

A Short Synopsis of the Educational Philosophy Explained in This Book

'As soon as the soul spots truth, the soul recognizes it as her first and oldest friend.'
'The repercussions of truth are great. Therefore we must not neglect to correctly judge what's true, and what's not.' —Benjamin Whichcote

1. Children are born persons—they are not blank slates or embryonic oysters who have the potential of becoming persons. They already *are* persons.

2. Although children are born with a sin nature, they are neither all bad, nor all good. Children from all walks of life and backgrounds may make choices for good or evil.

3. The concepts of authority and obedience are true for all people whether they accept it or not. Submission to authority is necessary for any society or group or family to run smoothly.

4. Authority is not a license to abuse children, or to play upon their emotions or other desires, and adults are not free to limit a child's education or use fear, love, power of suggestion, or their own influence over a child to make a child learn.

5. The only means a teacher may use to educate children are the child's natural environment, the training of good habits and exposure to living ideas and concepts. This is what CM's motto 'Education is an atmosphere, a discipline, a life' means.

6. 'Education is an atmosphere' doesn't mean that we should create an artificial environment for children, but that we use the opportunities in the environment he already lives in to educate him. Children learn from real things in the real world.

7. 'Education is a discipline' means that we train a child to have good habits and self-control.

8. 'Education is a life' means that education should apply to body, soul and spirit. The mind needs ideas of all kinds, so the child's curriculum should be varied and generous with many subjects included. [pg xxx]

9. The child's mind is not a blank slate, or a bucket to be filled. It is a living thing and needs knowledge to grow. As the stomach was designed to digest food, the mind is designed to digest knowledge and needs no special training or exercises to make it ready to learn.

10. Herbart's philosophy that the mind is like an empty stage waiting for bits of information to be inserted puts too much responsibility on the teacher to prepare detailed lessons that the children, for all the teacher's effort, don't learn from anyway.

11. Instead, we believe that children's minds are capable of digesting real knowledge, so we provide a rich, generous curriculum that exposes children to many interesting, living ideas and concepts.

12. 'Education is the science of relations' means that children have minds capable of making their own connections with knowledge and experiences, so we make sure the child learns about nature, science and art, knows how to make things, reads many living books and that they are physically fit.

13. In devising a curriculum, we provide a vast amount of ideas to ensure that the mind has enough brain food, knowledge about a variety of things to prevent boredom, and subjects are taught with high-quality literary language since that is what a child's attention responds to best.

14. Since one doesn't really 'own' knowledge until he can express it, children are required to narrate, or tell back (or write down), what they have read or heard.

15. Children must narrate after one reading or hearing. Children naturally have good focus of attention, but allowing a second reading makes them lazy and weakens their ability to pay attention the first time. Teachers summarizing and asking comprehension questions are other ways of giving children a second chance and making the need to focus the first time less urgent. By getting it the first time, less time is wasted on repeated readings, and more time is available during school hours for more knowledge. A child educated this way learns more than children using other methods, and this is true for all children regardless of their IQ or background. [pg xxxi]

16. Children have two guides to help them in their moral and intellectual growth—'the way of the will,' and 'the way of reason.'

17. Children must learn the difference between 'I want' and 'I will.' They must learn to distract their thoughts when tempted to do what they may want but know is not right, and think of something else, or do something else, interesting enough to occupy their mind. After a short diversion, their mind will be refreshed and able to will with renewed strength.

18. Children must learn not to lean too heavily on their own reasoning. Reasoning is good for logically demonstrating mathematical truth, but unreliable

when judging ideas because our reasoning will justify all kinds of erroneous ideas if we really want to believe them.

19. Knowing that reason is not to be trusted as the final authority in forming opinions, children must learn that their greatest responsibility is choosing which ideas to accept or reject. Good habits of behavior and lots of knowledge will provide the discipline and experience to help them do this.

20. We teach children that all truths are God's truths, and that secular subjects are just as divine as religious ones. Children don't go back and forth between two worlds when they focus on God and then their school subjects; there is unity among both because both are of God and, whatever children study or do, God is always with them.

[pg 1]

A Philosophy of Education

Introduction

These are stressful times for those involved with education. WWI is over, and we rejoiced in the strength, bravery and devotion shown by our soldiers. We recognize that these things are due to our schools, and to the fact that England still breeds 'very valiant people.' It's nice to know that the whole army was remarkable. The natural heroism of our officers benefitted even more from the education that every boarding school boy gets, and from organized sports where they learn habits of obedience and leadership. But what about the pathetic ignorance we saw in the thinking of those many men who chose to stay home? Is it our fault? I guess most of us feel like it is. Those men were educated by the methods we thought were correct. I mean, they can read and write and think through an argument, although they're unable to detect a fallacy. Perplexed, we wonder, why do so many people seem to have no impulse to be generous, no logical patriotism, no ability to see beyond their own narrow concerns? It's because those things come only with the proper education. Those things distinguish a well-educated person. When millions of the men who should be the strong backbone of the country seem to feel no duty to serve their fellow man, we have to ask, 'Why [pg 2] weren't these people educated? What have we given them instead of an education?'

If we've erred in education, the problem has stemmed from our concept of what the mind is. The theory which has trickled down to teachers is the outdated notion that the mind is made up of different 'faculties' that have to be developed. This notion comes from the idea that thinking is nothing more than a function of the brain. And that notion is the only explanation for the scanty curriculum that most of our schools provide, and for the tortuous way teachers give lessons, and the disastrous idea that 'it doesn't matter what the child learns, all that matters is how he learns it.' We teach a lot, but the students learn very little. So we comfort ourselves with the belief that we're 'developing' one 'faculty' or another of his mind. The nation that understands that it is knowledge itself, and not developing faculties, that education should concern itself with, will have a great future. The mind needs the daily food of knowledge.

Teachers are searching for a sound theory. Such a theory must be convinced the the mind plays an active role in education, and what conditions the mind needs to do this. We need an educational philosophy that realizes that only thoughts can appeal to the mind, and that thoughts give rise to more thoughts. All of the activities of the senses and muscles that supposedly train the mind as well as the body must be put in their proper places. *This point is very important.* Understanding that the mind feeds on thoughts and ideas, and isn't developed with physical exercises, isn't just something that needs to be understood as part of education, it's *all* of education. This relates to vocational training, too. Our newspapers scornfully ask, 'Is book-learning the only good education? Isn't the boy running a farm, or fixing computers, also getting an education?' The public lacks the courage to say with conviction, 'No, he isn't,' [pg 3] because the public doesn't have a clear understanding of what education is, and what makes education different from vocational training. But the people are beginning to understand. They are beginning to demand that their children receive the kind of education that prepares their children for *life*, not just to earn a living. As a matter of fact, the man who has read and thought about all kinds of subjects and also has the training he needs, will be the most capable, whether his skill is with handling tools, drawing plans, or accounting. The more of a well-rounded, whole *person* we succeed in making the child, the better able he'll be to fulfill his potential, live his life and serve society.

There has been a lot of talk about what caused the break-down in character and conduct in Germany [*in WWI*]. The terror of war was just one symptom, and the symptoms have been traced to the kinds of thoughts that the people had been taught to think for three or four generations. We've heard a lot about Nietzsche, Treitschke, Bernhardi and the rest, but Professor John Henry Muirhead helped us to see that it goes even deeper. Darwin's theories of natural selection, the survival of the fittest and the struggle for existence, came at the moment Germany was ripe for such an idea. The ideas of a super race, the super state, the right for the strongest country to disregard treaties and destroy weaker countries, and to recognize no law except what serves its own interests—these come from Darwinism as surely as a chicken comes from an egg. The concept that 'might makes right' actually predates even Darwin—Frederick the Great wrote, 'Let those who have power take, and whoever is strong enough to keep power is entitled to it.' Perhaps Darwin, an Englishman, gave Germany a logical reason to do what it wanted to do anyway. Human nature tends to prefer natural laws over spiritual laws and to get its code of ethics from science rather than God. And that's why the Germans took Darwin's theories as justification to be brutal. [pg 4]

Here are a few examples of how German philosophers add to what Darwin said: 'All natural and spiritual powers dwell in physical matter. Matter is the foundation of everything that is.' 'What we call spirit, thought or knowing, is merely natural forces in peculiar combinations.' Darwin himself protests against the idea that, in man's higher nature, the struggle for existence is the most driving force. He never intended to make education purely materialistic any more than Locke intended his essays to bring about the French Revolution. But men's thoughts have more power than they think. Darwin and Locke both directly influenced world-changing ideas. Germany had had 25 years of materialistic thought, so they accepted Darwin's ideas. His theories freed them so that they no longer felt limited by morals. Darwin's follower, Ernst Haeckel, thought that the concept of natural selection made it acceptable for Germany's lawless action [*since they were merely a country struggling to survive*] and led to the notion of a superman. 'The principle of natural selection is very elite.' Buchner also simplified Darwin's theories and made them more popular. 'All the things the brain does that we think of as physical activities are only functions of the physical brain. Thought is to the brain what gall is to the liver.'

However Germany has used Darwin's teaching, good or bad, wouldn't concern us (except for the war), except that Germany has influenced our educational thought with the fallacy that the brain has various faculties that need to be developed. English psychology hasn't come to any firm conclusions yet, but it has progressed far enough to deny the myth of brain faculties. The concept of [pg 5] 'mind' may be debated, but all psychological writers write about it [*thus confirming its existence?*] At least, that's what the Encyclopedia Britannica says under Psychology, and they are qualified to know. We have mind and we have matter. If, as we're told, psychology rests on feeling, then what about mind and physical matter? Is there something else?

II

The body needs healthy food and can't thrive on just anything. We don't realize that the same is true for the mind. The war [*WWI*] taught us that men are spirits. The soul, spirit and mind of a man is something more than just his physical body. A person's spirit is the person. His physical body lives and breathes merely as a vessel for his thoughts and feelings. Now we recognize that man is a spiritual being. And so we need to make sure that the education we give the next generation is made up of the great thoughts and great events that influence the way our nation thinks.

The educational thought we hear about most is based on various Darwinian presumptions. And from Darwin's theories, people have come to think that all that matters is physical health, and being trained with a marketable skill. Those things may be important, but they aren't the most important thing. In the 1700's when Prussia lost their war against Napoleon, they discovered that it wasn't Napoleon who was responsible for the country's ruin, but the ignorance of their own citizens. Some philosophers worked together to bring history, poetry and philosophy to the people, and it saved the nation. Studying those things develop the whole person: his character, cooperative community spirit, and personal initiative. Those were the qualities that Prussia needed most. Those are also the qualities that make individuals happy and successful. But, on the other hand, when [pg 6]

Germany switched to a utilitarian style of education, that was the beginning of its moral downfall. History repeats itself—there are rumors such as one where students in Bonn, Germany burned French novels, art prints and other luxury items in a solemn procession. This is just the kind of thing that ruined Germany before. Its youth should have saved Germany, both then and now. Will Germany have another Tugenbund? [*Tugenbund is an organization compared to the KKK; based on the teachings of philosophers such as Voltaire and Rousseau, it originated under the name Order of the Illuminati. Its original purpose was to advance secular philosophy and eliminate monarchy, religion and religious morality. Their goal was for The Order to take over the world.*]

We need an education that will nourish the mind as well as provide physical and vocational training. In other words, we need a philosophy of education that works. I believe that the PNEU has found such a philosophy. Over the last thirty years, we have tested and made adjustments to our theory, and had success with thousands of children. I've written about this theory in the other volumes of the Home Education Series, which have been published at various intervals over the past 35 years. I'll summarize just a few of the most important points that set it apart from current education:

(a) It's the children, not the teachers, who are responsible for being educated. Children exert their *own* effort to do the work of learning.

(b) The teachers encourage and sometimes help explain or guide, but the actual work is done by the students.

(c) In each 12-week term, students read 1000-3000 pages, depending on their age and level, from a variety of scheduled books. Such a large amount of material allows only enough time for a single reading. Comprehension is tested by narration, or by writing on a test passage. By the time term exams come up, so much material has been covered that reviewing it all would be impossible. But the children know and retain what they've read. They can write about any part of it easily and clearly with dramatic style. They usually spell well. [pg 7]

Many feel that 'mere book learning' is inferior, that people should focus on the practical aspect of living. But I'd like to point out that, whatever weaknesses have been found with using books don't apply to our method. As far as I know, this method has never been used before. Has there ever been a wide-spread attempt to get students to know many pages from lots of books after a single reading, and to know it so well that they can write about any part of it freely and accurately, even months later?

(d) Lessons, books and passages aren't selected for school based on the child's whims. The best available book is used and read through consecutively, sometimes over two or three years.

(e) Children study many books on different subjects, but that doesn't seem to cause them confusion. Bloopers on tests are almost nonexistent.

(f) Students find that, as Bacon said, 'studies are delightful.' This delight doesn't rest in entertaining lessons, or a pleasant teacher. It rests purely in a love for their books.

(g) Whenever possible, well-written, literary books are used.

(h) Grades, prizes, placement, rewards, punishment, praise, blame, or other inducements aren't necessary to get a child to pay attention. Students pay attention willingly, immediately and very effectively.

(i) Success in disciplinary subjects such as math and grammar depends on the ability of the teacher, although the students' habit of attention helps here, too.

(j) No diverting rabbit trails are followed to capitalize on student interest. The knowledge the children get is consecutive. [pg 8]

The children show unusual interest in their lessons and pay close attention. They have varied and fairly accurate knowledge of history, literature and some science. These results have made people take notice and assume that these children are tutored in privileged homes where education and culture is valued. Nobody believes that these results aren't the norm for all tutored students. But soon it will be apparent that all children are capable of this kind of success. Then there will finally be hope that even children of lower socio-economic classes, or children of working parents, can receive this kind of varied, generous education.

We believe in cause and effect, and our results make it evident that we have stumbled onto previously unknown truths about how education works. At any rate, we have discovered truth in Comenius's Golden Rule: 'Teachers shall do less teaching, yet students will learn more.'

Now let's outline a few of the educational principles that are responsible for our success.

III

Principles That Have Been Unrecognized or Disregarded Before Now

I've discussed some of the ways in which our work is extraordinary. I hope to convince readers that our results—students doing so well both in classrooms and home correspondence schools—are based on principles that have been unrecognized until now. Recognizing these principles should give our country's education an intelligent foundation and should make students more stable, content and ambitious.

I'd like to add a couple more arguments to my reasons for implementing this kind of education. [pg 9]

This education doesn't just work for unusually smart children. It works for average and handicapped children, too.

Schools using this plan take less time to do a day's work than ordinary schools, even though the number of subjects is the same.

There's no need to do reviews, complete work at night, cram for tests, or catch up in subjects. So there's more time to use for vocational training, outside pursuits, or hobbies.

All bookwork is done in the morning so that afternoons are free for outdoor nature study, drawing, handicrafts, etc.

Even with these limitations, students produce a surprising amount of good intellectual work.

There is no homework.

It isn't that we PNEU workers are such geniuses, but, like William Paley's man who found the watch, 'we have stumbled onto a good thing.'

'Any benefit that I experience should be shared.'

We feel that the country and, in fact, the whole world, should know about educational discoveries that can make people more moral. We are experiencing the Renaissance as if for the first time, except we don't have its pagan lawlessness.

Let me share the steps that brought me to these conclusions. When I was a young woman, I spent a lot of time with a family whose half Indian children were living at their grandfather's house and being raised by their aunt, who was a good friend of mine. The children impressed me. They were generous and sensible, intelligent, creative and able to discern moral issues with understanding. Their imaginativeness and moral insight were illustrated one day when the five-year-old girl came home from her walk silent and sad. After leaving her alone for awhile, some careful questioning brought out sobs as she struggled to get the words out— [pg 10] 'a man—no home—nothing to eat—no bed to sleep in,'—and then she collapsed into tears. Such incidences may be common in most families, but it was new to me. I was reading a lot about educational philosophy at the time because, like any enthusiastic young teacher, I thought that education should change the world. I worked at an elementary school and a church high school, so I was able to observe children in varied age groups. But children aren't as open at school as they are at home. Being with my friend's children taught me to view them as persons, and I began to suspect that they are more than we adults are, except that they haven't learned everything they need to know yet.

I did find one limitation with these children. My friend claimed that they couldn't understand English grammar. I disagreed and said that they could. I even wrote a little grammar book for children aged 7 and 8, which is not quite ready to publish. But I found that my friend was right. She let me give my lessons with as much clarity and freshness as I could. But it was useless. No matter how hard I tried, they couldn't understand the nominitative case. Their minds rejected the abstract concept, just like children reject the idea of writing an essay about 'Happiness.' But I had learned something—a child's mind accepts or rejects new knowledge according to what it needs.

Once I had established that fact, the next step in logic was obvious. In accepting and rejecting knowledge, the mind is actively seeking what it needs. The mind needs nourishment to grow and be strong, just like the physical body. But the mind can't be measured or weighed. It's spiritual. Therefore, its food must also be spiritual. The mind needs the nourishment of ideas—what Plato called images. I came to understand that children are equipped with all they need to deal with ideas. [pg 11]

Explanations, comprehension questions, drawing out points, are unnecessary. They bore children. Children are born with a natural hunger for the kind of knowledge that is informed with thought. Like the stomach's gastric juices digesting food, children use their own imagination, judgment and what some people call 'faculties' to digest a new idea. This discovery was enlightening, but a bit startling. All of the teacher's hard work to present vividly, illustrate accurately, summarize and draw out by questions were nothing but obstacles. They intervened between the children and their mind diet of ideas. On the other hand, when children are presented with the right idea, they go to work on it with the focus and single-mindedness of a hungry child eating his dinner.

The Scottish school of philosophers explains this with their doctrine of desires. It seemed to me that those desires could stimulate the action of the mind so that it seeks invisible nourishment, just like appetites do to keep the body alive and continue the human race. This was helpful. It seemed to me that, of all the desires, the desire for knowledge (curiosity) was the main tool of education. This simple desire *to know* can be paralyzed, or rendered as powerless as a deformed arm if other desires are allowed to come between a child and the knowledge that's appropriate for him. Placement can encourage competition, prizes can encourage greed, special privileges can encourage ambition, praise can encourage vanity. Any of these can be a stumbling block for the child. It looked to me like, without even realizing it, teachers had created a complex system to ensure that students would behave and be enthusiastic about their lessons through the use of grades, prizes, etc. Yet, in doing that, they have eliminated the children's natural thirst for knowledge, which is incentive enough.

And then I asked myself, Can't people do just fine with a bare minimum of knowledge? After all, how much is really necessary? My young friends gave me an answer. Their insatiable [pg 12] curiosity showed that the whole world and its history was barely enough to satisfy any child, unless spiritual malnutrition had made him apathetic. My next question was, What is knowledge? Ages of intellectual thought haven't answered that question yet! But perhaps all we need to know is that the only knowledge a person has is what he has digested when his mind has actively chewed on it.

Children's natural inclination to learn, and their eagerness to know everything, made me conclude that the areas made accessible for children to learn about should never be artificially restricted. He has a right to as much and as varied knowledge as he's able to take in, and he needs it. Any limitations on his curriculum should only depend on what age he leaves school. In other words, a common curriculum up to age 14 or 15 should be the right of every child [*regardless of social class*].

We no longer believe that old medieval notion that intelligence is only born in children of the privileged classes, or that intelligence is inherited or can be developed by artificially manipulating the environment a child grows up in. Of course, inheritance plays a part, but so many factors come into play in genetics. Environment can make a child's learning fun or stressful, but learning is a spiritual thing of the soul, and can't be forced by making the child look at things or making him manipulate his fingers. Things of the mind are what appeal to the mind. Thought gives rise to more thought, and *that* is how we are educated. This is why we owe it to every child to put him in touch with great minds so that he can have access to great thoughts. Then he can be in communication with the minds of the people who left us great works. The only essential method of education seems to be that children should read worthy books, and lots of them.

But some will say that schools have libraries, and children have access to their public libraries and that they *do* read. Or, some will protest that the literary language of well-written books is too challenging for children of the lower classes. But [pg 13] we know that, although haphazard reading is fun and can even teach a thing or two—yet it isn't education in the sense of obtaining knowledge. If a person reads casually, then he isn't really applying his mind to work at making the knowledge 'his own.' If we don't actively read to know, then we won't be much better educated, even if we read a lot.

Why insist that books be written with literary style? My many years of experience have shown me too many circumstances and considerations to describe here, but I have seen that it comes naturally to us to enjoy well-written words—until our 'education' kills our taste for books.

It's difficult to explain how I figured out how to solve the problem of getting students to focus their attention. Observing many children, things I read here and there, remembering my own childhood and considering my own current mind habits, has taught me that there are certain laws that relate to the mind. By adhering to those laws, the focused attention of children can be guaranteed all the time, regardless of their age or social class. And they can keep their attention focused even with distractions. It's not due to the winning ways of their charismatic teacher, since hundreds of different teachers working both in homes and PNEU elementary schools and junior high schools are able to secure the attention of students without really trying. And it isn't because their lessons are so entertaining. The students do find their lessons interesting and enjoyable, but they're interested in a lot of different subjects, and their attention doesn't wander during the dull parts.

It's not easy to summarize those principles that the mind acts on naturally in a few sentences. I've tried to relate those principles as they apply to a school curriculum. The main idea is that children are already persons when they're born, which makes them affected by the same motivations to behavior that [pg 14] we adults are. One of those is the desire for knowledge. Everyone hungers to know, because curiosity is natural to everybody. History, geography, what other people think, which is humanities, are things that we all like to know about, and it's good for us to know about them. Science is, too, since we all live in this world and want to know more about it. Everyone needs beauty and wants to know how to evaluate it, so art is something worth knowing about. Ethics and social studies teach us how to act in life. And everyone needs to know about religion, because all men, not just those on the battlefront, hunger for God.

Since all children have that thirst to know, their unspoken demand is to have a wide and very diverse curriculum. They should learn something about all the many different issues that humans should know about. The various subjects included in their curriculum should never be curtailed because of convenience or time constraints.

Considering the wide range of things that children have a right to know about because they are persons, how can we get them to learn those things? What should they learn in the few years they go to school? We have discovered answers to those two questions. I say *discovered* rather than *invented*, because there's only one way to learn. Intelligent people who can talk about any subject, and experts who know a lot about a specialized subject, both learned in the same way—by reading to know. I have discovered that this method of *reading in order to know* is available to any child, whether homeschooled or in a large classroom.

Children are born with all they need to deal with knowledge, in the same way that they're born with all they need to deal with digesting their food. They already come pre-wired with a hunger to know and an enormous, almost unlimited ability to focus their attention. Their ability to remember seems to be related to their power of attention [pg 15] in the same way that the stomach and intestines are related to the total digestion of food. Some might say, 'Yes, children have natural curiosity and they're capable of paying attention when they're interested, but they can only be coaxed to attend to their lessons part of the time.' But isn't that the fault of the lessons? Shouldn't lessons be planned carefully around the needs of the child's mind, just as his meals are planned around the needs of his physical body? Let's consider the way the mind works. The mind is concerned only about thoughts, imaginings, and reasoned arguments. It doesn't assimilate facts unless they're in the form of appropriate mind food. The mind is always active. It tires quickly of passive listening. A child's mind is as bored by the rambling twaddle of a prattling teacher as we adults are by twaddly small talk. The mind prefers something literary. When presented with something in literary form, the mind is curious and will attend to a great variety of topics.

I say that these are things of the mind because they seem to be true of the minds of everyone. I've observed these things, as well as a few other points about how the mind works. All I needed to do was to apply what I had discovered to a trial curriculum for schools and families. Lectures were mostly eliminated. Lots of books from many subjects were scheduled for reading during morning school hours. So much work was scheduled that there was only time for a single reading. All reading was tested by narrating either part of the selection or the entire reading, either orally or in writing. Students doing this kind of work know what they read, even months later. Their ability to focus their attention is remarkable. They don't have trouble with spelling or composition. They mature into well-informed, intelligent people. (The small test school related to The House of Education, with students from ages 6-18, tests the schedule of schoolwork sent out each term and the end-of-term exams. The work in each form/grade is easily finished in the hours of morning school.) [pg 16]

But someone might say that reading or hearing different books read out loud chapter by chapter and then narrating is merely memory work. But that can be easily tested. Before turning off your light in bed, read a newspaper article or a chapter from Boswell or Jane Austen, or an essay by Charles Lamb. As you go to sleep, narrate silently to yourself what you just read. You'll be disappointed with the results, but you'll find that the act of narrating requires every power of your mind. Points and details that you didn't notice come into your memory. The whole thing is visualized and brought into focus in an unusual way. What's happening is that the particular scene or argument has become part of your personal experience. You have assimilated and know what you read. This is not memory work. In order to memorize, we repeat a passage or series of points or names over and over, inventing little clues to help us. We can memorize a string of facts or words this way, and that memory is useful in the short term, but it isn't really assimilated. After its purpose is served, we forget it. That's the kind of memory work students use to pass exams. I won't try to explain (I don't even understand!) this power to memorize. It has its temporary use in education, I'm sure, but it must never take the place of the main tool, which is the ability to focus the attention.

Long ago, a philosophical friend used to quote this saying: 'The mind can know nothing except what it can produce as an answer when it asks itself a question.' I haven't been able to trace the saying to its author, but over the last forty years, I've become more convinced of its importance. It implies that questions shouldn't come from [pg 17] without (this doesn't include the Socratic method of questioning to draw out students' thinking for the purpose of teaching morals). This internal questioning is necessary to be certain of something intellectually, to really own the knowledge. For example, if we want to get the details straight in our memory after a conversation or incident, we go over it again in our minds. That 'going over' process is the self-questioning I just mentioned. When someone narrates something they just read, this is what happens: The mind asks itself, 'what happened next?' to remember each consecutive detail. This is why it's so important that only one single reading be allowed. Trying to use rote memory techniques weakens the power to focus the attention, which is exactly what the mind needs to do. If the teacher wants to ask questions so that certain points are emphasized, they should be asked after the narration, not before or during.

Some advanced psychologists agree. They declare that the key is 'not a group of mind faculties, but one single subjective activity, which is attention.' And, again, there is 'one common factor in all mind activity, and that's attention.' (I'm quoting from the Psychology article in the Encyclopedia Britannica.) I would add that attention is unfailing, prompt and steady—so long as the material set in front of students is suited to their intellectual requirements, and so long as the material is presented concisely, directly, and simply, as all good literature should be.

Another thing to keep in mind: the intellect needs a moral motivation. We tend to rouse our minds to action better when we know, somewhere in the back of our minds, that there's a reason that we must. For students, that reason is that they'll be required to narrate or write from what they just read, and they'll have no opportunity to look things up or otherwise refresh their memory. Children enjoy narrating so much that the teacher hardly ever has to coax students to do it. [pg 18]

What follows is a complete list, a chain, describing the educational philosophy that I've tried to work out. If nothing else, what it has in its favor is that it's been successful in practice. I've adopted and applied a few hints, but I hope that I've succeeded in methodizing the whole thing and making education what it should be—a system of applied philosophy. Even so, I have been careful not to use philosophical terms.

Briefly, here's how it works:

A child is a complete person with all the spiritual needs and abilities of any person.

Knowledge nourishes the mind in the same way that food nourishes the body.

A child needs knowledge just as much as he needs food.

He already has:
The desire for knowledge (curiosity).
The ability to take in knowledge by paying attention.
As much imagination, reflection, judgment, etc. as he needs to deal with knowledge, without the need for outside props.
Natural, inborn interest in all the kinds of knowledge that he'll need as a human being.
The ability to retain and articulate that knowledge, and assimilate what he needs.

He needs most of his knowledge to be communicated to him in literary form. When he articulates knowledge from a literary source, his version will be touched by his own unique personality, so that his reproduction becomes original.

The natural ability for making use of knowledge and digesting it is already sufficient. No external stimulus [reward, threat, entertainment] is needed to make a child learn. But some kind of moral motivation is needed to prompt students to pay attention. [pg 19]

The moral motivation is knowing with certainty that he will be required to tell what he read. Children have a right to the best that we have. Therefore, their school books should be the best books we can find.

Children get tired of lectures, and bored with comprehension questions. They should be allowed to use their schoolbooks for themselves. If they need help, they'll ask for it.

Children need a variety of knowledge—about religion, humanities, science, art. Therefore, they should have a broad curriculum with a set amount of reading scheduled for each subject.

The teacher should give the student some direction, sympathy in his work, an encouraging word sometimes, help with things like setting up experiments, and the usual help they need in languages, experimental science and math.

When education follows these conditions, 'lessons are enjoyable,' and seeing daily progress is exhilarating to both the teacher and the students.

Some readers might say, 'I already knew all of this before and I've always acted more or less on these principles.' All I can say is, the incredible results we've had didn't come from adhering to these principles 'more or less,' but by following them strictly in practice. Joseph Lister must have had this same difficulty to contend with. Surgeons in his day knew that their instruments should be sterile, but it was only those who actually acted on that knowledge and sterilized their instruments each time with his chemical solution who saved millions of lives. That's the difference between scrupulously following exact principles, and casually using them 'more or less.'

It remains to be seen whether my method is the only right way to educate. There needs to be more proof than [pg 20] the thousands of students who have used it. But one thing is certain—today's current education is feeble and unclear because there are no sound principles being put into action and applied exactly. It's time to decide. We've trusted in 'civilization' and we've taken pride in our modern progress. Of all the painful things that war has brought us, perhaps the most difficult is the total breakdown of the civilization that's always meant education to us. We've learned our lesson and we're once again relying on our human instinct and God's divine rules. The part of a person that can be educated is his mind. The senses and muscles aren't educated, they're trained. The mind, like the rest of the body, needs quantity, variety and regularity in its diet. The mind, like the body, has its own appetite: the desire to know. The mind, like the body, is perfectly capable of taking in and digesting its food via attention and reflection. The mind, like the body, doesn't like limp, dull and unpleasant food. It wants its meals to be in literary form [*such as, in stories*]. The mind's diet is restricted to one thing: it can only absorb ideas and facts when they're connected to the living ideas on which they hang. Children who are educated this way respond in a surprising way. They develop ability, character, self-control, initiative, and a sense of responsibility. Even as children they are good, thoughtful citizens.

In this book, I've tried to show the principles and methods that this kind of education is based on, and that's so successfully being carried out. I've added chapters to explain the history of our movement, whose aim is, as Comenius says, 'All knowledge for all men.' I've been given permission to use the comments of various teachers, Directors [pg 21] of education, and others about the practical application of this method.

It is a cause for celebration that we have the opportunity to give students from all socio-economic classes a foundation of mutually shared thought and knowledge. This includes familiarity with a common collection of literature and history, which has an interesting way of bonding people together. Also, it's a wonderful achievement that children of lower income families, even with their limited opportunities, will have access to this kind of education. They will have equal opportunity to develop the stability of mind and nobleness of character that are the result of a rich, bountiful education.

In this book, I'll limit myself to clarifying and illustrating some of the points I tried to make in this introduction.

Book 1

Chapter 1 - Self-Education

[pg 23]

The title, 'self-education,' may bring some familiar images to mind, images of rhythmic movements, independent action, various kinds of interesting self-expression. Isn't that what self-education means? Most of these measures are fine and shouldn't be neglected. They're useful to train the limbs to be graceful and limber, to train the fingers to be skillful and precise, to train the eye to truly see and the ear to hear, to train the voice to interpret. Today, we know that all of those skills enhance life and should be available to every child. We eagerly anticipate the kind of citizens that children educated in all those things will become.

Although we PNEU workers use some of those very methods and others, our point of view is different. We seriously doubt that those activities will have any impact on the child's character and behavior. A person isn't built up from without, but from within. He is a living creature, and any attempts to apply education to the outside of him will be mere decorative ornaments, and won't be a vital part of him.

This sounds so obvious. But consider what the conviction that 'a child is already a person' and that a [pg 24] person is, first of all, a living being, implicates. Nothing that is applied to the outside of any living creature will sustain life and promote growth. Bathing in wine and wrapping in velvet will have no impact on the physical health of the creature, other than being a hindrance. The creature's life has to be sustained by what it takes in, not by what's applied to its surface.

Perhaps the only accurate analogy with the human mind is the physical body, especially a human body. That's what we know the most about. The familiar analogy comparing a child to a plant in a garden is misleading, especially since it always seems to involve a gardener who directs the direction in which every twig grows, and the position of every leaf. But even without a gardener, the child as a garden plant doesn't hold up. It fails to recognize something that plants don't have, but that every child has—a unique, individual personality. So let's use the body analogy and compare it to the mind. The body lives on air, grows with food, needs exercise and rest, and thrives on a carefully selected diet that has plenty of variety. The same is true of the mind (by mind, I mean the entire intellect, soul, feelings, everything that isn't physical). The mind breathes in air, needs activity and rest, and thrives on a diet that has plenty of variety.

We talk about the mind, and go around it as if it was a house—but we rarely go into the House of the Mind. We offer mental gymnastics, but we don't see that what the mind really needs is food. And what little food we do give is so meager, it's like trying to live on one bean a day! Everyone is so anxious about nutrition for the physical body, but no one thinks to ask, 'I wonder if the mind needs food, too, and regularly scheduled servings? And what is a proper diet for the mind, anyway?'

I have asked myself those very questions and worked for fifty years to find answers. I'm anxious to share what I've found out, but it can't be expressed in the form of a list of things to do. Instead, I'll invite you to consider some things. It's only when we have the right frame of mind that we can understand the right thing to do. [pg 25]

The living mind needs the nourishment of ideas to survive. A mind doesn't have intellectual life if it isn't receiving several ideas as often as every day. But surely science experiments, the beauty of nature, field observation, rhythmic movement, exercises for the senses—aren't those all ripe with ideas? Generally speaking, yes, they are. They present ideas in invention, discovery, and even art. But, for the moment, consider the ideas that influence life: character and behavior. It appears that these kinds of ideas pass directly from one mind to another. They aren't hindered by 'educational' props, but they aren't helped, either. All children get lots of these ideas by word of mouth, from family traditions, sayings that pass on a way of thinking. This might be thought of as oral literature. But, to get back to the body/mind analogy—we understand that bodies need three square meals a day. In the same way, a mind fed on a casual diet of ideas will be poorly nourished and weak. Our schools graduate students who are clever enough, but who lack ambition, the power to reflect on thoughts, and the kind of moral imagination that helps them understand what it's like to be in someone else's shoes. All of those qualities thrive on a good diet of ideas. But those kinds of ideas don't come in regular school textbooks or lessons, at least not very often. I'd like to focus on *quality*. That's just as important for the mind as it is for the physical body. Both mind and body need regular, balanced meals.

It's not so easy to give a healthy diet to the mind. Some say that children don't have brains, or have inferior minds, or other harsh things. But many of us have seen the intelligence of children first-hand when they're fed the proper diet for their minds. Unfortunately, teachers don't usually bother to find out what a healthy mind diet is. And so, we come dangerously close to what Plato condemns as a 'lie of the soul,' which is the corruption of the highest truth. Protagoras was guilty of that corruption when he [pg 26] said, 'Knowledge is what can be discerned with the senses.' And we say the same thing when we use educational methods based only on sensory learning. Knowledge is not sensation, and it isn't developed through the senses. We feed on the thoughts of other minds. When we reflect on those thoughts, we add on to those thoughts, and we become more thoughtful people. We don't need to be encouraged to reason, compare or imagine. We do it naturally. The mind, just like the body, has everything it needs to digest its food. But, if it doesn't work at digestion, it atrophies and stops working.

But children 'ask for bread' and we 'give them a stone.' We give them dry facts about things, and their minds don't even try to digest them. Instead, their minds vomit them out (perhaps in the form of answers on a test?) But, if information relates to a principle and if it's inspired by an idea, then it will be devoured enthusiastically. And that information will be used to build onto the spiritual nature in the same way that food builds physical tissue in the physical body.

Lord Haldane of Cloan once said, 'Education is a spiritual matter.' And that is very true. Yet we continue to apply education to the outside, like one would do with physical activity, or by coating the body with scented oils. But we're beginning to understand. If no one can understand the hidden things of a person except his own spirit, then the only real education is self-education. As soon as a child begins his education, he begins learning as a student. Our role is to make sure he has plenty of food for his mind. He needs intellectual nourishment of good quality, and he needs lots of it. Each of us naturally has a limited amount of ideas in our minds, but we know where to get more. The best thoughts that the world has are stored in books. We must introduce our children to books—the very best books. Our concern as educators is to have abundance and orderly serving of them.

I want so much for children. Every modern educational trend tends to underrate their intellectual ability, especially a recent brilliant idea to nourish normal young minds with the kind of meat paste that is supposed to help mentally ill patients. [*possibly referring to Montessori.*] George Bernard Shaw said, 'All wildly popular [pg 27] fads inevitably come to sudden death, never to live again.' If he's right, then there's no need for me to even mention a certain popular form of 'New Education.' It has been rightly said that education should be removed from psychology and sociology. But, once education is freed from them, it would be a disastrous mistake to ally education with pathological science.

For various reasons, I feel that I must take some unpleasant action. It's time that I stood up and presented some educational principles and practices that would benefit the general public. Like the lepers of 2 Kings 7:9 who feasted on spoils while the rest of the city starved, I feel ashamed. In my previous books, I have tried to explain a system of education that meets every requirement. It even satisfies Plato's demand that it should, 'meet every objection and be ready to answer them with absolute truth rather than opinion.' Some of my educational ideas are new, but a lot of them are not. Like mercy, it's always there and there's enough to go around. It is twice blessed—it blesses the one who gives it and the one who receives it. Both teachers and students using this method are known for their radiant expressions. Yet there are no dramatic testable results to attract the world's attention.

Professor Bompas Smith gave an inaugural address at the University of Manchester and said, 'If we have a thorough, comprehensive theory to guide us, we will widen our experience because we'll try things that never would have occurred to us otherwise.' I know of such a thorough, comprehensive theory, and Professor Smith is correct. With this theory as a guide, many teachers do try things that wouldn't have occurred to them otherwise. A person discovers something just because it's there. No rational person [pg 28] would take credit himself, as if it belonged to him. Instead, he says what King Arthur said: 'These jewels that God led me to are for the benefit of the public.' For many years, we have had an Aladdin's Cave open to us, and I long to open it up to the world 'for the benefit of the public.'

Here is a list of some of the advantages of this theory:
It's appropriate for all ages—even Shakespeare's seven ages of man!
It effectively educates brilliant children, and develops the intelligence of even the slower children.
Children concentrate with focused attention and interest without any effort from them or their teachers.
All children taught this way express themselves in confident, well-spoken English, and use a large vocabulary.
Children are calm and stable.
Keeping the mind busy with things to think about seems to make children's minds and lives pure.
Parents share their children's interest in their schoolwork and enjoy the company of their children.
Children enjoy their books, even when they aren't picture books, and they seem to really love learning.
Teachers don't have to work so hard making corrections.
Children taught this way do very well no matter what school they attend.
Students don't need grades, prizes, etc., to motivate them.

This isn't just quack medicine, although it might seem like I'm trying to sell some miracle formula at $29.95 a bottle.

Over thirty years ago I wrote Home Education (Volume 1) about teaching and training children at home. People wrote and asked how all my suggestions could be carried out perfectly without the help of Mary Poppins. I realized that a specific suggested curriculum might be created that would be in line with my principles and make students less dependent on their teacher. In other words, their [pg 29] education would be mostly self-education. So we set up a correspondence school. Our school motto was, 'I am, I can, I ought, I will.' That motto has been very effective in making children aware of the possibilities, capabilities, duties and their power to decide whether to do right or wrong. They have all these things simply because they're human.

'Children are born persons,' is the first tenet of my educational creed. I was surprised by 6-18 year-old children's responses to this kind of education. Yet they only displayed the ability to focus their attention, thirst to know, clarity of thinking, good discrimination in books and capability of handling many subjects at the same time— things I already knew they could do. I won't say any more about Knowledge than what I've urged in other books, but I propose a test. Read a 6-10 year old child a vivid, concise account of some incident and ask him to tell it back. He will relate it detail by detail in his own words, adding his own delightful touches. In fact, months later, he'll still be able to talk about it because he has visualized it in his mind and made that knowledge 'his own.' A rhetorical passage written like a newspaper article won't even make any impression on the child. A passage read a second time may get a more accurate narration because the child has memorized some of it, but his narration won't have the stamp of his own individuality. An older child might read one of Bacon's essays or something from De Quincey and they might write or tell about it with flair right afterwards, or even months later. We've heard how Mr. Fox recited an entire pamphlet by Burke at a college supper even though he probably read it only once. This is the result of attention, interest, literary style, wide vocabulary, love for books and skill at articulating. We all feel that these things should be included in an education that begins at school, but continues to be a way of living for the child's whole life. This is something we all want. But how do we get those things? [pg 30]

That's part of a hidden truth that I'm working to present to the world for the benefit of the general public.

I'm anxious to show the world a successful educational experiment. The time is right, since we are being told by an authority that 'education needs to appeal to the spirit if it's going to interest the student.' My suggestions for education are as interesting and fascinating to parents, teachers and students as fine art.

In the last thirty years, thousands of children educated this way have grown up loving knowledge and being able to judge all things correctly when their wide curriculum supplies them with the proper information.

I think children should get familiar with the practice of learning from books even before they learn the mechanical skills of reading and writing. And this is fun for them. They fix all their attention to a paragraph or page being read aloud, and then they're able to tell it back point for point in their own words. But it takes literary English to draw this skill out of children. They can't learn to get knowledge from books with anything less. Children begin learning from books at age six, the same time they begin to learn phonics and handwriting. A child loses nothing by taking his time and spending two years on the mechanics of decoding text to learn to read, or learning to write, because, during this time, he is still getting knowledge from books in history, geography, stories and the Bible because his books are read aloud to him. He pays close attention and has a wonderful ability to reproduce the information in his narrations—which amounts to him translating the material to himself in a way he can understand. Meanwhile, the books he listens to are giving him a large vocabulary and the ability to tell things in order. In other words, he is an educated child right from the beginning. His skill at dealing with books, even when there are several books on different subjects in a day's work, will increase as he gets older.

All children are different. They are as different from each other as adults are. A couple months ago, I had a five-year-old boy in our correspondence school. His records said that he could read anything in five languages. He was currently teaching [pg 31] himself the Greek alphabet and could locate places on Bradshaw's Continental Railroad map. He was a sturdy, active little boy, and he brings all of these attributes to school with him. He is as exceptional as even a man would be who could do all those things. I think that all children bring many of their own capabilities to school, but their teachers miss it. In particular, their intellectual ability is usually ahead of their physical ability. But teachers tend to drown children's minds in a flood of over-explanations, or they dissipate children's intellect with busy work that wastes their time but doesn't teach them anything.

People naturally fall into two groups: those who read and reflect on what they've read . . . and those who don't. Schools should be making sure that all their students belong to the first group. It is wise to remember that, when someone is focused on the content and idea of what they're reading rather than just the words on the page, thinking and reflecting will inevitably follow.

The students I've been talking about aren't just into books. They're busy with real things, too. After all, 'Education is the science of relations' is the foundational principle of their curriculum. A child goes to school with many interests and tendencies, and school should give him the opportunity to explore as many of them as possible. Children should learn a lot about science since they have no problem understanding basic principles, although technical details will be over their head. They should practice different crafts so they know what it's like to work with wood, clay and leather and how fun it is to handle tools. They can then form their own relationships with materials. But it's always the book or what he's learning or what he's making from clay that's on his mind, not how well he's doing at it. [*His focus is on the work, not on himself.*] I'm afraid that open-minded teachers who want to try our suggestions will need some knowledge of the theory behind our method, because underlying principles affect every detail of the classroom. For example, it would be easy to [pg 32] experiment with our booklists without giving it much thought. But in education, just like religion, motive is what counts. A student who does his lesson for a good grade might memorize it perfectly, but he hasn't really owned the knowledge. But our principles are obvious and simple. Current education is chaotic because there's no unifying theory to make it work together. We see that current education has no thorough theory of education that agrees with the latest thought and is useful in every situation. Why not try a theory that's practical to put right to use, always pleasant, and has proven itself by producing lots of able, useful people who have good judgment and willing minds?

In urging that we replace what pretends to be education with my method of self-education, I'd like to consider what a relief this would be to teachers. They are self-sacrificing and overburdened. The difference in educational principles is like the difference between driving a car that's smooth and responsive, and one that seems to have a mind of its own. The first one covers the distance easily and pleasurably, and the driver goes along very happily. The teacher who allows her students freedom in the world of books is free to be their guide, philosopher and companion rather than just a public servant whose job is to force-feed lessons.

[pg 33]

Chapter 2 - Children are Born Persons *(Principle 1.)*

1. The Mind Of A Child

As soon as the soul spots truth, the soul recognizes it as her first and oldest friend.'
'The repercussions of truth are great. Therefore we must not neglect to correctly judge what's true, and what's not.' —Benjamin Whichcote

It shouldn't be any great surprise that a chapter written to show a great truth should open with the meaningful words of the wise Benjamin Whichcote. But truths get old and wonders cease to amaze us. We're no longer entranced about the stars in the heavens, or new buds on the trees in spring, or the clever way that birds build their nests. Even babies are no longer miracles, except to their parents and siblings. The completeness and perfection of their newborn brother is what children marvel at most—his toes and fingers, his ears, and all his other tiny little perfect parts. His parents have some understanding of babies. They know that his most important task is growing, and they feed him with just what he needs most. Wise parents give him freedom and space to wiggle and stretch and play, and that strengthens his little muscles. His parents know what he might become, and it gives them hope that he may do something to benefit the world. But, for now, he needs food, sleep, shelter and lots of love. We all know that much. But is the baby anything more than a 'huge oyster'? That's the question before us, and, in the past, [pg 34] educators have been inclined to say, 'No, the baby is just a huge oyster.' Their notion is that, with a push here and a pull there, compressing something somewhere else, they will turn out a person according to the pattern they had in mind.

The other view is that the infant's body is the setting for a jewel so valuable that, if you put the child on one side of a scale and the whole world in the other side, the child would outweigh the world. One poet, Thomas Traherne, looked back on the hazy memory of his infancy and remembered this:

'I was entertained like an angel with God's creations in all their splendor and glory. Isn't it strange that a baby should be the heir of the whole world and see mysteries that even scholars' books don't reveal? The cornfields seemed like great, immortal plains that would never be reaped and had never been sown—I thought they had been there from everlasting to everlasting. The dust and pebbles in the street seemed as precious to me as gold. The green of the trees enchanted me. Their sweet, unusual beauty made my heart leap. Boys and girls playing in the street looked like moving jewels. I didn't know that they'd ever been born, or would ever die. It seemed like the streets were mine, and the people were mine— their clothes and jewelry and coins were just as much mine as their sparkling eyes, fair skins and shining faces. The sky was mine and so were the sun, moon and stars. The whole world was mine and I was the only spectator to enjoy it.'

Only a poet like Traherne could remember and reproduce such vivid memories, although maybe all of us can remember when we felt like we were spectators at the show of life. Perhaps we can remember happy times before we knew how to speak to say what we thought. Punch [*the magazine*] had an amusing feature where a baby commented on his perception of his nurse and his surroundings, especially the pulling and pushing that he was subjected to. But, in reality, babies aren't critics. Their business is to take it all in, and they keep busy at this every day.

We suspect that poets say more than they really understand, [pg 35] express more than they really see, and that their version of life needs to be taken with a grain of salt. But perhaps the truth is, that, no matter how hard they think, they can't find the words to explain what they know and remember. So Wordsworth, Coleridge, Vaughan and the rest can do no more than hint at the glory that exists in childhood. We are not poets, and that sometimes makes us inclined to discount what poets say. But even the most ordinary of us have witnessed the surprisingly alert and tuned-in mind of a child. Consider that, in their first two years, children have managed to learn more than they will in any other two-period of their lives. Suppose an outer space alien were to land on Earth. Imagine all the things he'd have to learn to be able to get by here! Our concepts of hard/soft, wet/dry, hot/cold, steady/unstable, far/near would be as foreign to him as they are to an infant who reaches out his hand and thinks he can grasp the moon. We don't know how aliens get around, but it seems reasonable that the ability to run, jump, climb stairs, and even sit and stand would take as much resolve and practice as the years someone puts in to learn to skate, dance, ski, fence, or any other sport. And yet, a baby does this in just two years! He learns the properties of all different kinds of matter, colors, some ideas about size, the difference between solid and liquid. By his third year, he has learned to communicate with surprising clearness. Not only that, but he has learned a language, or maybe even two, if he's had the opportunity. I know a three year old who has mastered three languages, one of which is Arabic. He has mastered it so well that he can say anything he needs to say in any of those three languages. Don't we all wish we had this kind of fluency when we travel to other countries! [pg 36]

Lady Mary Wortley Montagu writes about children she knew of in Constantinople who could prattle in five different languages, and knew a good bit of each language. Even if we aren't convinced that children are born with minds as complete and beautiful as their perfect little bodies, we at least have to admit that they have as much mind as they need, to do all the things and learn everything they need to. In other words, a child's mind is like the instrument that education plays upon; his education doesn't produce a mind in him. His mind was already there and active before he ever entered the classroom.

Who can measure the limits of a child's thoughts? His constant questions about God and speculations about Jesus are more than idle curiosity. They are symptoms of a God-hunger that we're all born with. He may be able to comprehend as much about the infinite and the unseen as we complacent adults. Is it possible that our ways confine him, and that he needs fairy tales as a joyful escape to places where all things are possible? We hear that children have no imaginations and that they need to see and touch and taste to know. Infants devote themselves to learning the different properties of things by touching, pulling, tearing, throwing and tasting. But when children are older, they need only a glance to size up new things, even things that have complicated structures. Life is a continual progress for children. They don't go over and over the same things, they love to move on to new things. Quoting Traherne again:

'One sad, lonely evening I was alone in a field. All was still and silent, as if everything was dead. Suddenly a horror came upon me. The dead heaviness of the place, the loneliness, the wildness terrified me. Fear surrounded me. I was only a small, weak child and I'd forgotten that there were any other people alive in the world. Yet, a kind of hope and expectation comforted me from all sides.' [pg 37]

Traherne never forgot the lessons he learned. He goes on:

'This taught me that the world of people was where I belonged. The beauties of the world were made to entertain me. The presence of cities, churches, and kingdoms would sustain me, because being alone in the world is a desolate and miserable experience.'

Reason is just as much a part of children's minds as imagination. As soon as a child can speak, he lets us know that he has wondered the 'why' of things, and he asks us a thousand questions. His 'Why?' is endless! And his logic isn't as senseless as we might think. Look how early a toddler manages to charm his daycare giver or mother to get his own way! He will feel out her moods and play on her feelings. It is born in him to be like a tyrant. His daycare giver says, 'he has a will of his own,' but she is wrong. His passionate displays of greed, stubbornness and temper are not really signs of his will. It is only when the little boy is able to stop all these and restrain himself with a quivering lip that his will comes into play. For he also has a conscience. Before he even takes his first step, he knows the difference between right and wrong. Even an infant in-arms will blush when reprimanded by his daycare giver. His strong will acts in direct proportion to his learning the difficult art of obedience. After all, no one can *make* a child obey unless he wants to—unless he *wills* himself to. [*You can force compliance, but not willing obedience.*] And we all know how even the tiniest rebel can cause mayhem at home or in the classroom.

2. The Mind of a School Child

It's time to leave the young child, at least until he's grown old enough for school. I've tried to show (in Volume 1) what parents and teachers should do for the young child teaching himself about everything he sees and hears, and growing stronger [pg 38] with everything he does. This Volume is mostly concerned with the formal schooling part of education, but I was anxious to be sure that teachers understand that the child who comes into their classroom arrives with a mind that has amazing potential. He has a physical brain, too, of course, which is a part of his mind, like an instrument. Like a piano that is not music but is merely the instrument for music, a child's brain is the instrument for education. I don't think we need to concern ourselves with the way the brain, as a physical organ, has the same needs as the rest of the physical body—it's fed in the same way the body feeds, rests in the same way the body rests, needs fresh air and healthy exercise to keep it strong. But the brain depends on the mind [*the intangible, invisible spirit and soul of a person*] to do its functions.

The world has been obsessed with psychology lately. Psychology concerns itself with 'the unconscious mind,' that place beyond the influence of nerves and blood (which we'd do best to leave alone) that we tend to ignore in our educational efforts. We neglect the mind and focus instead on a set of physical symptoms. But the mind is spiritual. It doesn't suffer fatigue like the physical body does. If the brain is adequately nourished along with physical body, and gets fresh air and rest, it also shouldn't get fatigued. With these two conditions, we have a vast field of possibilities for education. But it's up to us to come up with a theory and practice that recognize the role of the mind. A saying that we normally associate with religion also applies here: What is born of the flesh is flesh. But we forget this when we teach children. We make lessons seem like play, and, although play is good and necessary, it isn't the path to the mind. We strive to make a child's environment perfectly appropriate, which is good, but it's not the path to the mind. We teach children beautiful physical motions, and that's fine, since the physical body also needs training, [pg 39] but we are mistaken if we think that these things approach a child's mind. It is no less true here that what is born of the spirit is spirit. The way to the mind is quite direct. Mind must connect to mind via ideas. 'What is mind?' asks the old riddle, and the answer is still the same: 'No matter.' We teachers need to realize that physical, material things have little effect on the mind. There are still schools where all the work is physical and technical, where lessons are given with blocks of wood or scientific equipment. One elementary school teacher wrote, 'Yesterday the father of one of my pupils told me, 'You've certainly given me some work to do. E. wouldn't let me alone until I promised to set up my microscope and get some pond water to look for monad protozoa and other wonders.' That is what should be the correct order: what was born of the spirit (the idea) came first and was compelled to confirm and find examples of it. We wonder how these things can be, and the answer isn't obvious.

Like faith, education is the evidence of things not seen. We have to begin with the notion that the body's task is to grow. It grows upon healthy food, which is itself made up of living cells. Each cell is, in fact, a perfect life in itself. Analogies are never adequate or accurate, but, in a similar way, the only proper nutrition for the mind is ideas. And ideas, like the single cells of physical tissue, appear to go through the same stages and functions as a life. We receive ideas with appetite and some interest. Ideas seem to feed in an odd way—for instance, we hear of some new treatment for AIDS, or a poet's latest thought, or the new direction that some school of art is taking. We take in the idea, we accept it, and, it seems, for days after that, everywhere we turn, every magazine we pick up, every person we talk to, brings food for the notion we've just received. The casual reader might say, 'You can't prove that.' But [pg 40] watch how your own minds acts towards any idea in the wind. You'll see that the kind of process I've just described will happen. And it's this same process that needs to be considered when educating children. We can't continue taking things as casually as we've been doing. Our job is to give children the great ideas of life—ideas in religion, history, science, but it's the *ideas* they need, although they may be clothed with facts. And we must give the child space to deal with them in his own way.

For example, this might be how a child deals with geography:

'When I heard about any country across the sea, I would envision the glory of that place. That vision would rise up in me until the whole thing filled and expanded me. I saw its goods, its rivers, meadows, people. I felt like I owned the vision of that place, as if it had been prepared just for me. That's how much joy I had in my vision. When I heard the Bible being read, my spirit felt like it was really there in another time. I could see the light and splendor of those ages, and the land of Canaan, the Israelites entering in, the ancient splendor of the Amorites, their peace and wealth, their cities, houses, grapevines and fig trees. I saw and felt all of this in such a real way that it seemed as if these places could only be entered into by the spirit. I could physically stay in the same place, yet visit and enjoy all these other places in my mind. No matter how long ago something happened, even a thousand years ago, it could always seem to be right there in front of me.'

I'm quoting Traherne again because I don't know of any other writer who still has such a clear memory of his infancy. But Goethe gives an equally thorough and convincing account of his early experiences with the Bible (see Volume 5). I use the word 'experience' with caution because the word implies the process children use to get to know something. They 'experience' everything they hear and read about. In this way, ideas feed their minds quite literally!

What about our geography lessons? Do they take our children there in their spirits? Do they feel like they're experiencing and living in the story of God's calling to Abraham? Or the story of the blind man who was healed on his [pg 41] way to Jericho? If they don't, it's not the teacher's lack of sincerity or intention to blame. The fault is the teacher's lack of confidence in children. He doesn't have an accurate assessment of a child's mind, so he bores his students with a lot of talk about things that they're quite able to understand for themselves—in fact, they understand it better than he does. How many teachers know that children don't need any pictures except the paintings of great artists, which serve a different purpose than illustrating? Children can see in their minds a picture more glorious, and usually more accurate than we, with our jaded experience, can envision. They're able to read between the lines and add in all the details that the author left out. A nine-year-old who'd been reading Andrew Lang's *Tales of Troy and Greece*, drew a picture of Ulysses on the Isle of Calypso cutting down trees to make a raft. A ten-year-old who was enjoying *A Midsummer Night's Dream*, drew the Indian Princess bringing her beautiful little boy to Titiana. Meanwhile, we adults are content just to know that 'Ulysses built a raft,' or, 'the boy's mother was an Indian princess.' This is how the mind of any child works, and we need to make sure we aren't starving these fertile grounds of intelligence. Children need intellectual food, and they need a lot of it, and all different kinds. They know perfectly well what to do with it themselves—we don't need to bother coming up with separate exercises for each of their minds' 'faculties.' The mind is one and it works as one unit. Reason, imagination, reflection, judgment, etc., are all like worthy seamen summoned by the captain. They all swarm on deck when it's time to unload the cargo. The cargo is that rich, fragrant bounty of ideas, and the boat is the child's mind waiting to receive. Don't we want every child to say, or, at least, feel, 'I was wonderfully broadened' by a geography lesson? Then let him 'see' a place through the eyes of those who have seen or conceived it. Barometer charts, temperature graphs, contour lines, relief [pg 42] maps, section cutaways, summarized sketches, etc., won't do it. When a child looks at a globe, his mind should be so filled with the panorama of images of places he's collected that he'd rather ponder them than go out to play. And it's so easy to give him this life's joy. Let him learn about the world in the same way we prefer to learn about it when we travel. Let him learn about its cities and people, its mountains and rivers, and his lesson will leave him with a piece of the place he has just read about, whether it's a county or country, sea or shore, and the place he pictures in his mind will seem like 'a new room prepared just for him, he'll be so broadened and pleased with it.' Truly, all the world is the child's possession prepared just for him. If we keep what's rightfully his away from him with our technical, financially-minded, or even historical approach to geography, or with attempts to make geography illustrate our own pet theories, then we cheat the child. What the child really needs is the whole world, every bit of it, piece by piece, and each piece a key to the next piece. When he reads about the Bore [*surge wave*] of the Severn River, he feels that he would know a Bore anywhere. He doesn't need to see a specific mountain to feel like he knows it. In his mind, he sees all that is described to him with a vividness that we adults underestimate. It's as if the only way to those places is in the spirit. Who can accurately assess a child? The genie of Arabian Nights isn't as marvelous as he is. Just like a genie, a child can be freed from his bottle and let out into the world. But woe to us if we keep him imprisoned in his bottle.

We've established that children have minds and we know that a person's mind is needed to earn a living. But there's much more to it than that. The working class will have more leisure time in the future, and there is a lot of discussion about how this leisure time will be spent. No person can use his leisure time well if his mind isn't used to being active daily. The routine duties of life don't supply any intellectual food, and only a little bit of monotonous mental exercise. Science, history, philosophy, and literature must [pg 43] no longer be luxuries of the educated classes. *All* classes need to be educated. They need to partake of these things just as they do their daily meals. They need to have the pageants of history, the wonders of science, the intimate acquaintances of literature, the speculations of philosophy, and the assurance that religion offers to every person. Education should be preparing people to wander in these realms of gold.

How should we prepare a child to use the sense of beauty that every child seems to be born with? His education should familiarize him with entire galleries of mental pictures by great artists from the past and present, such as Jozef Israels' Pancake Woman, his Children by the Sea; Millet's Feeding the Birds, First Steps, Angelus; Rembrandt's Night Watch, The Supper at Emmaus; Velasquez's Surrender of Breda. In fact, every child should leave school with at least a couple hundred paintings by great artists hanging permanently in his mental gallery, as well as great buildings, sculpture and beautiful forms and colors that he sees. It would also be good to supply him with a hundred lovely landscapes, too, such as sunsets, clouds and starry night skies. Anyway, he should have plenty of pictures because imagination grows like magic. The more you put in, the more it can hold.

It isn't just a child's intellect that arrives at school fully furnished. His heart does, too. How many of us can love as a child can? He showers love on Mommy, Daddy, sister, brother, neighbors, friends, the family pet, an ugly stump of a broken toy. He's so generous and grateful, so kind and simple, so empathetic and full of goodwill, so loyal and humble, so fair and just. His conscience is always alert! He demands to know if a story is true, or if a person is good. These are important questions to him. His conscience reprimands him when he misbehaves, and, little by little, as he learns, [pg 44] his Will begins to help him and he learns to have self-control over his own life. We teach the child to say his prayers without realizing how real his prayers are to him.

3. Motives For Learning

Now put a teacher in front of a class full of little persons who each have their own beauty and their own wide soul. The teacher will wonder, 'What do I have that I can offer them?' His boring run-of-the-mill lessons are seen to be as useless as dust when he realizes what children truly are. He won't be able to go on offering them his stale lessons. It feels wrong to bore them, or to use unworthy goads like greed or competition to motivate the very minds that his lessons have dulled. He must not be like Timon, who sent invitations to a feast where he served only warm water. The teacher knows that children's minds get hungry regularly, just like their bodies. But their minds don't hunger for dry facts and information, they crave real knowledge. The teacher knows that his own collection of knowledge isn't enough to satisfy them. His own lectures don't have enough substance, and his interjections disrupt the child's train of thought. In other words, the teacher isn't enough.

Yet, children lack an extensive vocabulary, and the background of concepts gained from familiarity with culture, especially children from the inner city. Children's minds have been compared to a large pitcher—roomy enough to hold a lot, but with a narrow neck that only lets in a trickle at a time. And so education has tended to dilute teaching so that it's as sparse as lukewarm dishwater. And, as a result, the pitchers go away still unfilled.

But now that's all changed. During the war [*WWI*], we saw large hearts and patriotic spirits revealed in our soldiers. In the same way, our schools have revealed that each child is a person of infinite possibilities. When I say 'each child,' I include mentally challenged children. They are not an [pg 45] exception. I am familiar with some experiences of the Parents' Union School. I have just seen selected exam papers from tens of thousands of children from elementary schools, secondary schools, and homeschools [*correspondence schools, many using CM-trained governess/tutors.*] The children have relished knowledge! Their answers are so good and interesting! They spell and write so well! We don't need their teachers to tell us how much the term's work was enjoyed. Their enthusiastic narrations speak for themselves. Every one of these children knows that life offers hundreds of interesting arenas for the mind to roam in. The children are good and happy because care has been taken to understand what children truly are and what they need. This care has been very amply rewarded by results that change the entire outlook of education. In our Training College [*Scale How, where teachers and governess/tutors learned how to teach and train children*], student teachers aren't taught how to hold children's attention, how to keep order [*crowd control*], how to grade papers, how to discipline with punishment or even rewards, how to manage a large classroom or a small one-room school with children of all different grades. When teachers understand what children are capable of and what they need, these things take care of themselves. To hear inner-city children telling about *King Lear* or Scott's *Woodstock*, by the hour if you let them, or describing Van Eyck's *Adoration of the Lamb* or Botticelli's *Spring* in minute detail, is a surprise. It's a revelation! We stand amazed—we had no idea it was in them, whether we're parents, teachers or onlookers. And with this feeling of awe, we'll be better prepared to think about how children should be educated, and what resources should be used. Let me add that all the claims I make have been substantiated with thousands of instances just in our experience alone.

[pg 46]

Chapter 3 - The Good and Evil Nature of a Child

Principle 2. Although children are born with a sin nature, they are neither all bad, nor all good. Children from all walks of life and backgrounds may make choices for good or evil.

1. Well-Being of Body

A well-known educational specialist has accused us of bringing up children as 'children of wrath.' He's probably exaggerating, because the opposite view, perceiving children as perfect little angels, is just as dangerous. The truth is, children are very much like ourselves. They aren't that way because they've become so. No, they were *born* that way. They have tendencies and dispositions towards good and evil, just like us. And they have an interesting intuition about what's right and wrong. This indicates some influence of education. There are tendencies towards good and evil in body, mind, heart and soul. The hopeful task before us is that we might strengthen the good in us so that the evil is crippled. This can be done only if education is subservient to religion. We are no longer merely concerned about saving our own souls, but our religion is more open-hearted and responsible. Our religious thought now encompasses our whole community, nation and race. It's time for our education to reflect that. [pg 47]

When we acknowledge that education is the birthright of all children simply because all humans deserve to know, rather than thinking of just our own child, or the privileged children of the upper classes, we have a sense of openness. It's as if we can breathe more freely. The prospect is exhilarating. Recognizing the potential in every child, regardless of his social status, should revolutionize education and make the weary world rejoice.

Doctors and physical specialists say that all newborns [*except those born with birth defects?*] begin healthy. A baby may inherit a predisposition for lung disease, but he is not born sick with the disease. It is our job to see that conditions keep him from ever realizing the disease that he has a tendency toward. [*Having a predisposition for TB doesn't doom you to actually ever having TB!*] In the same way, all possibilities for good are contained in the child's moral and intellectual capacity. But every potential for good may be hindered by a corresponding tendency to do bad. We begin to see what we need to do. It's up to us to know our child, to know what his passions and weaknesses are. We need to discern the pitfalls that his traits might lead him to, and the wonderful possibilities he might have if his better tendencies are allowed free reign to make his path through life smoother. No matter how disappointing or repulsive a child's failings might be, we can be encouraged with the certainty that, in every case, the opposite tendency is there. We just need the wisdom to figure out how to bring it out in him.

Mothers come by this kind of wisdom more naturally than outsiders, such as teachers. Of course everyone knows of at least one exception—there's always one parent who can't do a thing with their child and hopes that the teacher can whip him into shape. But how often we're surprised to see that Robert and Polly are more themselves at home than they are at school! Perhaps that's because parents know and love their children better than anyone else. Therefore, they believe in them more, since our faith in possibilities, both divine and human, grows as we know more. For this reason, it's good for teachers to get some understanding of the human nature that's in every child. Everyone knows that hunger, [pg 48] thirst, rest, and virtue are given by nature to help the body grow and function. But every child has tendencies to greed, restlessness, laziness, and corruption. Any one of those vices, if allowed free reign, can ruin the child, and ruin the man he'll become.

Even the five senses need some guidance and practice. Smell in particular can be developed to give subtle pleasure by being taught the habit of discriminating the wonderful smells of the field, garden, flower, fruit just for their own enjoyment, and not indulging a child's personal preferences. Pampering the sense of taste too much can rule a person and limit what he enjoys. But there isn't a lot of new information to learn about the body and its senses. Education already trains children's muscles, cultivates their senses, orders their nerves. And it does this for all children, both rich and poor, because, in our day, we understand that development is good for all children. If there's any lack in the physical side of education, it's in the area of steadying the nerves. We forget that the nutrition, rest, fresh air and exercise that benefit the whole body are good for the nervous system, too. The undue stress from a small child being pressured to carry a cup of tea without spilling, or, later, cramming for an exam, may be the cause of a nervous breakdown when the child is older. We are becoming a nervous, stressed nation. Although golf and baseball may do something for us, a careful education that stays alert to avoid every symptom of stress from too much pressure will go a long way in making sure that every child has a healthy body and good amount of endurance.

One trap that brilliant teachers can fall into is not realizing that an overwhelming personality can exhaust children. Children are such enthusiastic, affectionate little souls that a teacher who gives them approving nods, coaxings and insincere smiles may lure them like the Pied Piper. [pg 49]

But the teacher needs to beware. Relying on the teacher's personality to win over students is likely to suppress and subdue the personality of the children. Not only that, but children can become so eager to live up to the demands of their teacher that they become stressed under the influence of the charming personality of a teacher. This kind of subjection was the subject of a recent novel about the German *Schwarmerei*. In this story, an unscrupulous but fascinating mistress used her charm with disastrous results. But the danger isn't with extreme cases. A girl who adores her teacher so much that she kisses her door, will forget that teacher someday. But the parasitic habit has been formed, and she will always need to have some person or some cause to give her life purpose. It isn't just female teachers who do this. Ever since the Greek days when youths would hang around their masters in the walks of the Academy, there have been teachers who have undermined the stability of the boys they were supposed to be devoting themselves to. Were Socrates' countrymen entirely wrong about him? The most noble minds who have the most to give seem to have a tendency for this kind of weakness. Therefore, it's important for those of us who teach to have a general understanding of human nature.

2. Well-Being of Mind

We tend to believe that we have an inalienable right to say whatever we want, and think whatever we want. We think that, although the body is limited by physical laws [*such as gravity*] and our affections, love and justice are under moral laws, our mind is ours and ours alone. Maybe this is why we tend to neglect our intellect. We don't realize that the mind, like the rest of us, has its own tendencies towards good and evil, and every inclination it has towards good can be hindered [pg 50] by a corresponding inclination towards evil. I'm not talking about moral evil. I mean the intellectual evils that we're slow to define, and careless about dealing with. Teachers need to realize that, no matter how dull and inattentive a student may seem on the outside, his intellect is alive inside him. Every child in the classroom is capable of being stirred by the wonders of science. Every child is interested in the stars of the winter sky. One teacher said, 'Child after child writes to say how much they loved reading about the stars.' An eleven-year-old girl says, 'Sometimes when we're walking at night, I tell my mother about the stars and planets and comets. She says she thinks that astronomy would be very interesting.'

But we take a fascinating topic like astronomy, and teach it by emphasizing heat and light, using devitalized text books, diagrams and experiments that seem like white magic to children. The invisible microscopic world fascinates children as much as the universe. They love learning about the behavior of atoms and ions as much as they enjoy fairy tales. History, with its collection of interesting characters, is as good as a story because children can picture the scenes in their minds. We make a big deal about the costumes, tools and other details about historic periods. But children just need a few appropriate and exact words about the subject and they can envision it in their heads. In fact, with the lively imagination that comes with their intellect, they can picture long movies about it!

Children are amazing in the way they can take examples offered to them, and make them their own. When a child hears that Charles IX was 'feeble and violent,' he'll always remember that characterization, and he'll learn a lesson about self-control. We shouldn't point out the moral of the story. That needs to be done [pg 51] by the children themselves, and they do it on their own every time. What we think may be too difficult doesn't seem to affect them. One teacher wrote about her eleven-year-old students, 'They can't get enough of Plutarch's *Life of Publicola*. They always groan when the lesson is over.'

I've said a lot about history and science, but math appeals directly to the mind and, although it's as challenging as scaling a mountain, it can be just as rewarding. Good math teachers know not to drown lessons in too many words. What about literature? Introducing children to literature is like planting them in a rich, glorious kingdom, or like bringing a continuous vacation to their doorstep, or laying an exquisite feast before them. But the way they need to learn about literature is to be familiar with excellent examples from the beginning. A child's relationship with literature needs to be with good books, the best available. We've always known that this is the best thing for children of the educated classes, but what about children who live in situations where books aren't commonly owned? One wise teacher in Gloucestershire said that, in dealing with this problem, we need to realize two things—

'First, defining and explaining hard words is a distraction and an annoyance to the child. Second, explaining may not even be necessary. Even though a child may not know the exact meaning of a word, he may have no problem understanding the sentence or paragraph. He may be able to get enough from context to even use the word correctly in his narration. I saw two examples of this last term. One boy in Form IIB [*about grade 4*] was never considered an unusually intelligent child. In fact, by his age [*maybe 12?*], he should have been two Forms higher. Last term, during the story of Romulus and Remus, I noticed that in his ability to narrate, and his degree of understanding by sensing a paragraph and converting it to his own words, he was ahead of his class, and even ahead of most students in the next higher Form.' [pg 52]

The Headmaster of A. said, 'What has surprised us most is the prompt way in which the boys absorb information and get interested in literature, and I mean the kind of literature that used to be considered inappropriate to teach to elementary-aged students. A year ago, I would never have believed that boys could read Edward Bulwer-Lytton's *Harold: The Last of the Saxon Kings*, Charles Kingsley's *Hereward, the Last of the English*, or Sir Walter Scott's *The Talisman*, and enthusiastically enjoy it. Or that they could understand and enjoy studying Shakespeare's *Macbeth*, *King John* and *Richard II*. But experience has shown us that we have underestimated the abilities and tastes of the boys. We should have known them better.'

That's the most serious accusation against most schools. The teachers under-estimate what their students will like, and what they can do. As far as intellectual things, children have extraordinary possibilities for good—even mentally challenged or learning disabled children. The possibilities are so great that, if we were smart enough to let them use their heads, the children would carry us along as easily as a gushing stream.

But what about the opposite intellectual tendencies—the possibilities for evil? One of those tendencies dominates many schools in spite of teachers' best efforts to rouse the slumbering minds of their students. But, the harder the teacher works, the more careless the students become. So the teacher prods them with grades, competition for first place, and the threat of exams is always dangled in front of them. The result is some haphazard effort, but no living, vital response. Although the students may enjoy school, and like their teacher, and look forward to lessons, they don't really have a passion to know just for the sake of knowledge—yet that's the kind of enthusiasm that schools ought to be producing. I can think of two sure-fire ways to guarantee carelessness in a class. One is a teacher who constantly lectures and won't stop talking. We all know someone in person who bores everyone by always explaining and clarifying. What makes us think that children aren't just as bored by that? They try to tell us that with their wandering eyes, listless expressions and fidgeting hands. They're using every communicative aspect of their body language to tell us, and kindly adults simply assume that it means the children just want to play or go outside. But it isn't play [pg 53] they need; they only need to play some of the time. What they really need is knowledge expressed in literary language. The chatter of their smiling, pleasant teacher leaves them cold. And there's another practice that we think makes learning easier, but that unwittingly contributes to mental lethargy. We take pride in reviewing and going over and over the material to be sure that the students get it. But that kind of monotony is deadly to children's minds. One child wrote, 'Before we had these living books, we had to keep reading about the same things again and again.' Isn't that true? In the homeschool, children are still using the same books that their grandparents learned from, and public school text books might be bought used with the names of a half dozen previous students crossed out! And what about compilations used in elementary schools that aren't living books, but aren't textbooks either? No wonder Mr. Fisher, when he opened a public library, said that he'd been surprised and distressed when visiting elementary schools, that he didn't see anything in them that he would call a book. He couldn't find any books that could charm, enlighten or expand the imagination. And yet, he said, the country was full of artists and writers. If we want them to really grow, we need to realize that they aren't like cows who chew the cud—not physically, and not mentally. They can't be continually rehashing the same tired old material without deadening and paralyzing their minds. Intellectual life and growth requires continual forward progress and new information.

When it comes to the mind, habit is useful as a tool, but shouldn't be the rule that drives curriculum. It has been trendy to focus teaching on specialized skills [*such as magnet schools that focus on specific subjects like science or math?*], but that's a bad idea. It's not good for people to focus too long on one topic. For example, we shouldn't be too preoccupied with our daily affairs and routines to broaden our minds with outside interests and pursuits. And it's possible for a person to become interested in some great subject [pg 54] and to throw himself into it until he's so focused on that subject that he can't function outside of it. Darwin, for instance, lost himself in science to such an extent that he couldn't enjoy anything else. He couldn't read poetry, or appreciate art, or meditate on the things of God. After a lifetime of focusing on science, his mind was unable to think about anything else. In the great and free age of the Renaissance, great things were done, great pictures were painted, great buildings were designed, and great discoveries were made. One single man might be a painter, an architect, a goldsmith, and a scholar at the same time. And all that he did was done well, everything he learned was assimilated into his daily thinking and enhanced his enjoyment of life. Giorgio Vasari wrote about Leonardo Da Vinci:

'He had a divine and wonderful mind. Since he was excellent at geometry, he was able to sculpt and prepare many architectural plans. He designed mills and other engines powered by water. Painting was his life, and he studied drawing by observing real objects from life.'

Leonardo knew nothing about our recent popular phrase, 'art for the sake of art.' Neither did Britain's Christopher Wren, who was also a great mathematician and knowledgeable about many things. Architecture was just one of his many interests, yet he built St. Paul's Cathedral in London. How sad that his idea to plan London so that it would be beautiful and spacious was rejected because it would cost too much to carry out! And we also reject the minds of our country's children because we're too stingy. Their minds could make their lives more fulfilling, more useful, more filled with beauty, with very little cost to us. It's good for us to realize that education is something that continues throughout life. We must always be learning more and increasing our knowledge.

Of all the ways we hinder mind growth, perhaps the most subtle way is with comprehension questions. It's no different than expecting a child to show us [pg 55] how his food is being digested at all different stages after dinner! Requiring that of a child wouldn't help his digestion. In fact, he would starve! The mind is the same. It needs its food, and it needs to be left alone to assimilate and digest knowledge on its own. If a child seems capable, we assume he has more depth than he really possesses, and we ask him ridiculous questions that bewilder him: 'If John's father is Tom's son, how are Tom and John related?' A shallow child can guess the answer and impress everyone. Yet we use tests like this to produce youth who are quick at trivia, but have no ability to reflect and no intellectual pursuits. All they know is how to look cool.

The imagination can become like the filthy cave that Ezekiel mentioned. There were all kinds of ugly, evil things in there. It might be like a temple where the Self is glorified, or a chamber of horrors. But it doesn't have to be, it might also be like a beautiful house. The imagination stores all kinds of images. Do we want its walls to be adorned with images from the movies, cheap novels, shocking pictures? Or great art, and visions inspired by the works of Homer and Shakespeare? One man's imagination became obsessed with the Sphinx!

These days, uneducated people admire Reason above everything else, and their reason leads them to make mistakes. Students need to be able to spot faulty logic. Even more important, they need to know that Reason is man's servant, not his master. A person can take any idea and, once he decides to believe it, his reason will find logic to justify his choice—even a bad choice, like mistrusting a neighbor, being jealous of his wife, doubting his faith, or even having contempt for his country.

When we understand this, we can see how men found plausible logic to justify going on strike after two workers were denied access to a [pg 56] meeting. We can see the unfairness of denying the men access, but people tend to confuse reason with what's right, and the workers thought that one unfair incident gave them the right to protest by striking. The only way to keep a nation morally and economically strong against fallacies that threaten to undermine it, is to provide education for everyone, the kind of education that encourages them to reflect and compare while providing enough information on which to base sound judgments.

What about what Coleridge called the aesthetic appetite? Much of the appreciation for culture depends on it. But it is vulnerable. Without beauty to feed on, it becomes empty and dies. It needs to feed on beauty—beauty in words, art, music and nature. The purpose of our beauty sense is to open a paradise of beauty for our enjoyment. But what if we grow up admiring the wrong things? Or, even worse, what if we grow up believing in our arrogance that only we and those just like us know how to discern and appreciate beauty? An important part of education is being exposed to lots of beauty, and learning to recognize it and being humble in its presence.

3. Intellectual Appetite

The physical body has natural appetites. Undue indulgence on any one appetite can ruin a person, but keeping them in balance brings health and strength. In the same way, our souls have natural appetites whose purpose is to make sure that we get the nourishment we need for spiritual or intellectual growth. Current educational practices make a serious mistake by latching onto these natural desires in inappropriate ways. Every child wants approval. Even a baby wants praise when she wears her new red shoes. Every child likewise wants to be first, to get some of whatever is offered, to be admired, to lead and manage others, to have companionship with peers and adults, [pg 57] and, finally, to satisfy his curiosity to know. Those normal desires are there, ready to act when needed. It's our job to work with them to educate the children. And we do make use of them—a little too well, and in all the wrong ways! We use children's desire to be first in a competitive way, so that the most assertive student, rather than the most capable student, takes first place. We use children's desire to get what is offered by offering public acclaim, rewards, prizes, and scholarships as incentives— which encourages children to be greedy. We play upon a child's vanity and desire to be liked by the teacher, and we create stress because the child tries too hard for approval. One might wonder what harm there can be in using the tools that are already there in the child's make-up. Even an athlete can damage the muscles he was born to use if he over-does it too soon. A boy whose ambition or tendency to admire is unduly stimulated will become a careless and weak person. But that's not the worst of it. We all crave knowledge as much as we crave bread. We all know how giving more exciting food can kill a child's desire for wholesome bread. The worst thing about tapping into other desires to motivate children to learn is that it kills the natural desire to learn for the love of knowledge. The excitement of finding out which should carry children eagerly through their school careers, and which should enhance them all their lives, is choked out. Instead of enjoying the pure act of learning, children cram to pass tests without really internalizing the knowledge. They do pass their tests, but they still don't really know. The God-given curiosity that should have sustained their learning for their entire lives doesn't even survive elementary school.

It has been proved that the joy of knowledge itself is enough to carry a child successfully and happily through all twelve years of school. Prizes, first place standings, praise, blame and punishment aren't needed to guarantee enthusiasm and an eagerness to work. The love of knowledge is enough. All of those other desires should play a [pg 58] part, but it seems like one or two desires are manipulated in excess of the others. The area of conduct gives all students an opportunity to excel, especially in team sports, where most of the natural desires are at work. But even in play, we need to be careful that a competive spirit doesn't overshadow the more important feelings of love and fairness. In class, the pure stimulation of knowledge itself should be enough to motivate students to pay attention and persist in completing their work. A student who is constantly winning prizes for being at the top of his class may be displaying greed, not a love of learning.

4. Misdirected Affections

Those of us who deal with children sense that they have more than intellectual minds and physical bodies. Whether we call it 'soul' or 'emotions,' we find ourselves appealing to that spiritual part that makes us who we are. We've probably never even taken the time to analyze and name the different emotions, and we might never have figured out that they all fit within the headings of love and justice. It is a glorious gift to be able to show love and justice in any situation. When such a situation arises, we have all the love and sense of justice we need to deal with it, we never run out.

This divine gift is something that teachers should consider. And they do, but in the wrong way. They point out the moral of stories with numerous clichés. They lead, teach, illustrate—and thus bore the delicate, sharp minds of their students. The area of feelings is where teachers should be more careful—they should be hesitant to praise or blame children in the area of feelings because students will either disregard their praise and blame, or else they will focus on it to the extent that it becomes their only motive for doing things—they [pg 59] won't choose to do something because it's the right thing to do, they'll do it to gain someone's approval.

Moral education, the education of the feelings, is too delicate and too personal for teachers to take on by trusting their own resources. Children can't be fed morals with predigested food as if they were pigeons. They need to pick and eat for themselves, and they do this by observing or hearing how others act. They need a lot of mental food dealing with conduct, and that's why so much poetry, history, fiction, geography, travel, biography, science and math are made available. No one knows which particular bit will ignite a spark in a child. A small boy of eight years old may come downstairs late for breakfast because 'I was thinking about Plato and couldn't button my shirt.' Another child may find his sustenance in Peter Pan! We don't know what will feed any particular child, but all children have complex, multi-faceted natures, so all children must read widely, and they must 'own' what they read in order to nourish their moral being.

What about morality lessons? They are useless. What children need is a lot of excellent moral food of many different kinds, and they'll extract moral lessons from it themselves. Every child is gifted with *Love* and is able to express it in all its possible manifestations: kindness, goodwill, generosity, gratitude, mercy, empathy, loyalty, humility, gladness. We adults are amazed when the most common child showers one of those manifestations of love on us. But all children have been provided with enough love to last their whole lives. Yet we adults are aware of how we've been tainted and tend to be ordinary and common. So, when it comes to teaching children morals, we don't trust ourselves. Instead, we draw on the rich resources of the best we can find in art and literature, especially the Bible, to teach children's delicate spirits about these most important issues. [pg 60]

St. Francis of Assisi, Collingwood, Hawaii's Father Damien, or one of our soldiers who was awarded for bravery, will inspire children more than any lectures and clichés of ours.

And there is another gift to help us live right which even the most neglected person or the remotest savage is born with: a sense of fairness. Everyone has justice in his heart. Even an unruly mob demands fair play, and everyone knows how children pester us with their accusation of, 'it's not fair!' It's important to realize that every person has, not only enough love to live a good life, but enough justice. Discontent and unrest in the masses, which grows as the result of wrong thinking and making judgments incorrectly, is not so much the fault of bad conditions as a misguided sense of justice with which every person is born.

Justice is another area that needs to be educated. But, all too often, schools fail to educate properly. The sense of justice is so strong that no amount of neglect or bad teaching can kill it, but if it's choked from its natural course, it spreads devastation instead of helping the child live a good life.

One of the most important tasks of education is teaching students to distinguish between their rights and their duties. We each have our rights, and others have duties towards us, just like we have duties towards them. But it's not easy to make someone understand that we have the same rights as everyone else and no more, and that others owe us only as much as we owe them. That principle is born within each of us, so it's within us to understand it and adjust our perception. But it doesn't come naturally—our eyes must be taught to see. And that's where education comes in. But if education isn't teaching students to understand justice as it relates to others, then it's useless. To think in a way that's fair and just takes knowledge as well as reflection.

Students must also learn that their thoughts are not their own. More about this is in Volume 4, *Ourselves*. What we think about [pg 61] other people can be just and fair, or unjust. We owe everyone we deal with a certain manner in the way we speak to them, and not saying the things we should amounts to being unjust to our neighbors. Truth, or justice in our words, is due from all people. It's a wonderful tool to be capable of discerning truth, but that tool is only available to those who are careful about what they think. Francis Bacon wrote, 'Truth, which only judges itself, teaches that questioning truth (which is the wooing of truth), or knowing truth (which is the presence of truth), and believing truth (which is the enjoyment of truth)—this is the highest good of human nature.'

If it's important for all students to learn justice in word, it's even more important to learn justice in action (integrity). Integrity on the job won't allow a worker to turn out shoddy work. A skilled worker without integrity will try to do as little as possible in his work time. A student may not be receiving a salary, but he does receive a reward in the form of support, the cost of his education and trust from his teachers and parents. He must not be careless and hasty with his work, or dawdle, or postpone, or cheat or otherwise shirk from his work. He must learn that his duty towards others is to resist stealing. Whether a man is a servant, a workman, or a wealthy white-collar worker, he should understand that justice requires that he have integrity in his honesty, and not have the kind of common honesty that 's dishonest when no one's looking. A good example of honesty and values is illustrated by George Eliot's character 'Caleb Garth' from *Middlemarch*.

There is one more area where broad-minded citizens of the future need to be taught justice: the area of opinions. Our opinions reveal how much integrity we have in out thinking. Everyone has many opinions, but whether our opinions are our own through the sincere process of working them out in our own minds, or popular notions we picked up from the media or our colleagues, shows how much integrity we have. A person who thinks out [pg 62] his opinions conscientiously with a realistic assessment of his own abilities, is doing what he ought. He is doing his duty as much as if he saved a life, because no duty is any more or less important than another.

If children need guidance to get them to think justly so that their opinions will be trustworthy, how much more do they need guidance so that they'll have just and fair motives—or, what we call sound principles? After all, principles are simply the motives that we give priority and allow to lead our actions and thoughts. It seems like we absorb our principles casually—we rarely even have any definite consciousness of them. Yet our very lives are ordered by them, for better or worse. This is one more reason why wide, carefully planned reading is useful. There are always buzzwords in the air: 'What's the use?' or, 'Nothing matters in the end,' and others. A vacant mind will latch onto these and make them the basis of thought and behavior. They will become the worthless principles that guide the person's life.

And this is one more reason why nothing in the world of literature is too good to educate children. Every wonderful story, enlightening poem, informational history, every glimpse into travel books and every discovery in the world of nature, is there to teach children. Maxim Gorky said, 'The earth belongs to the child, always with the child,' and there is truth in that.

We believe that the PNEU has benefited education by discovering that all children, including the mentally challenged, know what they need and are desperately eager to get the nourishment they need. They don't need to do any exercises to prepare themselves to take in this nourishment. A limited vocabulary, underprivileged home life, or lack of familiarity with books isn't a hindrance. In fact, those challenges can be strong motivators in the same way that the hungrier the child, the more readily he eats his dinner. This statement is not some idealistic [pg 63] opinion. It has been well proved in thousands of children.

Students in a poor school in the inner city are eager to tell the whole story of *Waverly*, and their tellings capture the beautiful language and style of the author. They talk about the Rosetta Stone and other artifacts in their local museum. They discuss Plutarch's *Coriolanus* and conclude that his mother must have spoiled him! They know every detail of a de Hootch painting by heart, or a picture by Rembrandt or Botticelli. They're capable of grasping the march of history, the flow of drama, the subtle sweet inspiration of a poet. But they won't learn anything that isn't presented to them in literary form.

Whatever they receive in literary form, they absorb immediately. And they prove that they know it by being able to tell about it confidently, clearly, and with charm and spirit. And these are the children who have been expected to learn from nothing but the three R's for generations! It's no wonder that juvenile crime is increasing. An intellectually starved child has to find some kind of food for his imagination, and outlet for his intellect. And, like an exciting movie, crime offers brave adventures.

5. The Well-Being of the Soul

Now we leave the outer courts of the mind and body, the holy places of the affections and the will (we'll return to the will later). Now we'll enter the holy of holies inside the person, where he serves God. We may wonder what education can do for the spirit of a child. 'What can outwit a man's understanding? What is out of the range of a man's thoughts, or out of the reach of his aspirations? It's true that his own ignorance baffles him. Even the wisest man is full of ignorance. But ignorance doesn't mean he can't learn. The wings of a man's soul beat impatiently against the bars of his ignorance. He wants [pg 64] out, he wants to be free to go out into the universe of infinite thought and infinite possibilities. How can a man's soul be satisfied? Kings have sacrificed their crowns because they want something greater than kingdoms. Profound scholars are frustrated by the limits that confine them to only dip their toe into the deep ocean of knowledge. No great love is satisfied with only loving. There is only one thing that can satisfy the soul of man. The things around him are finite, measurable and incomplete and his soul can reach farther than it can grasp. He has a desperate, relentless, unquenchable thirst for something infinite.' [*from Volume 4, Ourselves*] 'I want, I am made for, and I must have a God.' We need God, not the mere outer form of religion. Inside all of us we have an infinite capacity for love, loyalty and service, and we can't expend these on anything but God.

How do we plan education to prepare children to seek the God they need, the Savior who is all the help they'll ever need, the King who gives them all the joy they can hold, and who is worthy of their complete adoration and loyalty? Any words or thoughts we might have will be poor and insufficient. But we have a resource—a treasury of divine words that children can read and know with satisfying pleasure, and that they can tell about with beauty and relevance: The Bible.

One ten year old who read many books said, 'The Bible is the most interesting book I know of.' Little by little, children get what they need to know about God in order to fulfill St. Chrysostom's prayer, which is a part of the Episcopalian liturgy: 'Let us know Your truth while we're in this world.' Everything else that children learn gathers around the truth of the Bible and illuminates it.

Here's an example of how this kind of knowledge grows. I listened to a class of thirteen year old girls read an essay about George Herbert. The essay included three or four of his poems. None of the girls had ever read the essay or any of the poems before. They narrated what they [pg 65] had read, and, while narrating, gave a complete paraphrase of *The Pulley*, *The Elixir* and one or two of his other poems. They remembered every point that the poet had made, and they used his original words pretty freely. The teacher commented about one or two unusual words, but that was all. If she had tried to explain or enforce (in a way that wasn't reverently sympathetic and showed that she cared) then it would have been meddling. Interestingly, hundreds of students the same age in classrooms and home correspondence schools read and narrated the same essay and paraphrased the poems easily. I felt humbled by these children. I knew I could never immediately and quickly understand so many pages of a new book, especially if it included poems that were obscure and vague. This is how the minds of great thinkers enlighten children and help them grow in knowledge, especially the knowledge of God.

And yet this most important part of education is often drowned in a flood of words, or tedious repetitions, or chiding and reprimanding—all kinds of ways that result in the mind becoming bored, and the affections deadened.

I have tried to outline some of the possibilities for good in children, but, at the same time, corresponding possibilities for evil that are in every child. Children desperately need guidance and control, but, even more than that, they need the influence of knowledge to help them develop internally. I've avoided using technical terms and have used the more common words—body, soul, mind, spirit—because these words represent concepts that, although we can't define, we all can grasp. These ideas need to be the foundation of how we think about education.

We also need to be familiar with the raw material we have to work with if our education is going to be effective. So we need to know about children, and what [pg 66] they need—but not their needs based on how we can make them useful cogs in society's wheel, or based on the standards of the current culture. We need to know their requirements based on their personal potential and unique needs. We don't want to educate them towards 'self-expression.' After all, a young child doesn't have much to express yet, except what he's already learned from lessons or experience. Even if he's not yet accomplished at expressing originality, what he *can* do is take in and digest knowledge, and give it back in his own individual way because his unique mind has modified it and re-created it and made it 'his own.' This unique originality can be produced from the same mind food that everyone else is getting. It becomes original as it reacts on the unique mind of each particular child.

Education implies that the mind is taking in knowledge from the outside world. But if something causes the mind to draw inward for introspection or in self-consciousness, intellectual progress stops. You may have been disappointed that I haven't delved into current psychology. Undoubtedly the subconscious mind does exist somewhere between mind and body, where the mind submits to the physical body. The mind, by definition, is always and forever conscious, so talking about a subconscious or unconscious mind sounds contradictory. But psychologists mean that the mind is able to think in ways that we aren't conscious of, and they say that we need to look deep within ourselves and make ourselves aware of the nature of our subconscious and how it works. But that much introspection and self-occupation isn't healthy. So far, the results of this kind of study are not encouraging. They seem to be trying to tell us that the best that's within us originates in 'complexes.' We have a sensory complex, erotic complex, greed complex, etc. Even if these possibilities are safely hidden away within us, it seems dubious to nourish the mind so that the seed of base desires will bear beautiful fruit. This kind of research is undoubtedly fascinating, and may eventually contribute to education [pg 67] by adding a few interesting facts about the mind to our store of knowledge. But so far, such research hasn't improved the field of education. It's possible that the mind, like the body, has certain regions that were never meant to be touched. If we simply stick to those areas of the mind that we do know about, we may have enough information to come up with something we don't have yet: a Science, or, even more accurate, a *Philosophy* of Education.

[pg 68]

Chapter 4 - Authority and Docility

Principle 3. The concepts of authority and obedience are true for all people whether they accept it or not. Submission to authority is necessary for any society or group or family to run smoothly. (The third of Charlotte Mason's 20 Principles)

Since WWI, new discoveries don't excite us as much as they used to, but before the war, we were amazed at the wireless telegraph. To think that a message could travel through space unseen and unheard, and arrive almost instantaneously at another place seemed unbelievable. We were wise enough to value the discovery for its own sake, not just for its practical application. We were in awe at discovering a law that had always been there, but that we never knew about before. In a similar way, we were awed when our common soldiers fighting in France displayed amazing heroism—it had always been there, but now it was revealed to us. And now, discoveries just as exciting are waiting for us in the field of education. Any educational worker might be the one to make some startling new discovery that will enrich the world. In the Bible, the citizens of Genneserat made a startling discovery: they found out that Jesus spoke with authority, not like the scribes.

It's not for us to speak with that kind of authority. That supreme authority belongs to God. Yet, we do have some authority given to us. A person can be 'an authority' on a particular subject if he has studied the subject so much that he's made it 'his own,' and he has the right to speak about it. The ability to accept delegated authority seems [pg 69] to be imbedded in everyone, ready when needed. Benjamin Kidd once said that the London Police was the very embodiment of authority. Even strangers were surprised at how implicitly they were obeyed. Every king, every commander, every mother, older sister, school official, work foreman and team captain finds something within himself that ensures he will be faithfully obeyed—not on the basis of his own assets, but on the basis of the authority that goes with his role. Without this principle, society would fall apart. Practically speaking, there's no such thing as true anarchy (absence of authority). Rather, what we think of as anarchy is really just transferring authority, even if the anarchist finally submits to no other authority but himself. Some people say that authority leads to tyranny, and that compliance, whether willing or forced, is kin to slavery. But that isn't so. Without authority, there can be no freedom. Unless authority is abused, it exists in happy harmony to those placed under it. We're made so that, by nature, we like to be under some kind of order, even if it's circumstances that order our lives. Servants take pride in the orders they receive. Our badge of honor is called an 'order.' It's true that 'order is heaven's first law' [Alexander Pope] and order is the result of authority.

The principle working within us that makes us submit to authority is docility, or compliance, or teachableness. It is universal. Even if a man is too proud to submit to any other authority, he will still submit meekly to his fate, or his destiny. It appears that the very act of submission is as natural and necessary as reason, or imagination. The two principles of authority and docility are at work in each person's life to do the same thing as the two forces that keep the earth in orbit. One force draws the earth to the sun, the other pulls it into space. Between these two forces, the earth maintains a middle course and the world goes on. [pg 70] The principles of authority and docility are at work in every child. One draws him to an ordered life, the other pulls him towards rebellion. The key to raising children is to find the middle ground that will keep him in his proper orbit. The solution we have these days is freedom in our schools. Students should be governed, but so cleverly that they don't realize they're being governed. They should feel like the rule is, 'Do what you like,' but the moving force is really, 'Do as you're told.' The result is an ordered freedom. That kind of ordered freedom defines the lives of 999 out of 1000 citizens of the world. The only drawback is that, when indirect methods of securing compliance are used, children aren't really learning to be subject to authority. It just looks like they are. They're not learning the habit of proud subjection and dignified obedience, which is what sets great men and noble citizens apart. Undoubtedly, it's nice when children are natural and free to get up and wander around, or sit still, or play if they feel like it. But it's important for them to learn conscious, willing obedience. A great part of their happiness (and ours!) depends on obedience being pleasant and peaceful.

It's up to the teacher to secure willing obedience, not so much to himself, but to the school's rules and whatever the situation at hand calls for. If a student is supposed to read a certain passage, he obeys the bidding of that duty before him. He reads his passage with full attention and is happy to do so. We all know the sense of importance we have when we say, 'I have to be at Mrs. Jones's by 11:00.' 'It's necessary that I see Mr. Browne.' A person who doesn't obey the necessities of such situations has his life out of orbit and is useless to society. It's necessary for us to follow an ordered course. Children, even babies, should begin in the way they should continue to go. Fortunately, they come prewired with two inherent forces, centripetal and centrifugal. Those two forces bring about [pg 71] their freedom (self-authority) on the one hand, and 'proud subjection' on the other.

But parents and those who care for children have a delicate task. There must be subjection, but children should feel proud to submit. It must be a distinction, an accomplishment. The way to do this is to avoid coming between children and the laws of life and behavior that ultimately rule us all. The higher the authority, the greater the pride in obeying it. Children are quick to spot the difference between a teacher exercising his own arbitrary will and pleasure, and the submitted authority who is himself under a greater authority. The final tragedy for any country, family or school is when subservience replaces docility. Docility implies equality. There's no huge chasm between the teacher and student that makes one superior to the other. They are both pursuing the same ends. They are busy with the same task, enriched by mutual interests. It's possible that the pleasant quest for knowledge gives the only real freedom there is for both the teacher and student. 'He who the truth makes free is truly a free man.' The steady pursuit and delightful acquiring of knowledge give us freedom day by day. 'The mind is a world unto itself,' they say, 'it can make itself a heaven or a hell.' And what is a heaven of the mind, if not continually growing and expanding in an ordered freedom? And what hell is more restless and irritating than continually chafing against natural righteous order?

As far as the superficial freedom of sitting or standing or coming or going as one pleases, that usually settles itself, like all relations between teachers and students, once children are allowed to have some part in their own education. Their education isn't a benefit we bestow on them. It's a feast for them to take and enjoy. Our main concern, whether for the mind or for the physical body, is to provide a carefully planned table with plenty of delicious, healthy and varied food. [pg 72] Children will take what they need and deal with it for themselves in their own way. But their food must be served in its natural state, and without being predigested so that it's sucked dry of all of its stimulating, life-giving properties. No force feeding or spoon feeding is allowed! Hungry minds will come to such a table with the greediness of hungry little children. They absorb it, digest it, and grow and are enlarged at an astonishing rate as compared to children in schools where they regurgitate textbook lessons. When teachers avoid exhorting with lectures, students change their physical position if they need to, but they're usually so intent on their lessons that they sit still and are less inclined to mentally wander. But the physical body does get the exercise it needs because the teacher makes sure to include physical movement, whether it's games or calisthenics. But schools already know about physical education, so I'll just add that, although mental activity is good for the body's physical functions (an American discovered that people can live 160-1000 years if they continue to use their minds!!), the reverse isn't true—physical activity alone doesn't have the same effect on the functions of the mind.

These days, it seems like educators are mostly concerned about making it easy for the mind to work. But I must urge that, while physical activities like hand crafts, gardening, dancing, etc., are useful to train the nerves and muscles to be ready and responsive, *physical exercise does nothing to keep the mind alive*. We also must not put the focus of children's education on drama—even when it's Shakespeare—or poetry—even when it's beautiful, lyrical poetry. Yes, children need these things, but they come into the world waiting to connect with lots of different things. They need to establish relationships with places far and near, with the expanding universe, with the long-gone days [pg 73] of history, with current social economics, with the earth we live on and all of its delightful plants and trees, with the affectionate families who love them, with their home country and foreign countries, and, most of all, with the highest of all relationships—their relationship with God. With all these things to learn about, only the most ignorant teacher will let his students spend most of their time on math, or crafts, or singing, or acting, or any one of a hundred specialized subjects that try to pass for a complete education.

Children need to have a sense of *must*. It's a mistake to give children the impression that they're the only ones who have to obey a higher law, while grown ups can do whatever they want. The teacher or parent whose children pester for permission to do this or that, even though it's against the rules, has only himself to blame. He has given the impression that he, as a person, has the authority, rather than given the impression that he's a person *under* authority. Therefore, children think that it's okay to break the rules so long as their well-being isn't jeopardized. In order to guarantee proper submission to authority, two things are required. If these two requirements are met, there is seldom a conflict of wills between adult and child. The conditions are (1) The adult can't be rigidly arbitrary, but must give the impression of being so much under authority himself, that the children sense it and understand that he, too, has things he has to comply with. In other words, they need to see that the rules weren't made for the adult's convenience. (I'm assuming that everyone who is entrusted with the teaching of children recognizes that we are all under God's authority. Without that recognition, I don't see how it's possible to establish a healthy relationship between teacher and child.) (2) Children should understand that they have the freedom to [pg 74] put to use whatever they learn in any way they choose, without the teacher's interference. Children will choose, and they will be glad to do their work. Therefore, there's no need to use coercion or pep talks to try to gain their cooperation.

But the principle of docility/authority is inborn in children. When teachers use tact and judgment to help students put this principle into use properly, children will be prepared for their future duties as citizens of society and contributing members of their families. The trend to have students serving in positions of authority in their schools [*such as elected class president*] shows that schools recognize the importance of teaching students about docility and authority. It allows children to become familiar with the idea of representative authority because they are governed by chosen members of their own group. It's a form of self-government. To make full use of the educational opportunity of this practice, the student officer should be elected and voted on by the children, and they should be encouraged to think carefully about their choice. But this allows only a few to experience what it's like to be in a position of authority. Even more should be done to teach children this concept. Every classroom should have small offices that can be rotated for students to vote on. Many times, a person will rise to the office he's given, and, often, even incompetent students will do very well at the duties they're given.

All school work should be done in such a way that students are aware of their responsibility in their own education. It's their job to know what's been taught. We all know from experience how we tend to skim halfheartedly over daily news when we know it will be repeated in a weekend edition. And if there's a monthly review, we only skim the weekend edition! These crutches make us feeble-minded, unable to remember and prone to wandering attention. In the same way, repeating and reviewing lessons shifts the responsibility of learning from the student to the teacher. It tells the child, 'I'll make sure you know it.' So students don't put forth any real effort to pay attention. And the [pg 75] same dry lessons are repeated again and again, and the children get bored and restless, and that's when they get into mischief.

Teachers tend to belittle their high position and obstruct the process of education because they cling to two or three fallacies. (1) They regard children as inferior, and themselves as superior beings. Why else would they be given the position of authority as a teacher? If they only realized that children's minds are as potent, or even more so, than their own, they wouldn't see their mission as spoon-feeding their students, or predigesting it to make it tolerably understandable for their students.

(2) Another way we belittle children is when we're convinced that they can't understand a literary vocabulary. So we explain and paraphrase to our heart's content—but it doesn't do them any good. Educated mothers realize that their children can read and understand almost anything. They don't offer explanations unless they are asked to. All this time, we thought that the children of educated parents were bright merely because they inherited intelligence.

(3) Another misconception we have concerns attention. We think that we have to capture children's feeble attention with persuasion, dramatic presentation, pictures and visual models. But the fact is, a teacher whose success depends on his charismatic personality is merely an actor who belongs up on a stage. We now know that attention is not one 'faculty' of the brain and it's not a definable power of the mind. It's the ability to turn on that power and concentrate [*it's not something the brain **has**, but something it **does***]. By attempting to capture a child's attention with gimmicks, we waste our time. The ability to focus the attention is already there in a child, as much as he needs. It's like a forceful river just waiting to obey the child's own authority to turn on. Yet it's capable of stubbornly resisting attempts to be coerced that are imposed from without. What we need to do is to recognize attention as one of the appetites. Then we'll [pg 76] feed it with the best we have in books and knowledge. But paying attention is something that children have to do on their own. We can't do it for them. It's not for us to be the fountain of all knowledge—we don't know enough, we don't speak well enough, we're too vague and random to cope with the capability of creatures who are thirsty for knowledge. Instead of pretending to be the source of their education, we must realize that books, the very best books, are the source, and we must put that resource into their hands, and read them for ourselves, too.

(4) One final fallacy that hinders our work as teachers is undervaluing knowledge. It's currently characteristic of the British to belittle knowledge. One well-known educationalist recently nailed up a thesis about what children need from education. The list included only two items: Children need to know a skill to earn a living, and children need to know how to behave as a proper citizen. The writer of the thesis apparently doesn't realize that the quality of a man's work is directly in proportion to how much of a complete person he is. The more broadened a person is, the better his work will be and the more dependable he will be. Yet we remove the humane influence of literature from common education, and it's that literature which results in efficiency. One school with 9,000 adolescent students has its students attend in batches of a few hundred at a time so that they can rotate and learn various skills and crafts. But in three years in this school, students don't spend even one hour learning any kind of humane knowledge. The reading and thinking that's left out is the very thing that should be making these students better people and better citizens!

But, to get back to the topic of attention, it's more than a convenient, almost miraculous way of covering the material and getting the students to learn a surprising amount of knowledge, and to retain it. All of this is very good, but employing attention is even more than that. It's a foundational principle that's vital to education. In focusing his attention, the child takes on responsibility for himself. He uses the authority [pg 77] within himself in its highest function: as a self-commanding, self-compelling force. It's delightful to find that we can use an ability that we have within us, even if that ability is only being able to toss and catch a ball in a cup a hundred times as Jane Austen did to amuse her nieces and nephews. To make yourself pay attention, and make yourself know—this is a remarkable power to have! And children feel even more delight in being able to do this because they have the double satisfaction of enjoying the knowledge they gain from lessons, which satisfies their inborn curiosity.

Here's a note that just arrived as I was writing this. It's from the mother of an eleven year old girl who's just spent a couple of days visiting London:

'My mother took her to Westminster Abbey one afternoon. I was tucking her in and she told me all the things she had noticed there that she'd been learning from her lessons about architecture that term. She loves architecture. She also said she was anxious to see the British Museum. She wants to see the things there that she heard about in her term's lessons [*probably from Frances Epp's book about The British Museum*]. So, the next morning, we went there. We spent lots of time in the Parthenon Room, studying the things there in great detail. She was such an interesting companion, and she taught me so much! We also went to St. Paul's Cathedral and Madame Tussaud's, where she was excited about seeing so many people from history. The modern people didn't interest her as much, except for Jack Cornwell and Nurse Cavell.'

Notice that this girl is educating *herself*. Her companions merely take her to places where she can see the things she knows about, and she tells about the things she's read. That's such a different approach from pouring information down the throats of less lucky children who are taken to these kinds of places.

Recently the King and Queen visited the British Museum, probably also to see the Parthenon Room. A group of London school children were there. They were as full of information and as interested as the girl in the letter. They had been doing the same kind of lessons as she had. It's wonderful when children know that the very things that interest them also interest their country's leaders. This is the kind of bond that unites societies. One of the main purposes of a [pg 78] 'broad education for everyone' is to form links between the educated and the uneducated, the rich and the poor, the elite and the common people. They can all share the strong affinity for the same knowledge, and it will give them something in common. Our public schools have done this by using classic literature. An occasional quote from Horace moves and unites the House of Commons, not just because the poetic words are moving, but because the quote is a key to other associations. If this can be done with a quote in a dead language, what possibilities for common thought and universal wellsprings of action might be the result of reading our own rich, inspiring English literature?

Imagine what this kind of power to pay perfect attention and remember everything could mean for every employer and leader! What an asset that would be for the entire country! This week I heard a Colonel say that his second-hand man was an old PUS boy (Parents Union School student), and we hear this all the time. There aren't too many people who don't struggle with the effects of inattention and forgetfulness in their employees. We envision a world of surprising achievement when all children have been trained to have quick comprehension and can remember instructions.

We must not masquerade in front of our children, or pride ourselves on collecting knowledge so that we can deliver it as if it emanated from ourselves. There are people who have earned the right to lecture because they've devoted their lives to some specific subject, or maybe written a book about it. Lectures from experts like that are full of insight, power and imagination, just like their books. But we don't have very many of those kinds of people in every school to lecture on every subject. Even if we did, it wouldn't be the best thing for the students. The teacher's personality would influence them to distraction so that they weren't able to focus fully on the pure delight of the knowledge itself. And it's the knowledge which is in itself enough of a compelling force to capture their perfect attention and settled behavior. [pg 79]

I'm not advocating a place like Samuel Butler's Erewhon, where citizens were forbidden to get sick. I'm not talking about some unreal Utopia in Dreamland. We of the PNEU seem to have discovered a very real force that's capable of sending forth a new generation with the resolve:

'I will not cease from mental strife
Nor shall my sword sleep in my hand
Till we have built Jerusalem
In England's green and pleasant land.'

So many schools are doing such amazing things. We are educating our teachers to have lots of enthusiasm and dedication. But what seems tragic is that, after 8-12 years of the most brilliant teaching that public education has to offer, students graduate and are content to let the latest movies, football games, or car races satisfy their need for mental stimulation. We are so sad when we see a war hero with a limp, useless hand or leg, or with a reconstructed artificial jaw or nose. But many of our young graduates go around even more seriously maimed than that. They have absolutely no intellectual interests. History and poetry bore them. The latest scientific research is only a little interesting. Their job and their social life are all that life has to offer them.

That kind of maimed existence where a person goes day to day without learning anything new or using his mind is a cause for concern to those who are interested in education. They know that education is second in importance only to religion. Education has to be the servant of religion.

[pg 80]

Chapter 5 - The Sacredness of Personality

Principle 4: These principles (authority and submission) are limited by the respect due to the personality of children, which must not be encroached upon whether by the direct use of fear or love, suggestion or influence, or by undue play upon any one natural desire.

All too often, children are used as pawns for pet agendas, which change all the time. We need a better method of education. We need an accurate understanding of children—we need to realize that, whether they're brilliant or slow, or advanced or challenged, they are first of all, complete persons. Gifted children's abilities will be nurtured and slow children will advance; all children will benefit from this kind of education, as I've said in previous chapters, regardless of their inborn intelligence. Our job is to seek a greater understanding of what the person is. What we *do* grows out of what we *think*, and which foundational concepts we adhere to. If we seriously consider personality, we'll come to see that we cannot allow ourselves to damage or crush or suppress any part of a person.

Yet we have many clever and even kindly ways of doing this, and they're all based more on less on ego. Our own conceit persuades us that we're superior only as long as the child is dependent on us. Everything we do for the child is out of our grace and favor, and we adults have a right to do whatever we want with our own children or students. But we need to consider that, in God's eyes, children have a higher place than adults. We are told that we need to [pg 81] 'become as little children,' they aren't told that they need to be more like grown-ups. The rules God gives us for bringing up children are mostly negative: Don't despise them, don't hinder them, don't offend them with our harsh, clumsy acts or lack of thought. The only positive rule we have is to 'feed' (or, 'pasture') 'my lambs.' We are to place them in the middle of an abundant supply of food. A Yorkshire County teacher renders this concept as, 'I left them in the pasture and came back and found them eating.' In other words, she left her classroom during a reading lesson, and, when she came back, they were still happily reading with interest. 'Our utmost reverence is due to the child' means more than we give it credit for. We think it means that we shouldn't do or say anything inappropriate in front of children. But it also suggests a profound, reverent understanding of what children are like and the possibilities within them.

We don't need to be discouraged at the task before us. Our greatest fault, the fault that makes us unable to treat children as we should is the one that the Bible warns about. We are not simple [*transparent and sincere?*]. We fill our roles and manipulate children in ways we shouldn't to motivate them. Perhaps the teaching sin we most condemn isn't the worst one after all. Perhaps the terror of 'Mr. Creakle' [*David Copperfield*] isn't so bad as the more subtle ways we use to undermine children's personalities. I'll only mention a few examples, but I think they'll give the general idea. For an example of using fear as a motive, the best example is David Copperfield (which is a great commentary about education). Mr. Creakle gives a great picture of fear in the classroom, and Mr. Murdock gives a great picture of fear in the home. But, possibly through Dickens' influence, fear is no longer accepted as the foundation of school discipline. Now we have [pg 82] more subtle methods than mere fear of breaking the rules. One of these methods is love. A teacher with a charismatic personality can charm students into doing anything for the teacher's sake. The children are affectionate and enthusiastic in everything. They're so submissive that their very personalities are buried, and they live for an approving smile, and are devastated when their adored teacher shuns them. Parents smile approvingly and think that all is well, but Robert or Melissa is losing that opportunity for growth that should be making them self-dependent and self-ordered. Day by day, they are becoming more like a parasite who can only go on when they're carried along. They'll be the easy prey of any fanatic or zealot. This intrusion on children's love turns the motive into 'do this for my sake.' Students avoid doing wrong so they won't grieve the teacher, and they do good to please her. To win the teacher's approval, a boy will learn his lessons, behave properly, be cooperative, display all kinds of virtues. Yet his very character is being undermined.

'Suggestion' is even more subtle. The teacher has become an expert about what motivates human nature, and knows how to make suggestions that relate to any one of them. He might not bribe with lollipops or scare with threats of a boogeyman. His suggestions have a more subtle, spiritual flavor. He can alter his suggestions to fit a particular child's individual idiosyncrasies. The method of suggestion is too subtle to illustrate well. Dr. Stephen Paget says that suggestion should only be used like a surgeon uses anesthesia [*in small doses*], but it's such an easy tool to use. Rash suggestions play on a child's mind like wind spins a weathervane. The poor child is doomed to be unstable, constantly changing. After all, how can a child have stability of mind and character if he's always influenced by constantly changing suggestions? But, someone might say, that may be true of rash, unconsidered suggestions. What about carefully planned suggestions that lead a child in the direction of producing perseverance, [pg 83] sincerity, courage, or any other worthy virtue? No, the child is even worse off in that case. When a specific virtue is used, he begins to hate that virtue, and to be disinterested in all virtues. He isn't developing any strength of character to stand alone. Instead, he waits for someone else to prompt him. Perhaps the most serious harm is that every time a person receives a suggestion, he's more likely to accept the next one. Respecting children's personalities will make us dread doing anything that might make them incompetent to live their lives well. We won't want to use such a dangerous method of motivating, no matter how attractive the immediate result may seem.

Influence is related to suggestion. It doesn't work so much by a well-directed word or coaxing action, as by a kind of atmosphere that comes from the teacher and surrounds the students. Late in the last century, moralistic books were written about influence—the beauty of influence, the duty of influence, learning how to influence. Children were brought up to think that influencing others deliberately was their moral duty. Undoubtedly, we all do influence each other. It's impossible for us *not* to affect one another, not so much by what we say or do, but by what we are. In that respect, influence is natural and healthy. We absorb influence from real and imaginary people, and we're kept strong by currents and counter-currents of influence we aren't even fully aware of. But submission to one single, constant, persistent influence is a different thing altogether. A schoolgirl who idolizes her teacher, or a boy who worships his school master, is deprived of the chance to live freely and independently. His personality fails to develop and he goes out into the world as a parasitic plant, always clinging for support to some stronger character.

So far we've considered unintentional ways of invading on a child's right to his own personality. But there some even more pervasive ways of [pg 84] stunting children's intellectual and moral growth, although they may not be as damaging. Our whole school ethic and school discipline rests on unfairly manipulating certain innate drives in children. Remember that the mind, like the body, has its own appetites, or desires. It is as important for the mind as it is for the body to be fed, to grow and to be productive. If the body never felt the pangs of hunger, it would never think to eat. In the same way, the mind needs those appetites to ensure that it seeks its food. So it's not such a bad thing for teachers to make use of children's natural desires in their education. The problem is when teachers stimulate the *wrong* desires to accomplish their end. There is the desire for approval, which even a baby shows. He isn't happy unless Mama or his daycare giver approves of him. Later, this desire for approval will motivate him to conquer a math problem, or climb a challenging hill, or bring home a good report card. All of those things are beneficial and help the mind to grow, because the people whose approval he wants have his best interests at heart. They want him to learn and know, to conquer laziness, develop habits of persistence in work, so that his inner self is as healthy as his outer body. But how unfortunate that vanity often goes along with the desire to be approved of. It can make a boy more concerned about impressing the cool young teen at the gas station than winning the approval of his respected teacher. In fact, this desire for approval may become such an obsession that he can't think of anything else. He feels that he *has* to have approval, whether it's from someone worthy of his respect, or someone totally worthless and lacking in character. Some acts of violence, robbery, even murder, happen just because someone wants infamy, in the same way that some good deeds have been done for the sake of fame. Infamy and fame are similar in that both mean being thought about and talked about by a lot of people. And we're all familiar with how the natural desire for approval is manipulated by the media. They report about a movie star one day, a [pg 85] spy the next day, or a hero or scientist for us to admire and applaud.

Emulation, the desire to be the best, can work wonders in the hands of a teacher. Indeed, this natural desire can be a powerful motivator to intellectual and moral effort. When two or more students are trying to outdo each other in virtue, the school gains a better atmosphere, and parents are justifiably happy to send their children to that school. But when it comes to academics, the desire to be first is dangerous. The worst thing that's happened to our schools is that many are practically ruled by grades, prizes and place ratings. A student can become so caught up with an obsession to win that he can't think of anything else. It isn't what he's learning that interests him, he's only doing his work to get ahead of the others.

But the competitive desire to win doesn't rule by itself in our schools. Another natural desire whose most straightforward name is avarice works alongside competitiveness. A small boy understands before he even enters kindergarten that his duty is to win a scholarship to an exclusive boarding school—perhaps justifiably, if his family won't be able to afford to send him to a good school any other way. Sometimes wealthy students get scholarships, but generally they go to those for whom they were intended, such as children of families who work for the ministry and have very little money. The scholarship program is really just a way for rich people to help out those less fortunate. Every prep school offers its own scholarships, universities have open scholarships and sometimes wealthy treasuries for the benefit of students. A free, or affordable education is available to most upper middle class students, if they're intelligent. No wonder every prep school and private boarding school for teens bases its curriculum on scholarship requirements. They know exactly what [pg 86] score in which subject will guarantee a scholarship to a particular school, they know precisely which students have a chance of winning the scholarship, and they arrange the term's work with that end in mind. It's hard to say what arrangement would be an improvement, yet I believe that deliberately 'teaching the test' is disastrous. It's inevitable that some students will suffer a lack in growth in their inner persons because of the limited intellectual study. They didn't learn because they loved knowing during their school days, and, as a result, in adulthood, they are shallow-minded and make judgments on a whim.

It's no use fighting a system from without when that system is somewhat effective at helping with the education of our future leaders and workers. But England needs to do to more. Many of the students could be more than they are. But change needs to come from within, from within the school, and what needs to happen seems obvious: make better use of the time allotted for 'English.' Most schools spend 11 hours a week in the lowest grades on 'English,' and 8 hours in the highest grades. 20 or 16 consecutive readings could be scheduled in that time, and the readings could be from a wide selection of books: literature, history, economics, etc. The books could be read with concentrated attention so that only one single reading would be necessary. Narrating from the readings might be useful for those students who need practice in public speaking. With just this one minor change in a way that wouldn't take any more time, our schools could graduate more students who are well-read, informed and better public speakers. Even if this kind of change were applied only to 'English' classes, then schools would no longer be places merely for cramming to pass exams. Students would be infected with a love for knowledge, and their natural inclination to collect things would be redirected. After all, what's more delightful to hoard than knowledge?

I won't take too much time discussing ambition, or the desire for power. It has a role in every life. But the teacher must [pg 87] be sure that it isn't over-emphasized. Power is useful when it's used to serve others, but it's dangerous when abused for the sheer enjoyment of ruling and managing others. Just like all the other desires, it can ruin a life if it's allowed to take over. Mis-used desire for power accounts for half of the disasters of mankind. A person who's ruled by ambition would just as soon lead others in riot and disorder as in a noble effort for a good cause. Who knows how much of our labor unrest is due to ambitious men who just wanted to lead others, even if only for the excitement of rousing others? It feels good to say, 'I have them wrapped around my little finger.' But the over-worked school principal needs to be careful. If one capable, power-hungry person is allowed to lead the rest, he is cheating the others of the right to manage their own lives. No child should be allowed to step aside feebly to make room for a more controlling child to take over. That isn't just to protect the rights of the more submissive child. The stronger child's welfare should also be considered. If he's allowed to muscle in, he could become a mean, manipulative person. The teacher needs to find him a healthy outlet. Perhaps with her guidance, he can strive to master knowledge as a way of exercising his power rather than bossing others around. This gives him plenty of opportunity to control without infringing on the rights of others.

Another desire that teachers can direct is the desire for society. Craving companionship can result in mischievous boys, delinquent youths and gossiping girls. It's pure fun to mingle with our peers, but a lot depends on the people we choose to hang out with, and why we choose them. This is an area where students benefit greatly from guidance. If they are taught in such a way that they love learning for knowledge's sake, then they'll want to make friends who share that passion. That's how princes are trained—they have to know a little bit about everything. They have to know something about plants to be able to chat with botanists, some history to [pg 88] talk to historians. They can't afford to be around scientists, adventurers, poets, painters, philanthropists or economists, and be too ignorant to talk about anything more than the weather. They need to know foreign languages so they can talk freely with men from other countries, and to be familiar with classical references. These are the things to be considered when educating princes. But doesn't every boy deserve the same education, so that he can hold his own in the company of people in knowledgeable circles?

Some people complain about the rigidity of society's class structure. But some of that is the fault of ignorance that limits most people so that they can only talk with those in their own clique—soldiers with other soldiers, teachers with other teachers, students with same-age peers. It's a worthy goal for a child to want to feel comfortable in the company of people in the know.

We've considered several desires that stimulate the mind and save us from the danger of mental apathy. Each desire has its purpose, but could lead to disastrous results if allowed to dominate. The final desire we'll talk about, the desire to know, is often pushed aside in schools, and replaced with a competitive spirit, the drive to be first, or a greedy desire to have wealth and things. The God-given curiosity that should create a thirst to learn is reduced to a desire to know trivial things: What did it cost? What did she say? Who was with him? Where are they going? How many postage stamps in a line would go round the world? And curiosity is content with a few disconnected, incomplete useless facts. That kind of information can never nourish the mind like real knowledge does. But our concept of education is so confused that [pg 89] we've convinced ourselves that children are repulsed by knowledge like bitter medicine, instead of craving it like they crave delicious food. So we resort to grades, prizes, games, entertaining presentations—any trick to disguise learning. But anyone who willingly depends on crutches will never develop his legs. A person who persists in going around blindfolded will never be able to tolerate sunlight. A person who lives on pre-digested liquid food will always have weak digestion. And a student whose mind depends on the crutches of competition and greed loses the only efficient power that can truly develop his mind. The loss of a love for pure learning is the price that students pay when we use inferior means to motivate them. They won't read unless a test is coming up [*or, unless they get Pizza Hut coupons as a reward?*] They're good-natured and pleasant enough, but they lack interest in a wide variety of things, they don't have any noble guiding purpose, and they don't have as much compassion for others as a good citizen should have. Great thoughts and brave deeds are unknown to them, although the potential for them is still within them. They may yet display great acts like those we saw and marvelled at during WWI. But we can't depend on a major war to draw forth such characteristics from our youth. The world can't afford to lose that many lives again. So the stimulus that the war gave to spur men to great deeds will need to come from the routine of their education.

Knowledge itself is fascinating. All of us have the kind of 'satiable curiosity' that Rudyard Kipling's Elephant had, although we often content ourselves with scraps of information from the daily headlines. Knowledge is like mother's milk. It helps us grow, and the very act of ingesting it is satisfying.

The work of teaching can be simplified once we realize that children, *all* children, want to know everything about human knowledge. They have a natural appetite for whatever is set in front of them. When we realize this, our [pg 90] teaching seems like less of an effort because our convictions give us confidence. Richeliu closed the colleges in France, both Jesuit and secular. He wanted to prevent the 'mania' of poor people educating their children instead of focusing their time on training for jobs and war. This same 'mania' is still with us, not just with parents, but with children, whose hungry souls yearn for mental meat. But we starve them, not by closing their schools, but by giving them lessons that no living soul can digest. How tragic that teachers and students complain that schoolwork is monotonous. It's commendable that some teachers try to make education less drudgery with entertaining methods. But the mind doesn't live and grow on entertainment. It needs solid meals.

Under Mr. Household's direction, the teachers in Gloucestershire have fully committed to using the method I outline. It's tempting to use their experience for most of my proof that the method works. But they aren't the only ones succeeding. Hundreds of other teachers have had similar experiences and shared them when given the opportunity. We have discovered a power that has been like striking a vein of gold in the mines of the wealthy country of Human Nature. Our great discovery is finding out that children naturally take to literary expression. They love hearing it, reading it, and using it in their own tellings and writings. We should have known this a long time ago. All the old ballads and songs of the ancient wild warriors and barbaric kings have been thought too complicated for anyone but highly educated people to enjoy. But we'll soon see that only minds like a child's could have produced such fresh, finely expressed thoughts. Children have a natural aptitude for literature. Their inclination for it can overcome [pg 91] the challenge of the vocabulary without effort. Knowing that should direct the kind of teaching we give. It should rule out our constant chattering and lectures. It should also rule out compilations and textbooks. Instead, it should lead us to put real books in the hands of students, only literary books that are crisp and spirited, as literary work should be. Children's natural desire to know will do the rest, and their minds will feed and grow.

Remember that every time inferior desires are stimulated, the love of knowledge is suppressed. A teacher who motivates with grades and first-place standing might get the students to do the work, but her students won't love knowledge for its own sake. They won't develop that relationship with learning that will save their mind from stagnation in their adult lives. Monotonous drudgery goes along with all schoolwork that's been motivated with grades and standings. It makes students work mechanically. The promise of rewards won't carry a student through twelve years of school. One Prep School teacher said, 'It seems to be the rule that average students coming into a new school are put in classrooms beneath their ability. It's a common occurrence. When we send up new students, even if they're gifted in math or literature, or language, it takes a couple of years before they're doing even the same work they were doing when they left our school.' Boarding school teachers have the same problem, he says. 'At twenty, a student is climbing the same pear tree he climbed when he was twelve.' In other words, when schools teach to pass a test, lessons have to be narrow and mechanical. How else can the questions be standardized and grading be absolutely fair? But that's not real education. Real education means definite progress, continual advance day by day, and no re-covering of the same old ground.

Some people are uneasy about providing a broad-minded [pg 92] education for everyone, as it appears will happen. They're concerned that it might cause the kind of social upheaval that took place in the French Revolution. But this fear is unfounded, it's based on a misconception. The doctrine of equal opportunity for everyone is dangerous. From an intellectual standpoint, it means 'survival of the fittest,' and we've already seen how terrible that can be in practice. Those who have uneasy, ambitious spirits force their way to the top and monopolize all the opportunities. They dominate everyone else and think that no upheaval is too great a sacrifice to advance themselves and their desires. These are the kinds of people who come out at the top when exams are the standard of measurement. After ambition (and maybe greed) comes perseverance. Someone said about Louis XIV that these kinds of men promote what they do as if it was a great scientific theory, and set up their own character as if it should be the principle of government. But they're just psuedo-principles, they're not real, and they rouse the masses because they promise that every person will have power and position in the government. But if each man has power and position, then each position can't be very powerful. I suspect that our current labor unrest is somehow related to student habits of working for prizes and good grades. A student whose motivation at school is to be at the top of his class and get something out of it, is less likely to be a calm, well-ordered citizen who will help to unite society and do whatever work the government needs.

Knowledge for its own sake is pleasing because it's so fulfilling. When you see evidence that a student in your class shares your delight in knowing, and shares your pleasure in expressing what he knows, and shares your affinity for some wise philosopher or brave hero, you both connect and share a kind of bond. A student who has that kind of satisfaction from learning is less likely to have a compulsive need to be better than everyone else. It may seem overwhelming for an intelligent, conscientious teacher to realize all the factors that go into raising up a well-rounded citizen, and everything that needs to be considered [pg 93] for each student in their care. It's true that,

'Our souls within us can't spare even the tiniest part.
The smallest public good needs to have dignity within its reach.
It needs the enthusiastic cooperation of everything it can find, and everything it needs, if men are going to be raised from the mire of vulgar activities and have their hearts freed from the enslavement of utilitarianism.
We need inspiring impulses from the past if we're going to do any good at all in the future.'

And Wordsworth is right. In the great work of education, we can't afford to leave out any part of the soul. But if we make knowledge for its own sake the goal of our education, then every faculty, or power, of the soul will work together to the same end. We find that children are ready and eager for this challenge, and what they can accomplish will surprise us.

[pg 94]

Chapter 6 - Three Instruments of Education

1. Education is an Atmosphere

Principle 5. The only means a teacher may use to educate children are the child's natural environment, the training of good habits and exposure to living ideas and concepts. This is what CM's motto "Education is an atmosphere, a discipline, a life" means.

Principle 6. "Education is an atmosphere" doesn't mean that we should create an artificial environment for children, but that we use the opportunities in the environment he already lives in to educate him. Children learn from real things in the real world.

Since we can't motivate with intimidation, misguided affection, prompting with subtle suggestions, deliberately using our influence to pressure children, playing on any one of a child's natural drives, or competition, we are limited. We aren't free to use any and all means to reach our desired goal of educating the child. There are only three means left to us. If we study them carefully, we'll see that they really are broader and fuller than they sound. Let's consider the first of these: atmosphere. For over ten years, we've put our confidence in providing the perfect environment to maximize learning. Some claim that the right environment accounts for nine tenths of a child's education, instead of one third. The theory goes, that if a child is raised in the perfect environment, its influence will be subtle, but those first impressions will be permanent. And the result will be an educated child. Schools can include Latin, math, or whatever else is in the official curriculum, but that's less important because the child's real education [pg 95] came in through osmosis. Selecting the best color scheme, the most harmonious sounds, beautiful objects, and considerate people will make a child grow up sweet, reasonable, and in harmony with his world.

'Peter's nursery was like a dream, a perfect place for his little soul to blossom. His walls were warm and cream-colored, and his father had decorated them with the most charming pictures of trotting and jumping ponies, dancing dogs and cats, leaping lambs, and carnival animals. There was a beautiful brass fireplace guard. All the tables had rounded corners so he wouldn't fall and get hurt on them while learning to walk. The floor was a soft cork carpet where Peter could play with his toys. There was a red hearth rug for him to crawl on. There were scales right in the nursery to weigh him every week, and a growth chart to check his progress. There was nothing casual about Peter's early years.'

That's what H.G. Wells wrote in his book about education, *Joan and Peter* [1918]. It's an accurate depiction of how parents try to prepare the perfect environment so that their children will be well-educated. Parents make great sacrifices to provide the most educational atmosphere. One couple spent more than they could afford on a statue to put at the top of their staircase so that their son's mind would be broadened by seeing beauty every time he went upstairs. This sort of thing has been going on since the 1880's or so. As usual, Germany surpassed everyone else in this, as she does everything she passes on to the rest of the world. Probably all the highly educated youths of Europe were raised like this. And the result is the kind of neo-Georgian youths we read about in Punch magazine who have an air of weariness, superiority and smug self-satisfaction. Indian scientist Sir Jagadis Chandra Bose concluded this about nervous impulse in plants:

'A plant protected from the outside elements by glass may look healthy and thriving, but its higher nervous system is stunted. When a series of [pg 96] electric shocks is delivered on this barren, overfed plant, the shocks themselves create nervous channels and deteriorate the plant even more. In life, it's the shocks of adversity that mature a person, not sheltering the person from life.'

We thought that the realities of the recent war inflicted enough blows, but current education still duly administers the 'beneficial' blows of adversity to students. Maybe overzealous teachers and parents are wrong. Maybe they've misread their list of duties, maybe they've over-rated their own roles, maybe, in their enthusiasm, they've intruded on the personalities of children. It's not a carefully controlled environment that children need, with everything artificially manipulated to relate to each other. They need a real atmosphere that hasn't been contrived and organized by specialists. The ideal atmosphere is everywhere, all around the child. It's what he lives and breathes in already, as naturally as the air around him. It gets tweaked and personalized by the people and things it includes, it gets modified by events, it's sweetened with the love of those he knows, and is regulated and kept healthy with some common sense. We all know the natural lives that children live at home. Their household routine is set by their mother. They play with their father. They're teased and shown affection by their brothers and sisters. They learn from bumps and bruises. They learn to sacrifice by having to wait until the baby's needs are met. They role play by pretending the couch is a boat, or by making tents with the table and chairs. They learn respect for the elderly by visiting grandparents. They learn how to get along with others by playing with friends in the neighborhood. They learn how to be intimate by sharing secrets and love with the family pet. They like discovering where buttercups grow, and they're ecstatic to discover where the blackberries grow! And they learn about consideration for people of all classes and races from relationships with their superiors, and with the man who comes to mow the lawn, or clerks at the store, or anyone who crosses their path. Children are expert at striking up these kinds of friendships, and it's a valuable part of their education. [pg 97]

They do need some watchfulness and guidance, though, to be sure their relationships are healthy ones. No artificially created environment could possibly compare to the natural atmosphere of real life, which blows like a fresh wind over the child.

It's fine to take advantage of a child's atmosphere to help along his education, but there must be limits. The limits are for us, not for the children. The most important limitation is that we may not artificially adjust the child's atmosphere to prevent him from feeling life's blows, or shield him from his own circumstances. Children need to experience the real world and face life. They aren't fooled, anyway—if their parents are anxious or upset, children sense it in the air. 'Mama, Mama, you aren't going to cry again, are you?' and a child offers a hug to try to take away the trouble. These are the kinds of things that prepare children to deal with real life. We should not shield them in glass boxes. If we do, they grow soft and delicate and will never be strong enough to handle problems effectively. But parents must remember their roles. The parents are the ones in charge, and the children need to submit to them. Also, it's wrong for more capable people to dump their heavy loads on those weaker than themselves. In the same way, it wouldn't be right for us to put young children in the position of making serious decisions for us. Decision-making is one of the most stressful tasks in life, and young children should be spared from that weight.

A school setting offers less opportunities for adding the element of real life to a child's atmosphere. But atmosphere applies here, too. School lessons can be so watered down and sweetened, and teachers can be so smooth and condescending, that they encourage lazy thinking and moral dullness that's difficult for a child to ever overcome. The strong brace of truth and sincerity should be in every school. Here, the common pursuit of knowledge by both teachers and students helps. It creates a current of fresh air that even a visitor to the school can see in the intellectual growth and working morality in the faces of both teachers and students.

But not all schools are striving out of a pure love for learning. Some are working very hard, but their effort is motivated by a desire for good grades. When that's the case, [pg 98] children's faces aren't calm and happy. Instead, they're anxious, restless and worried. The children don't sleep well and they're irritable. If anything goes wrong, they fall apart in tears of frustration, or get sullen. They're more difficult to manage in general. When this is the case, there's too much stress in the environment, their atmosphere is too over-stimulating, and they can't help reacting to the strain. Teachers come to the conclusion that the work is too challenging. They remove one thing or another from the curriculum. Or doctors may prescribe that a student relax for a year by being allowed to run and play instead of doing his lessons. The poor child! At the very time in his life when he needs knowledge to sustain his mind, he's turned away from lessons and left to pick up whatever he can learn on his own. So his nervous condition gets even worse and the child is labeled as having a condition of chronic nerves. But the problem was never the work. It was the atmosphere in which the work was done. Sometimes the teacher is so worried about her students doing well that the class picks up on her stress. 'I'm afraid that X can't do his test. He loves school, but he bursts into tears when I give him a test question. Maybe I've demanded so much that I've turned him into an over-achieving perfectionist.' This was said about a seven year old! The poor child was taxed into over-exertion because moral pressure was used to motivate him. But we envision better things. We foresee happy days for children when all their teachers understand that the only exciting motivation that's necessary to get high quality work from each child, no matter how big a classroom may be, is the natural curiosity in each child that makes him instinctively love knowledge. The calmness and pleasure of schools who use this principle is a surprise to any visitor who doesn't realize that this is as normal as the contentment a baby gets from nursing and taking in the nourishment he craves.

There are two possible paths for us: (1) We can create a fragrant but stale hot-house atmosphere by modifying and controlling conditions. In this atmosphere, children grow well enough from all outward appearances, but they are weak and dependent. (2) We can [pg 99] allow children to experience real life as it comes, but with enough care not to allow too much to batter them. For instance, we don't have to abandon them to evil influences by allowing them to have bad friends.

2. Education is a Discipline

Principle 7. "Education is a discipline" means that we train a child to have good habits and self-control.

Unfortunately, education doesn't 'just happen' by taking a casual, careless approach to school. Both students and teachers are limited, and both need to apply some deliberate effort. Yet, with my approach, we can have a totally new point of view. If we can only allow ourselves to believe it, we really don't have to manipulate children to learn their lessons. Nature has already taken care of that. If the lessons are the right kind, children will enjoy learning them. The most strenuous effort comes when instilling good habits. But, even then, there is relief. Good intellectual habits form themselves if the appropriate curriculum is followed in the right way. And the right way is this; children must do the work for themselves. They need to read the assigned pages and tell it back. In other words, they need to actively engage their minds with a concerted effort to 'own' the knowledge. We all know the tragic waste of the copious amount of reading we've done that was simply forgotten because we didn't actively work to know it while we read it. Yet this kind of effort is as natural as breathing, and, believe it or not, just as easy. The ability to focus the attention at will is the most valuable intellectual habit there is. It's also what distinguishes an educated person. With practice it can become second nature, and [pg 100] a good habit can overcome ten bad natures. Imagine how much our workload would be decreased if those who worked for us paid full attention to instructions so that they remembered the first time. Paying attention isn't the only habit that grows when one applies himself to learning. The habits of appropriate and prompt speaking, of obeying, of cheerful willingness, and an unbiased perspective all come naturally to a person educated this way. The habits of thinking right, making sound judgments, tidiness and order naturally follow when children have the self-respect that comes from the kind of education that respects who they are.

Physiologists say whatever thoughts become habit will make a mark on our brain tissue, although the mark may not be something we can visibly measure. Whether the mark is tangible or not, we do know for certain that one of the most fundamental jobs of education is to teach children the right ways of thinking so that their lives will result in good living, usefulness, clear thinking, enjoyment of beauty, and especially, a life lived for God. We can't understand how spirit, which is intangible and invisible, can influence a real, physical brain. But we know that it does happen every time we see a dark mood manifested in a scowling face. And we see it in—

'A sweet, appealing grace
Approval given with assuring looks.
There's comfort in the face of one
Who finds peace in the gospel books.'

We all know how forcing ourselves to smile can lift us out of a dark mood.

'The soul doesn't help the physical body any more than the physical body helps the soul.'

Both the soul and body are tools to help lay down the tracks of good habits that make life run more smoothly.

In the past, children have been abused and tormented by conscientious parents and over-zealous teachers who attempted to force good habits [pg 101] into children with severe punishment. And some adults exploited children for their own selfish gain. Now the pendulum is swinging the opposite way and parents are often too permissive. We've forgotten that people need good habits to live well, in the same way that trains need tracks to run on. It takes careful planning to lay railroad tracks, and it takes planning to develop good habits. Whether we plan or not, habits *will* be established one way or another. But if we don't resolve to make life easier by establishing good habits of thinking right and acting appropriately, then bad habits of faulty thinking and wrong behavior will establish themselves on their own. And, as a result, we'll avoid making decisions, which will cause us to procrastinate even more until we end up 'wasting our days crying over all the days we've wasted.' Most children are raised to have a minimum of decent, orderly habits that keep him from being a total misfit. Consider the amount of work it would take if every act of taking a bath, brushing teeth, sitting at the table, lifting fork and spoon to the mouth, had to be carefully planned and thought through just to decide what to do next to accomplish the task! Thankfully, that's not the case! But habit is like fire—it's a bad master, but an indispensable servant. A likely reason for our second guessing, hesitation and indecision is that we never learned good habits to begin with. Our lives weren't smoothed by those who should have laid down tracks of good habits when we were little so that our actions could run along them effortlessly.

I don't think we need to list the specific habits that we should try to form. Everyone already knows what they are, even if most of us don't actually do them. We admire the tall, straight posture of a soldier, but we don't have the discipline to produce it in ourselves. We admire a lady who can sit elegantly through dinner and who prefers a straight chair because her muscles are so accustomed to sitting straight from years of discipline. Discipline is the only way to form a good habit, although it's usually internal self-discipline [pg 102] that a person has over himself. A certain amount of deliberate work in establishing good habits is necessary because of the conflict between good and bad habits. An easy, bad habit is always pleasant and more tempting, and it's uncomfortable and difficult to resist it. But we can be sure of overcoming our bad habits because, built into us, we have everything we need to learn whatever good habits of body and mind that we deliberately attempt to. We entertain the general idea, and that gives birth to the act of actually doing it. If we do the action again and again, it will become a habit. We've all heard, 'sow an act, reap a habit. Sow a habit, reap a character.' But we need to go even one step further back—we need to first sow the *idea* or notion that motivates us to act in the first place. A lazy boy might hear the story of the Great Duke who wanted to sleep in a narrow bed while on the battle field so that, when he rolled over in bed, he'd have to get up. The story plants the idea of getting out of bed promptly. But his teacher or mother will instinctively know when, how often, and in what creative way to repeat the story before the habit of promptly getting out of bed is formed. She knows that the motivation has to come from the child himself, a desire to conquer his own self that becomes an impulse of chivalry that he can't resist. It's possible to sow great ideas casually, and this may be the kind of idea that needs to be sown informally because, as soon as a child picks up on his mother's deliberate attempts to influence him, he may resist the whole idea. When the parent or teacher has an air of expectancy that makes good habit seem like a matter of obeying authority, the child won't be so resistant. But if a child has been trying to start his lessons on time, and is late one morning, a good-natured teacher who doesn't rebuke or require a penalty is teaching the child that it doesn't really matter. And the child begins forming the habit of being late to class. The teacher's mistake is in thinking that being on time is difficult for the child, so he overlooks it. But, really, having orderly habits allows a person to be free and spontaneous. [*Think how much free time one has when they stick to a schedule, but how tasks can overwhelm a person who doesn't plan time to do them.*] The only hard work of having a habit is during the first few [pg 103] times that the habit is done.

Imagine how painstakingly wearisome life would be if it weren't eased with habits of hygiene, tidiness, order and courtesy. If we had to make a decision about every detail of getting dressed, eating, going anywhere, life wouldn't be worth living. Even the most lowly mother knows that her child has to learn habits of decency. Entire routines of etiquette are learned because a slip in the area of protocol is embarrassing and no child has the courage to face that kind of humiliation. Physical fitness, morality and manners are mostly a matter of habit. Even some parts of a devout life can become habit, and can become a pleasure that brings comfort and support as we try to be godly, sober and righteous. We don't need to be afraid that teaching children religious habits will doom their relationship with God to an empty, mechanical routine as long as they understand the concepts that make the routines worthwhile. Listen to what De Quincey thought about going to church when he was a boy:

'On Sunday mornings I went to church with my family. It was a building in the ancient British style. It had aisles, galleries, an organ. Everything was old and distinguished, and the proportions were majestic. Every time we entered, and the people were kneeling during the service, or praying for all sick people and prisoners, I would secretly weep and raise my eyes to the upper stained glass windows. There I saw the sun shining through, illuminating a spectacle that not even the prophets ever experienced. I saw pictures of the Apostles who suffered trials on earth, and the beauties of nature on the earth, and martyrs who had endured persecution. And behind it all, in the clear center pane, I watched white billowy clouds against a deep blue sky.'

And the young De Quincey had visions of sick children that God wanted to help:

'These visions needed no outside support. Just a hint from the church service, a fragment of the fleecy clouds and the pictures on the stained glass windows [pg 104] were enough. God also speaks to children in dreams and unseen messages. But in solitude, especially as a still small voice heard in a meditative heart while hearing truth at a congregational church service, God communicates with children undisturbed.'

With this kind of testimony, confirmed by our own memories, we can confidently believe that Divine service is appropriate for children. It will be more appropriate as they develop the habit of reading beautifully written books that sharpen their sense of style and their unconscious appreciation of the beautiful articulated words in the church liturgy.

We have discussed how important it is to have good habits of mind, morality, religion and physical development. We've seen the disaster of children or adults who learn to think in such a rut that the mere thought of a novel idea makes them shiver like a hesitant swimmer on the steps of a pool. This danger might be avoided by exposing children every day to the wise thoughts of great minds, and lots of them. That way they can gradually gain confidence in their own opinions, without even being aware of it. If we fail in this duty, then, as soon as our children gain some freedom, they'll follow the first fad that comes along, then discard that for the next one. The end result is that they'll be ill-guided and wavering in uncertainty for the rest of their lives.

3. Education is a Life

Principle 8. "Education is a life" means that education should apply to body, soul and spirit. The mind needs ideas of all kinds, so the child's curriculum should be varied and generous with many subjects included.

We've left the instrument implied in the last part of the phrase, 'education is a life,' for last. I say implied because life can't exist by itself or support itself. It needs nourishment—regular, planned rations that are suitable for it, otherwise it will die. Everyone knows this about life. Perhaps the greatest discovery of the twentieth century will be the realization that the mind needs the same thing or else it will die. Food is to the body [pg 105] what gasoline is to a car. It's its only source of energy. When we understand that the mind, in the same way, only functions when it receives its fuel, then we'll see education in a new light. If the body is fed with pills and artificial food, it starts to deteriorate. One glance at a bunch of couch potatoes at a football game makes us wonder what kind of mental food those guys have been living on. In spite of big, burly bodies, they seem to be empty and depleted of life. The mind is only capable of handling one kind of food: *ideas*. It lives, grows and flourishes on ideas and nothing else. Mere dry facts of information are as unpalatable to the mind as sawdust is to the body. The mind has no more faculties to deal with improper food than the body does.

'What is an idea?' we ask, and we find ourselves plunged in a question too incomprehensible to answer. Our greatest thinkers, including Plato, Bacon, and Coleridge, concluded that ideas are living things of the mind. We talk about how an idea 'struck us,' or 'seized us,' or 'took hold of us,' or 'impressed us.' If it's a big enough idea, it might even 'possess us.' In other words, ideas seem to have a life of their own.

If we ask a person why he has certain life habits, or intellectual preoccupations, or dedication to a particular cause, or obsession with a hobby, he'll usually say that some idea or another struck him. The power of an idea is something everyone recognizes. What phrase is more common, or holds more promise than, 'I have an idea!' We all perk up and listen in eager anticipation, like trout attracted to an alluring fly. There's only one place where the attraction of ideas seems to have no place—our schools! Just look at any publisher's list of textbooks and you'll see that they're all barren, carefully drained of the least hint of any idea, reduced to mere dry, dusty bits of fact. Private boarding schools do a little better. The diet that their curriculums offer may be meager enough to [pg 106] starve the average child, but at least they offer a few ideas. Though sparse, they do offer a few of the best thoughts from the best minds to nourish the minds of their students.

Samuel Coleridge, in his book *Method*, has done more than other thinkers to give us our current scientific perception of what an idea is. Psychologists define ideas as *insolens verbum* ["*haughty, arrogant word*"??], a term that Coleridge came up with, but Coleridge preferred to show the mind's reaction to an idea. Here is what he wrote about the progress of an idea in *Method*:

'The event in human history that most impresses the imagination is the moment when Columbus was adrift on the endless, unknown ocean and first noticed the change of the magnetic needle. Many other instances have happened in history when ideas that were always there in nature were suddenly noticed by men hand-picked by God, as if unfolded in a divinely-scheduled sequence of discoveries, and those ideas resulted in changes that improved man's lot in life. Columbus had a methodical mind and his logic led him from the magnetic needle on a compass to its foundational idea, entitling him to the title, *promiser of kingdoms*.'

This shows how the origin of an idea fits interestingly with what we know of great discoveries and inventions. It does seem that God specially selected men to give those ideas to. It not only matches our understanding of the ideas in our own lives, but the origin of practical ideas as mentioned in Isaiah 28:24-29:

'Does a farmer always plow and never sow? Is he forever cultivating the soil and never planting it? Doesn't he finally plant his seeds for dill, cumin, wheat, barley, and spelt, each in its own section of his land? The farmer knows just what to do, for God has given him understanding. He doesn't thresh all his crops the same way. A heavy sledge is never used on dill; rather, it is beaten with a light stick. ... The LORD Almighty [pg 107] is a wonderful teacher, and he gives the farmer great wisdom.' [*NLT*] Here is what Coleridge says about the kind of ideas that infiltrate the atmosphere of our lives, rather than suddenly illuminating the mind in a lightbulb moment:

'An idea can exist in an obvious, tangible form, like the idea of a circle in a mathematician's mind. Or an idea can be merely an internal instinct, a vague longing towards something, like an impulse that fills a poet's eyes with tears.'

These indefinite kinds of ideas should draw a child towards things that are honorable, lovely and admirable. [*Phil 4:8, NLT*] They should not be offered on a rigid schedule, but, instead, they should be a part of the mental atmosphere that surrounds him, breathed in like the air around him.

It's scary to think that our flawed words and ways should be grasped as inspiration by children. But recognizing that fact will make us even more careful to avoid any corrupt, unworthy thoughts and motives in our interactions with them.

Coleridge goes into more detail about the kinds of obvious, definite ideas that are ingested as food by the mind:

'From the originating idea, successive ideas grow, just like a seed that germinates.' 'The lively soul-stirring events and images in the outside world around us are like light, air and water to the seed of the mind. Without the presence of them, the mind would rot and die.' 'The path of any methodical course can take many varying twists and turns, but each path has its own particular guiding idea at the head where it begins. Ideas are as varied in importance as the paths that come from them are varied and different. The world has suffered a lot recently because the natural order of science, which is necessary, has overshadowed everything else. Science is limited to physical experience, and has no business requiring that reason and faith meet its standards. But reason and faith are not physical. According to the laws of scientific method, they owe no obedience to the physical arena of science. Progress follows a path that starts at the head with the originating idea. As it sets out down the path, the mind needs to be alert to keep it from going off on rabbit trails. That's why [pg 108] different orbits of thought need to be as different from each other as the originating idea themselves.' (*Method*, by Coleridge)

Biological science is making discoveries that shed new light on the laws of how the mind works. We are returning to Plato's doctrine that 'An idea is a distinct presence that exists without our approval or consent. It is in unity with the Eternal Essence.'

I've repeated these Coleridge quotes I used in Volume 2 [*Parents and Children*] because his opinion confirms our own experience. This should be enough to make us reconsider the way we teach. The whole subject is profound, but it is also extremely practical. We need to get rid of the wrong theory in our minds that says that education's function is mostly a gymnastic procedure of drawing knowledge from students, without also putting some in. Our current emphasis on 'self-expression' has given new life to this notion. Yet we know that there isn't much inside us that we haven't received from somewhere else. The most we can do is to give our own individual twist to an original idea that's passed on to us, or apply it in a new way. We are humble enough to realize that all we are is torchbearers, passing on our light to the next generation in the same way we received it ourselves. Yet even we invite children to 'express themselves' about a tank or a Norman castle or the man in the moon. We fail to recognize that the charming things children say about things they don't know are not profound manifestations of self-expression. They're just a hodge-podge collection of notions they picked up here and there. It's doubtful whether original compositions should be required of children—their consciences are so sharp, and they're very aware that their material is borrowed and not really original. It might be preferable for them to read whatever they want about the subject before they write about it, and then give them liberty to write what they like about it.

When a child is very young, it doesn't seem to make any difference what philosophical idea we had when we educated them, whether we had the notion of filling [pg 109] a bucket, writing on a blank slate, molding a lump of clay, or nourishing a life. But as the child grows, we'll come to find that the only things that are assimilated into who he becomes are the *ideas* that fed and nourished his mind. Everything else is tossed aside, or, even worse, becomes an obstacle that can even harm him.

Education is a life. That life needs ideas to keep it alive. Ideas come from a spiritual place, and God has created us so that we get ideas in the same way we pass them on to others: by expressing them in talk, or printed words, or the text of Scripture, or music. A child's inner life needs ideas in the same way that his physical body needs food. He probably won't use nine-tenths of the ideas we expose him to, just like his body only assimilates a small part of the meals he eats. He's very eclectic—he might choose this or that. We don't need to be concerned about what he chooses, we just need to make sure that he has a variety of things offered to him, and in abundance. If we pressure him, he will be annoyed. He resists force feedings, and he hates predigested food. What works best is a mental diet presented in an indirect literary form. That's the way Jesus taught when He used parables. What makes parables so wonderful is that they are unforgettable, every detail is remembered, yet the way they're applied might pass and leave no trace in an unworthy person, no influence at all in the person. Jesus took that risk, and we must. too. We just might offer children a meal of Plutarch's *Life of Lysander*, thinking that the object lesson will show what a good leader or citizen should avoid—but the child may love Lysander and think his 'charming' ways are admirable! But we have to take that chance, just like Jesus did when he told the parable of the Unjust Steward [*Luke 16*]. One note: it seems like we need ideas to be presented with lots of padding, such as the way we get them from novels, or poems, or history texts written with literary style. Neither a child's body, nor his mind, can survive on pills, no matter how much research goes into formulating them. From a big, thick book full of living ideas, he may only latch onto a half dozen that speak to his heart and nourish his spirit. And there's [pg 110] no predicting which ideas will ignite a spark in him; they tend to come from unexpected places and in forms we never would have guessed. No person can force a portion of Scott or Dickens or Milton to inspire him and feed his soul. It's as the Bible says, 'Stay busy and plant a variety of crops, for you never know which will grow.' [*Eccl. 11:6, NLT*] One of the rash things we do wrong is in offering our own opinions to students (and even to other adults) instead of ideas. We believe that an opinion expresses thought, and that, therefore, it carries an idea. Even if it once did, the very act of crystallizing it into an opinion kills any life it might have had. John Ruskin said that a crystal is not alive. It can't feed anyone. We think we're feeding children when we give them our church's convictions, Euclid's theories, or history summaries. And then we wonder why they never seem to retain what they learn. M. Fouillee, who wrote Education From a National Standpoint, thought that the idea was everything in philosophy, and in education. But Fouillee barely touched on education's role in forming physical, intellectual and moral habits. Here's what he wrote:

'Descartes said that scientific truths are victories. If you tell students the key point in the victory, the most heroic battles in scientific discoveries, you'll get them interested in the end results of science. By getting them excited about the conquest of truth, you develop a scientific spirit in them. Imagine how fascinating math might be if we gave a short history of the major theorems of math. Imagine if the student felt like he'd witnessed the work of Pythagoras, or

Plato or Euclid. Or imagine if he felt like he'd been there with modern intellects like Descartes, Pascal or Leibnitz. Great theories would no longer be lifeless, anonymous and abstract. They would become living truths, each with a thrilling history of its own, like a statue by Michelangelo, or a painting by Raphael.'

This is a way of applying Coleridge's 'captain idea' at the head of every train of thought. An idea shouldn't be some stark generalization that no child or adult could [pg 111] feed on. Ideas need to be clothed with both fact and story. That way, the mind can do its own work of selecting what it needs and initiating a new birth of ideas from a collection of colorful details. Dickens' David Copperfield says, 'I was a very observant child,' and, 'All children are observant,' but he doesn't just state the fact as a dull fact, he lets us come to that conclusion ourselves by telling us many charming incidents.

There is more than one way to get from point A to point B. Everything I've said should reiterate my point: that varied reading, and lots of it, as well as people's ideas expressed in the various forms of art, are not an optional luxury to be offered to children when we happen to think about it. It is their very bread of life. They need it regularly, and they need a lot of it. This, and more, is what I mean when I say, 'The mind feeds on ideas and therefore, children should have a generous curriculum.'

[pg 112]

Chapter 7 - How We Make Use of Mind

Principle 9. The child's mind is not a blank slate, or a bucket to be filled. It is a living thing and needs knowledge to grow. As the stomach was designed to digest food, the mind is designed to digest knowledge and needs no special training or exercises to make it ready to learn.

Principle 10. Herbart's philosophy that the mind is like an empty stage waiting for bits of information to be inserted puts too much responsibility on the teacher to prepare detailed lessons that the children, for all the teacher's effort, don't learn from anyway.

I can't resist presenting Herbart's psychology by quoting this humorous bit by John Adams:

'We haven't been able to explain ideas by the mind, so why not flip it around and try explaining the mind by ideas? That's not quite how Herbart put it, to be sure. He's a German philosopher. It's true that he starts with the mind, although he calls it 'the soul.' But don't worry, the concept is just as ridiculous. This 'soul,' as he calls it, is no more an actual soul than it is a crater in the moon. The way he defines it, the 'soul' has absolutely no substance. It isn't even a trap that can catch ideas! Ideas can slip in and out at whim, or, more accurately, at the whim of *other* ideas. The 'soul' has no ability to invite, create, store or remember an idea. The mind has no say at all.' [*The Herbartian Psychology Applied to Education*] 'The 'soul' has no power or means whatsoever to receive or produce anything. So it's not even a blank slate because [pg 113] you can't leave any marks on it. It's not a substance, as Leibnitz said when he spoke of the mind being capable of some activity. Herbart's 'soul' has no ideas, feelings or desires of its own. It has no intuition, no thought, no laws of will or behavior, not even the slightest hint of predisposed tendency towards any of these things. The pure nature of the 'soul' is an unknown mystery, and will never be known. You can't even speculate about its nature, much less do scientific research on it. [*Lehrbuch zur Psychologie*, by Herbart, Part 3: p 152-153] A strong force of inactivity is the only power that the mind has. Yet it is subject to the effects of other forces. The only thing that can attack the 'soul' is ideas. Therefore, the mind must be made up of nothing but the ideas that have collected there.'

We can imagine what a struggle must ensue at the mind's doorstep among the ideas all jostling each other to get in, and for those lucky enough to squeeze in, to get the most influential spot in the front of the mind. It must be like people who edge their way into groups when society is in a state of anarchy. This behavior of ideas jostling to get into groups has a name: Herbart called it 'apperception masses.' Whichever group of ideas struggles and becomes the strongest mass gets to have its way and dominate the mind. We won't spend a lot of time in this book analyzing Herbartian psychology, even though his ideas have been very influential to education in a serious way. Our interest is in considering how practical it is when worked out while teaching real children. But before we determine how it does when put to the test, let's read what Professor William James said about psychology in general:

'When we talk about psychology as a science, we shouldn't assume that it means psychology has been proved by science. In fact, the reverse it true. As a natural science, psychology is very fragile, and metaphysical critics find leaks in every point. All of its foundational assumptions and information need to be considered in relation to things beyond the realm of psychology, and translated into other terms outside of psychology. In other words, the term is used hesitantly and with trepidation, not arrogantly. That's why it's so strange to hear people talk about 'New Psychology' with an air of finality and triumph, and to write books about the 'history' of psychology—while the real substance of what 'psychology' means is still so vague. Psychology has a strand of raw facts, a bit of [pg 114] gossip and debated opinions, a little classification and generalizations in its foundational description. But after all the research and theories, not one single law, not one single proposal from which any result can be definitely predicted, has been found.'

Yet Professor James went on to write a whole book about psychology, a very interesting book. And we'll do the same thing, although our foundation is made up of nothing more than the common experience of mankind, at least as common as the experiences of mind can be to all of us.

Herbart's ideas about psychology are enormously satisfying and appealing to teachers. Like any other group of people, they're naturally eager to make their profession look indispensable. Herbart's philosophy shows that every child is a new creation, able to be molded completely by the teacher. If the teacher just learns how to do it, she can gather the best collection of ideas in the most effective sequence so that they form groups to the best pre-ordered advantage [*unit studies*]. Then the job is done. In the student's mind, the strongest and most powerful idea masses take over, and, if the teacher has selected beneficial ideas, then, viola, the student is made into a full-fledged, educated man.

Here's an example of a week's schedule, assembled by a teacher to make the best use of correlating subjects to manipulate ideas into apperception masses: 'Math (Decimal fractions, simple equations, parallelograms), Science (latent heat), Domestic Skills (nerves, thought, habits), Geography (Scotland, industries in general).' Here's one for another week: 'Math (metric problems, four rules of symbols, sum angles of triangles), Science (machinery), Domestic Skills (circulation), Geography (sculpture of Britain).' Apparently the ideas in these subjects of study are more clever and limber than they appear, and are able to recognize and leap towards each other to form apperception masses on cue!

One popular educational expert gave a valuable introduction to Herbartian education. As [pg 115] an example, he wrote a unit study series of lessons for elementary-aged children titled, A Robinson Crusoe Concentration Scheme. It starts with nine lessons in literature and language arts. The subjects are things like, 'Robinson climbs a hill and discovers that he is on an island.' Then there are ten object lessons, including The Sea, A Ship from Foreign Parts, A Life Boat, Shell Fish, A Cave. The lessons don't show how these objects are supposed to be produced. The third series is drawing lessons, probably nine or ten, drawing a ship, an oar, an anchor and so on. The next series is on manual work, all involving Robinson Crusoe, building a model of his island, his house, his pottery. The next course of studies is for reading. There are lots of lessons taken from selected portions of Robinson and from 'a general reader about the items studied in the object lessons.' Then there's a series of creative writing assignments, where students write a composition based on the object lesson. The children would come up with sentences, the teacher would write them on the chalkboard, and each student would copy the completed composition from the board. Here's a sample: 'Robinson spent his first night in a tree. In the morning he was hungry but he didn't see anything around him except grass and trees without fruit. On the seashore he found some shellfish and he ate them.' Compare that with the prolific output of six and seven year olds working in our Parents Unions Schools. They can write about any subject they're familiar with. In fact, they can dictate their own compositions from pages they've heard read aloud just once directly from Robinson Crusoe—and I don't mean a children's edition, but the original.

Arithmetic also has its lessons with lots of simple mental problems dealing with Robinson Crusoe. The eighth and last series was singing and reciting such things as, 'I am king of everything I see.' 'Each lesson lasted about forty five minutes. [pg 116]

Generally, a unit study based on a book like Robinson Crusoe would last the entire year. Students in England seemed as eager and interested in studying Robinson Crusoe as the students in our German schools. One can easily see the wealth of material in the story to develop even more lessons.' One certainly does! The whole thing must be fascinating for the teacher. Ingenious plans to amplify a thing are always interesting when you're the one putting the time and work into it. And no doubt the children were thoroughly entertained. The teacher was probably at her best developing as much as she could from a little bit by her own sheer force. She was like an actress putting on a show and the children were spectators, as they would be at a puppet show or a movie. But one thing we can be sure of. The children developed a loathing forever afterwards, not just for Robinson Crusoe, but for every other subject dragged in to illustrate his adventure. Another unit study uses an apple to base a hundred lessons on, including construction of a paper ladder to pick the apples. But, for all this, not one of the lessons suggests actually eating the poor apple. We won't name the author of the Robinson Crusoe study because, as a Chorus in a Greek play would say, 'we cannot praise him.' But he has followed the Robinson Crusoe study with one about the Armada.

The well-intentioned, clever, hard-working teachers who create these concentrated studies have no idea that each lesson is an offense to young minds. Children are eager and capable of a wide range of knowledge and literary expression. But these kinds of lessons reduce their learning to senseless trivia and insipid, pointless drivel. They develop apathy that stays with them, and the mere mention of learning makes them anticipate boredom. Thus their minds wilt and deteriorate long before their school career ends. I've spent so much time on this subject because I, too, believe that ideas are the [pg 117] only proper diet to grow children's minds. We are more clueless about the mind than about Mars! The only way we can draw conclusions is by looking at results. And the results conclude that the mind is a living thing, a spiritual organism. (I don't need to apologize for calling a substance-less thing an organism, since Herbart made a greater contradiction by speaking of 'apperception masses.') Just like the physical body, the mind needs regular and adequate nourishment. This nourishment comes from ideas that are assimilated when the mental diet is enthusiastically devoured, and growth and development are the result under this kind of diet. The fact that children like lame, uninspired talk and insubstantial, insipid storybooks doesn't prove that it's good for them. They like lollipops, too, but they can't live on them. Yet some schools are making a concerted effort to meet the intellectual, moral and spiritual needs of children with mental candy.

Like I said before, the kinds of ideas that children need to nourish their minds are mostly found in books with literary quality. If children are provided with these kinds of books, then their minds will do the work themselves to sort, arrange, select, choose, reject, and group the ideas together. Herbart has the ideas themselves doing this work after they push their way into the mind. This isn't just a trivial difference. As a philosopher, Herbart's thoughts influence universal perceptions. Most schools probably don't consciously know that it's his philosophy they're adhering to, but they are, in England and elsewhere. There are many reasons why. His theory throws the entire burden of educating on the teacher. With so much responsibility, the personality of the teacher becomes a major force in education. This gives challenging, creative, interesting work to teachers who are very intelligent, devoted and have a passionate hope to leave the world a [pg 118] little better than they found it by raising children to a higher level. Surely this vision will be appealing to teachers. It appeals to educational boards and school principals, too. Think how much influence teachers have if they're seen as the fountain of all knowledge, and all they need to do is turn on the spigot and let the information flow forth from themselves. Responsibility is placed fully on the teacher rather than the student. Lessons become entertaining and fun in order to hold the students' attention. The popularity of jigsaw puzzles shows how much people like to put unlikely things together—such as Robinson Crusoe and lifebuoys! The teacher is encouraged by small evidences of success every day, success that she has caused by her own cleverness, skill and drama in drilling some point into her students. I say 'her' because women seem to excel in this kind of teaching, although many male teachers do quite well at it, too. And what about the children? They are entertained and enjoy the amusement. They like their teacher because she puts so much effort into attracting their attention. While all of this is happening, it looks wonderful, who could fault it? But later, thoughtful people become dismayed and anxious about this kind of education.

A lot has happened in the decade since Alexander Paterson alerted us to oppressive conditions in South London in his book *Across the Bridges*. At the time, England was pleased with the resulting reform they brought about. What holds more promise than a freshly educated, eager school graduate ready to make his mark in the world? But the reality of the work world was horrible, conditions were terrible. Young men would be lured into promising-sounding jobs that entrapped them like blind alleys until they were let go to face a life of unemployment and poverty, and most lost their integrity and character. What's the solution? The issue of conditions after graduation is being considered. [pg 119] We already have adult educational classes so that, even if a graduate loses his job, he can continue to learn something that might help him. But Alexander Paterson thinks those classes don't prevent the best graduates from ruining their lives. What about a decent enough youth who gets a steady job and goes to a technical school to get a higher paying career? William Pett Ridge wrote about such youths. A young man may get a better job by going to a technical school, but the training does nothing to make him a fuller, better person. He may continue to have simple ideas about things, lack of moral principle, not be interested in much of anything and content with base entertainment. Yet, deep down inside, he's a decent person. What a waste! An enrichment school could have taught him to make the most of all the possibilities within himself, and to enjoy the challenge of using his mind. But schools give:

'Too much learning, without requiring any effort on the part of the student. The teacher works too hard to use all her training and experience, but the student does nothing. If education is made too easy, then students are robbed of the active mental challenge of learning. Learning can be a difficult challenge, but the exercise teaches students to concentrate and to work independently. The student should be left alone with the book so that he's forced to put his whole focus on the dull words in front of him. There shouldn't be someone right there to paraphrase or make the remembering easier with memory tricks. A promising youth who graduates might get a job with the railroad. He'll be required to sit and memorize Morse code. Perhaps the only school work he's done on his own is reading some exciting poem, which hardly trains the mind to persevere when the work seems hard. He'll find it difficult to learn the code . . . . Silent reading is sometimes scheduled for a half hour, but it should be regularly scheduled because reading to oneself is much more valuable than listening to a read-aloud.' [*Across the Bridges*, by Alexander Paterson] What good does our current curriculum do for students? Read what Mr. Paterson wrote:

'What do our schools strive to teach students by the time they graduate? What kind of person do they aim to graduate? A look at the scheduled curriculum [pg 120] should reassure every disgruntled critic who complains that his tax dollars are paying for the luxury of French and algebra and violin lessons for elementary students. The curriculum was carefully planned so that a graduate would have enough knowledge of reading, writing and arithmetic and enough familiarity with English, geography and history to allow him to vote or read the newspaper or know a bit about what he's doing. But that's only secondary to the three R's. Teaching the three R's occupies fully half of the scheduled blocks of time on the curriculum. That must be disheartening for both the teacher and the student since learning the mechanics of reading, writing and arithmetic doesn't train or teach anything. Those are just the elemental skills one needs to do any real learning. In many schools, students spend two years or more going over the fundamentals, even after they've learned all they need to enable them to read, write words and count. If an intelligent visitor looks at the work of an average classroom, he will be impressed by the accuracy and neatness, but he will find that this high quality is merely an outward veneer. The handwriting may look polished, half the boys may turn in compositions with flawless grammar and spelling. But the visitor might notice what's missing—their ability to think and reason independently, the curiosity that drives them to ask questions and use their imaginations, hasn't even been stirred up. In fact, the image of such perfection may make the visitor suspicious about the foundational principles of the government's official curriculum. In private boarding schools, boys aren't trained to be lawyers, ministers or doctors. They're trained to be men. Once they've been taught to work systematically and think for themselves, they're prepared to learn whatever trade or take on whatever kind of life they need to. But our public elementary schools seem to aim at making boys clerks. After all, it's only clerks who need perfect writing and spelling skills and nothing else.'

The teacher's best qualities are really her greatest obstacles. Her flaw is in doing too much. Quoting again,

'The mental capacity of the average ten to thirteen year old boy is wasted, and it's a great loss to our country. Ten productive years at school could make up for the drawbacks of home life, and could reveal a clever mind ready to learn. Many opportunities are lost in the early years of school. But if those years are wasted after age fourteen, the damage is irreparable. The mind probably won't be challenged again [pg 121] and will shrivel into nothing more than a center of automated responses to appetites and sensations. 'Asia' is nothing more than a hard-to-spell word, even though at school, he had to memorize its ports and rivers. It's likely that a forty year old man has less vocabulary than he had at fourteen. When the mind shrinks, it loses its ability to feed and grow from life experiences. For most boys, only half of their capabilities are used in the career they end up in after graduation. The other half curls up and goes to sleep permanently.'

And here we have a gloomy prospect of more tragic waste to come in the future. We all praise the Fisher Education Act of 1918 [which raised the age of compulsory education] because we think it's important for children to receive education until they're 16, or even 18. The nation feels generous, and employers don't mind supporting the new law. If they have to wait a couple of years for new workers, they feel that they'll be compensated with better workers.

But I see pitfalls ahead. The only way to make this plan really work is to make the students spend eight hours at a private school. As Mr. Paterson said, those schools don't train lawyers, pastors, stockbrokers or bankers, or even soldiers or sailors, with specialized training for their job skills. Their conviction is, that if you educate a person, cultivate his imagination, train his judgment, and open his mind to wide interests, then he'll be ready to master any profession. At the same time, he'll know how to make himself useful, and how to find pleasure in the skills of observation that his study of nature has given him. He'll have interesting ways to spend his free time and he'll be a good neighbor and good citizen. Besides being able to earn his living, he'll be able to truly live.

Private schools do this. Various [pg 122] career fields have their share of men who enrich their profession, and who sacrifice their free time and money to serve their fellow man as local judges, church board members, committee members, peace officers when needed, and as politicians. They consider it an honor to be of service, and are proud to wear those titles. The hours of voluntary service throughout the country as well as services done for very little wages, justifies the vision of private schools. In fact, training men to serve is important because many of the duties done by volunteers aren't interesting enough for anyone to aspire to do for money. Our great politicians, church leaders, civil servants and government workers have gone above and beyond the call of duty.

How can we interest men of all classes in this kind of service? We know it can be done because, during the war, we saw it happen all the time. Any soldier had the potential to be a hero. The Army became a kind of private school, offering our soldiers more knowledge, broader views, lofty visions, duty, discipline and wonderful physical culture. Our men made so much progress in personal growth that, rather than picking up where we left off, we need to be careful that those men don't regress physically, morally or mentally in a retrograde movement. The downward slope is steep and slippery. We all know how easy it is to slip backwards down the path of least resistance. We can't afford to have another great war just to educate our people, but we need to find some way of instilling private school elements in our youth. Mr. Fisher's Education Act of 1918 provides a perfect opportunity. His act gives four more years to schools to work with students, and four years is long enough to educate them. It gives enough time to influence them with goodness and light. But we need to limit this education to our ideal purpose of making broad-minded men. Specialized vocational skills should be off-limits. [pg 123]

Special training for engineering, textile work, etc. is unnecessary. After all, every company knows that a responsible, promising student is easily taught whatever he needs to be a good workman. Look at the women who worked during the war. Technical and vocational schools aren't esteemed all that highly by companies on their technical merit. Students hired out of vocational schools are usually hired, not because their technical skills were so impressive, but because they showed some intelligence and potential to be trained to make a good worker. This is a good reason to make adult continuing education schools more like private schools. They should avoid teaching money-making skills. Denmark and Scandinavia have both tried educating their youth to satisfy their natural curiosity to know and their inborn desire for knowledge, instead of training them for some specific trade. They teach history, poetry, science, art, which every man instinctively does, and for the hundred years they've been doing this, their system has been so successful that they've become a good example for the rest of the world.

But Germany has gone after a different vision. Germany has been driven by the ideal of utility, placing value only on what's profitable. WWI has shown us just how useless an education is when is doesn't uplift the moral and intellectual part of students. Germany's education had no higher purpose than using students' skills to their best wage-earning advantage, and to benefit the State. So the country became morally bankrupt (temporarily, we hope) not just because they were in the war, but because their educational system ignored the spiritual needs of the students. If they addressed the spirit at all, it was only mentioned vaguely in a curriculum designed solely to make students useful employees. We should enlarge our vision and make our Continuation Schools more like private schools. We should strive to have a broad-minded People's University with thousands of campuses, all called Continuation Schools (the name is actually very inviting) so that, no matter where you live, there's one close by. [pg 124]

But some will protest that private university schools educate with dead languages—Latin and Greek. Our own criticism is that, no matter how wonderful ancient Greek and Latin literature might be, it shouldn't displace our own English literature. Whatever lessons might be learned from Sophocles, Thucydides, Virgil can be learned just as well from Milton, Gibbon, Shakespeare, Bacon and other great English literary thinkers. Knowledge communicated in our own common language is more easily accessible than knowledge that has to be discovered among a text in a dead language. This fact will help us make more efficient use of the short time we have. If students apply themselves with perfect attention, then more can be learned in 400 hours per year. But that can only happen if we're convinced that students really do have an inborn craving for knowledge of humanities, and if they read with total focus so that they really absorb what they read. Narrating will help them prepare for public speaking, which is a skill that everyone should have these days.

What's the alternative? A coordinated unit study like the one about Robinson Crusoe, but based on what some corporation wants. It might be a year learning about soap—how it's made, what it's made from, the history of the soap business, how soap is shipped to buyers, ways to use soap, how to fill out a soap invoice, different kinds of soap, ad nauseum. Iron, cotton, nails, pins, engines, buttons— every industry will offer its own brilliant lesson plans for unit studies. Those who advocate utilitarian education will be thrilled. The students will be busy and learn some practical skills and gain some wit. And what will be the end result? Two hundred years ago, when there was a movement to educate Europe's youth after the devastation of Napoleon's wars, we English got in on that. The current of thinking [pg 125] went in two directions from the beginning. One branch favored practical, materialistic education. The other favored spiritual education to develop the whole person. England, already growing in manufacturing, went with the first branch, favoring utilitarian education. Germany, France, Switzerland also favored utilitarian education. But the Scandinavian countries chose something different. They listened to Denmark's poet, Grundtvig, who earned the title, 'Father of the People's High Schools.' He said, 'spirit makes strength, spirit reveals itself in spirit, spirit works only where there's freedom.' Munich schools are the epitome of utilitarian education, and Germany's army morale is its crowning glory. But we are slow to heed their lesson. We have let efficiency take priority over individuality. We obsess over how a youth might be made most useful to society. But we don't seem to care whether he's the most that he can be for his own personal development. We rationalize that, if a person is trained to get a job, then he will be useful to the world, and isn't that the best thing we can do for an individual? We forget that Jesus said, 'Man does not live by bread alone, but by every word that comes from the mouth of God.' Some of those words are the truths clothed in religion, poetry, art, scientific discovery, and literary expression. These are the things by which we live, and in which our spirit flourishes. Spiritual life and growth needs ideas for its food, like the body needs bread every day. We will find, as one Swedish teacher wrote, 'just as fertilizing the soil provides the best conditions for growing seeds, a well-grounded education in humanities gives the best foundation for developing the person, whether he goes on to be a businessman or a farmer.' But we don't need to go to Sweden to find an advocate. We have an educational prophet of our own, Mr. Fisher, in England, and I'll close by quoting him:

'What about the content in education? What should be taught? [pg 126] I'll answer in the broadest way. During my afternoon reading, I found a very fitting quote in the letters of John Stuart Mill. It said,

'Whether poor or rich, nobody needs to be taught someone else's opinions. The individual needs to be taught and encouraged to do his own thinking. Physical science doesn't teach this, no matter how thoroughly it's learned.'

'Our country's youth won't be inspired to greatness by learning about economic doctrine or physical science. They can only be raised to a higher moral level if they receive ideas that stimulate their imaginations, inspire their characters, influence their souls. It is the task of all good teachers to bring those kinds of ideas to their students.

'Sometimes I hear that you shouldn't teach patriotism in school. But I disagree, I think that patriotism should be taught in the schools. What I mean by patriotism isn't blind devotion. I mean an intelligent appreciation of noble things in adventure stories, both in literature and in the country's history. Youths should learn to admire what's great when they're still school-aged. And don't forget that, for poor people, school may be the only place they learn such things.

'What I want is patriotism, but in a much broader sense than is normally taught. Of course, no country is perfect, one can find reasons to criticize any country. It's important that schools teach students to look with a critical eye. But before they learn the flaws of their country's institutions, and learn to criticize everything that's wrong, they should learn to recognize and admire what's good. After all, life is very short and we only have one chance to live it. In the few years we have, we should try to fill ourselves with love, admiration and uplifting pleasures as we can. If education is only used to train students to be critical and bitter, then they'll lose all of the sweetness life has to offer. We will have made them miserable for no good reason. Life has enough sorrow and hardship. We don't need to introduce it to young people too early.'

Note: Some educational authorities may decide to spend an hour or two each week on physical exercise or handicrafts. In that case, there will be that much less school time [pg 127] for reading. I suggest that, with free evenings, communities offer classes at the local club [*or YMCA?*] for military drill, calisthenics, gymnastics, dancing, singing, swimming, carpentry, cooking, first aid, sewing, weaving, pottery, acting—anything that will stir up the minds of its citizens. Nobody would be forced to go. The way clubs are already set up, social attractions are already in place to motivate people to participate. They already have things like public recognition and prizes. Students who have spent part of their day at the adult continuation schools will bring their new knowledge to these classes, making them more interesting. Every community should also have outdoor sports on Saturdays.

I have urged the case for adult continuation schools as strongly as I know how. But there's one thing even better than continuation schools. These days, parents are doing well enough that they're able to let their children stay in school until they turn 17. Then those students are fully prepared to go to college, which is really what schools have been training them for since they were in first grade. If all children stay in school, the world will be a much different place. Every person will have received a broad, varied education. The ideas taught in school will become relevant to the real world. If, as Plato said, knowledge is virtue, and that knowledge is enhanced with religious teaching, then we shall see in our own lifetime how righteousness can exalt a nation.

[pg 128]

Chapter 8 - I. The Way the Will Works

Principle 16. Children have two guides to help them in their moral and intellectual growth—"the way of the will," and "the way of reason."

Principle 17. Children must learn the difference between "I want" and "I will."
They must learn to distract their thoughts when tempted to do what they may
want but know is not right, and think of something else, or do something else,
interesting enough to occupy their mind. After a short diversion, their mind will
be refreshed and able to will with renewed strength.

The most important aspects of life, indeed, even life itself, are beyond definition.
We are told that 'the will' is 'the only practical faculty that man has.' But who can
define the will? We are often told that 'a person is as much or as little as his own
will,' yet most people go through their entire lives without any definitive
determined act of their will. Habit, tradition, society's accepted norms have so
much influence over us that we get up, get dressed, eat breakfast, go about our
morning routine and evening leisure without even thinking about it, it's second
nature. One thing we do know about the will: its function is to *choose*. It decides
for us. It seems certain that the harder the act of [pg 129] making up our minds
becomes, the weaker our general will becomes. Opinions are spoon fed to us. We
absorb our principles second-hand, or even third hand. Our habits are whatever is
most convenient and accepted as mainstream. What more do we need for a
decent, orderly life? However, the one thing that's within reach of any person to
accomplish, and the one thing that's necessary for every person, is character.
Character is like wrought iron beaten into shape and beauty with the repeated and
habitual action of the will. We teachers must make ourselves understand that our
aim in education isn't so much conduct as it is character. We can get decent
conduct from students via various indirect methods, but good behavior is
worthless to the world if it doesn't stem from inward character.

Every attack on a person's flesh and spirit, no matter how subtle, is an attempt to
compromise his integrity or will. However, in these days, we're threatened with a
war upon us. This war is no longer indirect, but it's aimed deliberately and
directly at the will, which *is* the person. The only thing preventing us from
becoming a nation of idiots is that there will always be a few people with strong
wills among us who will resist the general trend. Our mission as parents and
teachers is to make sure that our children are in this group. It's a serious injury
when adults use suggestion to weaken a child's moral strength of character. When
we consider what this means, we won't want to do such a thing. After all,
consider this: whatever we do with a deliberate, conscious act of the will is
described as voluntary. Whatever we do *without* any deliberate, conscious act of
our will is called involuntary. The will only has one function: it chooses. And
with every deliberate choice, our character grows stronger.

From our infancy until the day we die, suggestions surround us, crowding upon
us. These suggestions help to educate us because we have to choose between
them, and that's a learning experience in itself. But a suggestion given
intentionally to influence us by someone we respect carries added weight. Few
are able to [pg 130] resist and make an unbiased choice when we feel like the
decision has already been made for us by someone else. Our human nature tends
to make us take the path of least resistance and just accept the decision someone
else has made. Of course, some of these kinds of decisions are made for our own
good, either for our health or to instill willing obedience to authority. People who
propose that suggestion be used as a means to educate a child forget that every

attempt to use suggestion to influence a child weakens the child's own power of choice, the very force that should be making him a person of integrity. The compliant creatures who let habits, principles and opinions be dictated to them by others may easily turn into criminals. All they need is some opportune popular mania to be carried into a wave of mob fury, as happened with the crimes of the Gordon Riots. We've had terrible examples of this kind of mad fury in our own day, although we've failed to find the root source. When people don't learn how to manage their own will, which should be their main function, it's easy to undermine their power of choice. A person's will is his safeguard against the unlawful intrusion and control of someone else. We're taught that offenses against the physical person of someone else is wrong and not to be tolerated. But who teaches us that it's just as wrong to intrude and influence someone else's mind and override their will? Who teaches us that it's immoral to let one person probe the thoughts of the unconscious mind of a child or adult? We should all be conscious of the fact that we make our own choices. The teacher's job is to provide each of her students with a full tank of noble, right thoughts to draw from. Right-thinking doesn't come from self-expression. It flows when an idea stimulates the thoughts. And the best place to get these noble, right ideas to fill a child's mind is from books and pictures and histories of individuals and nations. That's what trains a child's conscious and stimulates his will, and it's his will that makes the choice. One successful politician, Count Witte, wrote in his memiors recently how [pg 131] a great empire was reduced to nothing because its rulers were weak and they allowed others to influence them by tampering with their will-power, swaying their better judgement and manipulating their actions.

We don't need to be alarmed quite yet about our own country. But we should realize that one of education's primary purposes is to strengthen the will of students. If we acquaint ourselves with how the inner person works (I like to think of the inner person as 'the City of Mansoul') then we'll be better able to help students recognize at least some of the rich resources they have within themselves. They need to know the tools they have to help them as they live in and enjoy the world. We all have these tools as a gift from God to every human. All the beauty of the world and all the thoughts of its great thinkers are available to everyone. Everyone may take what he needs from what the world offers. Everyone has access to the heavenly places from which he gets a glimpse of eternity. But the student needs to know some facts about himself. He needs to know about his body's senses and appetites. He needs to know about his intellect, imagination and need for beauty. He needs to know how important it is for love and justice to control his moral nature. Mansoul has so much potential and possibility open to it. But it also has enemies that assault and endanger it. The child must understand that he has a duty to be in control of his own inner 'Mansoul.' The tools that give him the ability to direct himself are as much a part of him as his intellect, imagination and hunger. Those tools are his conscience and his will. The conscience can't do its job without regular, consecutive education. That's why we're so careful about including an ordered sequence of history, poetry, math and art in our curriculum. We want to train the child's conscience. Training is also needed for the will. People tend to assume that the will responds automatically. But nothing in 'Mansoul' acts all by itself and for itself. The will is like the president in the kingdom of 'Mansoul,' and manages all the other parts. A little knowledge about how the will works might help us to understand exactly what it does.

At the very least, a young teen should understand plainly that his life is in danger of drifting into complacency if [pg 132] he allows any of his desires or appetites to lead him, instead of allowing his will to lead and keep those desires under control. It's up to him to take responsibility and use the tools he's been given to will himself to act in the right way. He must be sheltered from fallacies. He's probably heard about what a strong will his baby brother has because he cries to play with the knife and insists on pulling the tablecloth off the table. He reads at school in history or literature how certain famous characters did famous deeds spurred by their own willfulness. He reads about Phaeton's rashness and thinks he's funny, he carefully analyzes Esau's character and decides he likes him better than Jacob, even though Jacob was more favored by God. He observes that Esau may be stubborn and willful, but Jacob is the one who has a strong will. With this and lots of other examples, he learns that having a strong will doesn't guarantee that you'll be good. It isn't the same as being determined to have your own way. As he reads, he begins to discern which characters are willful and stubborn, and which are self-governed as an act of their will. Yet even that doesn't define whether the characters are good or evil.

But dividing characters between willful and will-controlled does show which ones are impulsive, thinking only of pleasing themselves, seeking what's in their own best interest, and the characters who have a goal beyond and outside of themselves, even if their goal is as evil as Satan's in Paradise Lost. So he learns that he not only needs to have a determined will, but he needs to keep a goal beyond himself in view. He will recognize that, even though Louis XI wasn't very nice, he was a great king because his corrupt policies weren't to make himself richer, they were for the good of France. The will develops slowly but surely. It's nourished by the ideas offered to it, and all things work together for good to strengthen the will of a child who receives the proper education. Children should learn that unstable, untamed people are not controlled by their will. They're ruled by their impulses and passions. At the same time, a person can be calm and controlled by their will, yet have unworthy or evil ends. Or they might have a worthy goal beyond themselves, but get there [pg 133] through disgraceful means. A simple, conformed will, what Jesus calls 'a single eye,' seems to be the one thing we need to live right and serve others faithfully. And having a strong, focused will requires some goal outside of itself, whether good or bad. A child who understands this isn't going to accept self-culture as the ideal, or wonder if eastern religions have something to offer him, and will involve himself with the problem Browning raises in *The Statue and the Bust.* Little by little, the student will come to understand that, as kings have a duty to rule their kingdoms, all men have a duty to use their will to control their own inner kingdoms. A king is not a king unless he rules, and a man is less than a man if he doesn't use his will for a good purpose. It's a fact of life that the will, like most other things, has its ebbs and flows when it feels strong or falters. One of the secrets of life is discovering how to survive the times when the will is weak without compromising one's integrity.

Students have to learn that the will is subject to temptations from many areas—physical comfort, wanting material things and raising one's status in society. The will is just one tool and doesn't act all by itself. It takes all of a person's being to will oneself to do something. A person can exercise his will wisely, justly and with strength only if all of his powers have been trained and instructed. We have to have some understanding before we can set our will with any determination. Jesus asked the Jews, 'How is it that you won't understand?' And most of us are the same way, we refuse to try to understand. We look for undeniable proofs before we'll believe, failing to see that belief is a matter of our own will making a choice to believe. Thus, it's important to train ourselves to use our will properly. Then we'll do what's right and appropriate any time the occasion arises.

Unlike the other agents in our 'kingdom of Mansoul,' our will is free to do what it wants. Its function is to prefer one decision over another. Every day we're faced with decisions, and the duty before us is to 'choose ye this day.' It's the job of our will to make those choices. But the very act of being torn between [pg 134] two decisions is stressful and hard, whether we're trying to choose between two prospective spouses, or two dresses [*or two homeschool curriculums! ;-)*] A lot of people avoid this difficulty by just doing what everyone else is doing. They let magazines dictate how their rooms are decorated and what they wear. They let bestseller lists tell them what to read. They let TV commercials determine how they'll spend their leisure time and what movies to see. They even let popularity decide who they'll spend time with. Often, we're quick to know what the other person should do, but we resist thinking through and making decisions for ourselves.

What about obedience? Obedience is due to the head of the household first of all, then to the government and church, and always to God. How well we obey is the test of our character, but only when obedience is our choice [*not when forced compliance leaves no other option!*] Very young children need to be trained to have the habit of obedience, but only those children who have made a decision to obey by choice are truly noble-hearted.

That kind of obedience is the essence of chivalry, and chivalry is the opposite of a self-absorbed, self-serving attitude. An honorable person is a person of steadfast will. It's not possible to continue exerting the will continuously for reasons of personal gain.

It's important to understand what we're choosing between. Things are just things; they symbolize deeper ideas. Several times a day, we're faced with two ideas represented by things, and we have to choose based on right and reasonableness. We need to be on guard against letting ourselves be carried along and then calling it 'tending to our duty' instead of consciously making a decision. We need to guard against dishonest fallacies, like the erroneous idea that our duty is to get the best there is at the lowest price [*instead of the fairest price!*] And we don't just chase after the cheapest new fashions and home furnishings. We chase opinions and ideas with the same restless urgency and fickleness. We eagerly adopt any fad, any notion we read about in the paper. A man is no more than the strength of his will. The will's job is to choose. We can find all kinds of ways to get out of committing to a decision, but our duty is to 'choose this [pg 135] day whom ye will serve.' There are two ways we can go: we can serve God and others, or we can serve ourselves. If all we care about is making sure our needs are met, doing well for ourselves, getting as much comfort, luxury and enjoyment out of life as we can, then we're only serving ourselves. And serving ourselves takes no act of resolved will. Our own appetites and desires are always there to spur us to do whatever is necessary. But if we serve God and others, we always have to be alert to the choices that present themselves before us. What springtime is to a year, is like school days are to our lifetimes. We often meet a person whose only business in life seems to be eating, drinking, working out at the gym and boating. It's possible that he has a deeper side and another facet to his life than we're aware of. But, as far as we can see, he is living to serve his own self. Or we might meet another man in an influential position who does important work, and his ideas are what he remembers from his wonderful teachers at school and college. He's interested in Greek plays, is open to great thoughts, and is always ready to serve as a result of his education. Whatever we receive when we're young, we keep all our lives.

The will affects everything we do and what we think—yet what it actually does is a small action. It's confined to a very little place between the conscience, and the reason. That's where all ideas have to present themselves. Should we accept a new idea, or reject it? Conscience and reason each have their say, but the will is supreme and makes the decision. The will's behavior is determined by all the principles we've collected, and all the opinions we've formed. At first, we entertain the novel idea and ponder it. We vaguely intend to do something with it, then form a definite purpose about what to do, then we resolve. And the result is that we take action or change our thinking to embrace or reject the idea. We hear how Rudyard Kipling's great ambition and desire at one time was to have a tobacco shop. Why? Because then he'd be able to get in touch with men as they came to [pg 136] buy their weekly tobacco. Luckily for the world of literature, he did not keep a tobacco shop. Yet the foundational idea that drove him then continued to act on his life. He always had his men around him, and who knows how many of those young men he has inspired to become 'Captains Courageous' by talking with them, as well as writing books!

But what if an unworthy idea presents itself in the mind? Suppose the idea is supported by popular opinion, by logic, and even the conscience finds it acceptable? The will soon gets tired from fighting with sheer force, and what then? Should the will fight it out? That's how the medieval church handled the bad ideas that it called temptations. The lash, rough shirts, stone couches, starved bodies witness that they weren't very successful at these battles.

When the overstressed will needs a break, it can't relax so much that it gives in. But it can and should find some diversion, some kind of recreation (Latin provides beautiful words that say exactly what we mean!) A change of physical activity or a mental challenge is helpful, but if no diversion is available, then we have to *think* about something else, even if it's something trivial. A new pair of socks, the sweater we'd like to buy, a story we're reading, a friend we hope to see, anything at all, as long as we don't tell ourselves what we should be thinking about the thought our will is struggling with. The will doesn't want arguments and suggestions. It needs a break, some kind of diversion to do something else. In a surprisingly short time, it's able to go back to that matter and make a decision to be faithful to duty, even if that duty is boring, a bother, difficult or even dangerous. This is the 'way the will works.' And this is the secret to having the power to govern oneself that everyone should have. It not only makes it easier to do the right thing in a practical sense, and develops our spiritual growth, but it also helps our intellectual well-being. The phrase 'free will' is correct. Our will *is* free to choose right or [pg 137] wrong. It's all up to our will, and the will has complete freedom to make that choice on its own. But we tend to think that free will means free thought, so we allow ourselves to let our thoughts wander towards intellectual anarchy. We forget that our will also has the job of deciding what we'll allow ourselves to think about, as well as what feelings we'll nurse in our hearts and which lusts we'll allow our flesh. Our thoughts are not our own, and we are not free to think whatever we want. 'Choose ye this day' applies just as much to the thoughts we allow to nest in our minds. Our will is the one free agent in our 'kingdom of mansoul' that accepts or rejects. Therefore, our will is responsible for every intellectual dilemma or moral quandary that has ruined a man's sanity. We are not free to think whatever we want about anything, whether trivial or profound. An instructed conscience and a trained reason can help the will to make the right decisions, both great and small, that affect our lives.

Having a strong, firm will doesn't happen because one day we resolve it. It is the result of a long, ordered education in which we receive guidelines and examples from the thoughts and lives of great men in history and in our own time. These examples flow into our minds as unconsciously and spontaneously as the air we breathe. Training the will is a long process, but the moment of decision is instantaneous, and the will acts voluntarily. Therefore, the object of education must be to prepare us for those immediate choices and voluntary actions that will face us every day.

While we explain to students the secret about 'the way the will works,' we probably should be careful about presenting the ideas of 'self-knowledge, self-reverence, and self control.' Proper education needs to be outer-focused. The mind that's focused inwardly, on the good it's doing for itself, even though the good may be virtuous, will miss the higher, simpler secrets of living. Doing one's duty and being useful to others should be all the motivation that's needed to help a child develop the kind of will that will make good decisions without [pg 138] undue effort and stress. Slowly strengthening the will is hardly noticeable to the child, but the impact on his community or country can be great. A person's will, his free will, needs to be focused on something other than itself. Tennyson has said it well,

'Our wills are ours, we don't understand how;
They are ours so that we can make them Yours.'

[pg 139]

Chapter 9 - II. The Way Reason Works

Principle 18. Children must learn not to lean too heavily on their own reasoning. Reasoning is good for logically demonstrating mathematical truth, but unreliable when judging ideas because our reasoning will justify all kinds of erroneous ideas if we really want to believe them.

Principle 19. Knowing that reason is not to be trusted as the final authority in forming opinions, children must learn that their greatest responsibility is choosing which ideas to accept or reject. Good habits of behavior and lots of knowledge will provide the discipline and experience to help them do this.

Every person who is stopped in their tracks by witnessing their own reason in action is as much of a discoverer as Columbus. We normally let reason do its own work without really even being aware of it. But there are times when we stand in startled admiration as we watch our reason unfold arguments point by point in favor of buying one carpet instead of another, or defending our old friend against some rival. We see every argument that our reason presents for something opposed with another argument in the background. How else can we explain that there is no one subject that two people won't have very different opinions about—food, dress, games, education, politics, religion? The two people have opposite opinions, and each of them has infallible arguments that would convince the other—if he didn't have arguments just as valid to [pg 140] strengthen his own opinion. Every character in history and literature illustrates this. Probably the best way to train children to reason intelligently is to let them work out opposing opinions in their own minds and decide for themselves which has more validity.

Shakespeare's Macbeth returned as a conquering general after a brilliant victory. His head and heart were inflated. Was there anything he couldn't accomplish? Couldn't he govern a kingdom as easily as he had governed his army? His reason outlines some logical steps for him to accomplish great things—but the methods for doing them aren't all honorable. And just then, he meets the 'weird sisters,' who illustrate the way we all fall into fatalism when our conscience can't condone our actions. As he contemplates the prophecy of becoming Thane of Cawdor, he receives word that he is the Thane of Cawdor! He is also prophesied to be king. If it's decreed, how can he change it? He is no longer a free agent, he is merely a victim of fate. And many logical arguments present themselves to him, convincing him that Scotland, the world, his wife, himself, will be enhanced and flourish and be blessed if he has the opportunity to carry out the plans within himself. Opportunity? He's already been promised the opportunity, the thing is decreed. All he needs to do is figure out what steps to take to make it come to pass. He had a sensitive nature and shrank from the horrors he vaguely foresaw in the future. But reason stepped in and played out the whole bloody tragedy in a vision to his mind. At the beginning of the play, Macbeth has honors, lots of friends, and the trust of his king. The change is sudden and complete, and reason justified every step of the way. But, although reason convinced him during the process, it didn't begin with reason. His will had been tempted with ambition and had already accepted the concept of his own ascent to power and greatness even before the 'weird sisters' shaped his inner desire into prophecy. If his own will hadn't already opened his mind to ambition, then prophecies of fate couldn't have influenced his actions any more than they influenced Banquo's. [pg 141]

But that doesn't mean that reason is totally unworthy and always giving bad counsel. Nurse Cavell, Jack Coruwell, Lord Roberts, General Gordon, Madame Curie, are all examples of people whose reason led them to glorious deeds. We know how Florence Nightingale was obsessed with the feeling of pity. She welcomed it and reasoned it out, and was led through many difficulties in her work of saving sick, suffering soldiers in her country's army. She was even able to convince those in power with the same arguments that her own reason had used on her. The medieval church had a wonderful thought when they presented the foundational idea of each of the seven Liberal Arts by having each one represented by a person who was great in that field and who could convince others with the same reason that had convinced themselves. [*I think this is referring to the Santa Maria Novella fresco in Florence*]. Thus, Priscian is represented as being the one through whom grammar came to the world, Pythagoras is represented as teaching the world arithmetic, and Euclid represents the science that he applied his reason to. But reason isn't just for great intellectual advances, or discoveries, or events that change the world for good or evil. There is no gadget we use, great or small, that some person hasn't exhausted his reason on. A sofa, a chest of drawers, a box of toy soldiers, have all been thought out step by step. The inventor had to consider the pros and work out the cons to make his invention practical enough to be useful. Hardly anyone ever takes time to consider how the useful, or even beautiful item, came into existence. It's good to sometimes ask a child, 'How did you think of this?' when he tells you about a new game he's just made up, or a country he's named in his imagination, complete with people and a government. He'll probably tell you what first put the idea into his head, and then how he reasoned it out step by step. And after he's considered the question, 'How did you think of it?' it will occur to him to ask the same of other inventions— [pg 142] 'How did he think of it?' And then he'll understand that there's a distinction between the first spark of inspiration that puts the idea into someone's head, and the reasoned steps that go into completing the object, or making the discovery, or writing a law. Sometimes a child should even be exposed to the psychology of a crime. He needs to see how reason can bring what looks like infallible proofs about how right the crime is. From Cain to the most recent convict, every crime has been justified in the opinions of every perpetrator by reasoned arguments that come all by themselves into their minds. We know the arguments that convinced Eve to eat the fruit when the serpent persuaded her like the weird sisters persuaded Hamlet. It's pleasant to look at, delicious, and it will make you wise so that you know right from wrong. Those are good, convincing arguments, deceptive enough to stand up to the protestations of Obedience. Children need to know that they will face this, too. Any time they're tempted to do the wrong thing, good reasons for doing it will occur to them. But, fortunately, when they want to do the right thing, reasons that are just as convincing will also appear.

After lots of experience in reasoning and following the process of reason in others either in real life or in their books, children will be ready to conclude that *reasonable* isn't the same as *right*. Reason is their servant, not their master. It's just one of the servants that helps to govern his 'kingdom of Mansoul.' But reason shouldn't be trusted to govern a man, much less a nation, any more than appetite, or ambition, or love of comfort. Logical reasons can be brought forward to prove a wrong course of action as easily as a good course of action. He'll see that reason works involuntarily. All the nice-sounding arguments follow one after another in his mind without any action from him. But that doesn't mean that he's a helpless victim hurried into sin by thoughts he couldn't help, because it never starts with reason. It starts when he allows himself to contemplate some [pg 143] course of action, like Eve standing by the fruit tree. That's when reason enters the picture. So, if he chooses to think about doing a thing that's good, then lots of logical reasons will rush into his head to convince him to do it. But if he chooses to entertain a wrong notion, it's like summoning reason to present a whole lot of logical arguments why the wrong thing is really a good idea.

Recognizing what Reason's job is should be a tremendous help to all of us in these days when fallacy is everywhere, and when our desire to be agreeable makes us willing to buy into public opinion about things, especially when those opinions are shared by people we respect. It's also good to remember that no wrong has ever been done, no crime has ever been committed that wasn't justified in the mind of the perpetrator with so many sound arguments from his own reason in such numbers that he couldn't oppose them. Has Shakespeare ever been wrong? Perhaps, in the case of Richard III, who recognized his own villainy and not only accepted it, but gloated over it. That's hardly human nature. But at least he wasn't a hypocrite! Richard may be the only exception to the rule—most men, when finally confronted with their own villainy, go out and hang themselves. Even Richard says at the end, 'I myself can't even find pity for myself.' It's enough for us and our children to know that reason will make any matter we propose look good and acceptable. Just because we're convinced that we're right doesn't justify anything, because there's no theory or action we can contemplate that our reason can't affirm. We can convince ourselves with many 'proofs' that Bacon really wrote the Shakespeare plays, and some ingenious person has devised an elaborate string of arguments that prove that Dr. Samuel Johnson wrote the Bible! And why shouldn't that be a valid opinion? Considering that [pg 144] France is known as a nation of logical thinkers, they made a curious blunder when they elected to give divine honors to the Goddess of Reason. But maybe they did it *because* they're a nation of logical thinkers. After all, logic is very close to reason, and just because something can be proved by logic, that doesn't make it true or right. It's no wonder that two equally honorable and virtuous men from any place will hold opposite opinions on almost any issue, and each will support his views with logical arguments. So we have people who cling to dogma in religion, and politicians who sway voters with emotional sentiments, and those whose understanding of science is nothing but dreams, and those who hope to stay one step ahead by keeping current with the latest popular opinions. But that won't happen to us if we've been raised to understand that reason is beautiful and a marvel, but that it has its limits.

We need to be able to counter popular current opinion, not with logical counter-arguments, but by exposing fallacy and then proving the merit of the correct position. For example, Karl Marx, who has been described as 'a very lovable, very exasperating, sincere but misguided zealot,' dominates today's socialist thinking. Point by point, for better or worse, his Marxian Manifesto of 1848 is gaining popularity. We are told that, 'the following measures might become general practice in the most advanced countries:'

1. 'Property and rent income will pass to the State.' We don't have time to examine this proposition in detail, but let's consider a single fallacy. It's assumed that rent income lines the pockets of property owners. But the records of the Duke of Bedford, to name just one example, shows that rent from his park property is barely enough to maintain the property and pay property taxes. [pg 145] Landowners generally employ many workers with fair pay and benefits, and most provide a public service by making their property a beautiful park for public use, maintained out of their own pocket.

2. 'Heavy progressive taxes.' The fallacy is this: the poorest working class citizens who are supposed to be helped by the Manifesto will have to pay taxes because they make up the bulk of society. In other words, the ones who will be most burdened by heavy progressive taxes will be the poor working class, whose very existence will be threatened as a result, as has happened in Russia.

3. 'Abolish all inheritance.' This is suppose to reduce everyone to the same economic level. Of course, eliminating class is the main aim of socialism. But the fallacy is the assumption that class is a permanent, stable thing. But, in truth, classes fluctuate like particles in ocean waves moving upward and downward with the tides. The man at the bottom of society may be at the top tomorrow, as we see in Soviet Russia and all other civilized countries. Trying to control this natural fluctuation of classes is like King Canute trying to tell the tide not to rise.

4. 'Confiscate property of rebels and emigrants.' It takes tyranny to maintain assumed authority. And the worst tyranny of all is penalizing people to intimidate them into powerlessness, as they do in the Soviet state. The fallacy here is in underestimating human nature. There is nothing that men won't sacrifice for an idea. Threat of losing property won't keep men from taking a stand for a grand idea, like freedom to think and move with liberty.

5, 6, and 7. deal with transferring factories and tools for producing things into the hands of the State. Since the Proletariat [the working class] makes up the government in a communist society, it's a way for Everyman to control all the wealth and means of getting wealth.

This is actually a logically thought-out similarity to [pg 146] a government of the people, by the people, for the people. But the fallacy here is that it results in a revolution that doesn't really bring any changes. It just results in a change of rulers, who might end up being better or worse. In the Soviet Republic, according to the law of perpetual social flux, new tyrants would work their way in because there are no longer precedents and customs in place to hinder them. And the children will have a great example of how the last stage of their country is worse than it was before.

8. 'All will be forced to work.' The original idea was to grant equal freedom and living conditions to everyone. But in reality, it means that everyone will have to serve in the army.

9. 'Agriculture and manufacture will be combined into one group.' The goal was to take away the difference and inequalities between towns and rural areas. It's a good idea, one we'd all like to see happen. But is it really possible?

10. 'Free public education for all children.' We are happy to see that this has come to pass with the added condition, 'for those who need or want it.' The downside is that the Soviet's concept of education is brainwashing the next generation in revolutionary propaganda.

To continue our examination of point number 10., the next clause (b) gets rid of child labor in factories 'in its present form.' We are glad to see child labor ended, but that clause could leave a loophole for something just as sinister. But, on the surface, everyone seems happy with this point.

(c) 'Education and production of goods will be united.' Motivated by motives of economy, England is copying this [pg 147] communist trend with its Continuation Schools. The fallacy affects us as well as them in our efforts to better educate the people. It assumes that a child who learns a specific trade at the expense of his overall academic education will do better in the future than a child who spends all his school time on educating his whole person. But employers themselves don't confirm this. On the contrary, if a child is fairly bright and willing, an employer will be happy to have him and can teach him the specific skills he needs on the job. The purpose of education isn't to train for a technical skill, it's to develop the whole person. The more fully a person meets his potential, the better his work will be, no matter what that work is. Like I said before, the concept of British Continuation Schools should be teaching humanities. By that, I don't mean a traditional classical education. Whether ancient classics are the best really isn't the issue. But our English language has a wealth of its own rich humanities to offer.

These ten maxims give us plenty of material—*not for lectures*, but for discussion. This gives an example of how current events should be used as opportunities to talk with our children. This kind of thing should be a part of the school curriculum. Students need to know how to follow an argument and detect fallacies for themselves [*rather than accepting our opinions and arguments.*] Just like every other function of the mind, reason needs raw material to work on, whether it comes in history or literature, or news of a strike or revolution. It's crazy to send youths out to face a confusing world with nothing but one specialized skill, such as the ability to solve math problems. An education that only trains a child to reason has its uses, but, really, children already have that ability. What they need is material to practice on.

A word of warning: reason, like everything else in a person, is subject to habit. It works on what it's used to handling. [pg 148] Plato formed a fair judgment about this when he wrote about Education of the Young in his Republic and perceived that math wouldn't help in the complex affairs of life, whether public or private.

I've shown why students' reading and current events need to be wide enough to provide opportunities for them to enjoy the kind of logical, methodical reasoning they need. When they find fallacies in one instance, it will sharpen their ability to detect them somewhere else.

Does that mean we should spend lots of time discussing every frivolous or profane premise they come across? Of course not. But we should give them some principles to help them identify what's frivolous or profane for themselves. A premise is idle and frivolous when it rests on a foundation of nothing and leads nowhere. And a premise is profane and blasphemous sin when it's irreverent and flippant towards God. We all know, without anyone telling us, that God is terrifying, wonderful, loving, just and good, as surely as we know that the sun shines or the wind blows. Children should be brought up understanding that a miracle is no less miraculous because it happens so continually and regularly that we call it a law of nature. For instance, sap rising in a tree, a boy born with his uncle's eyes, an answer we can identify comes to us while we pray in earnest. These things aren't any less amazing because they happen frequently, or even all the time, so that we take them for granted and cease to wonder about them anymore. That's the way it was for the people of Jerusalem when Jesus did so many miracles in their streets.

The guiding principle that should control people and countries is, 'My Father never stops working, so why should I?' [*John 5:17, NLT*] 'My Spirit will not put up with humans for such a long time' is a dire warning to every individual and every nation. God and Jesus work every day to hinder people and nations from doing the wrong thing and encourage them to do good. To the child [pg 149] who understands this, miracles won't be so unusual because all of life will seem like something full of wonder and adoration.

If we want our children not to get confused by all the trends and thoughts about religion, then we need to help them understand exactly what religion is. In *What Religion Is*, Bernard Bosanquet wrote:

'Will religion guarantee me happiness? Generally, we have to say, no. If we become a Christian just to attain personal happiness then we definitely won't find happiness.'

Here is a final and clear answer to the psuedo-Christianity that's offered so often to hesitating souls. It promises physical comfort, no more sorrow or anxiety, replacement of what's been lost, even going so far as to offer reuniting with loved ones who have died. We might call on mediums, go to séances, visit faith healers and put our faith in some man who only wants to manipulate us. We don't worry about sin or feel remorse for our past. We might live detestable lives, yet be satisfied and content with ourselves, totally oblivious to the anxiety and struggle of those around us. We think that we can will away sin, sorrow, worry and suffering through faith. In other words, we think that Christianity will guarantee us personal happiness. We use religion to make ourselves immune to every distress and misery of life, and we believe that this wonderful immunity is within the power of our own will. 'The only person who matters in my Christianity is me, and the only purpose for religion is to keep me from any physical or mental discomfort and keep me floating in some cloud of undisturbed Nirvana.' Is that what Christianity is? We must agree with Professor Bosanquet: absolutely NOT!

Real Christianity isn't about me, and any religion that does these things is idolatry, self-worship, concerned with nobody but myself.

To continue our quote: [pg 150]

'If religion doesn't guarantee my happiness, then what does it do? We value religion as being good and great, but if it doesn't do anything for me, then why should it be anything to me? But the answer changes if you word the question just a bit differently and ask, 'does it make my life more worth living?' And the answer to this is, 'It's the only thing that makes life worth living at all!'

In other words, 'I want, am made for and must have a God.'

Since children have a sweet faith and pure love, they have immediate access to God. Is there anything better than that? What more could a person desire? Children have complete trust that gentle Jesus is always with them, wherever they go, even while they sleep. Angels care for them and they enjoy all the immunities of the Kingdom. They have as much Reason as anyone else. A hundred years ago, there was a simple, straightforward way to give children a foundation for their faith. All the tenets of Christianity were outlined in a little catechism of 'Scripture Proofs.' That method had its good points. But today, if we use Scripture as our authority, we first have to prove that Scripture itself can be trusted. We also have to change tactics. We need to make it clear to children that the most important things of life can't be proved with conclusive evidence. We can't even prove without a doubt that we're living! So we must cling to what we know is true and doesn't need proof. We also know with conclusive certainty that our reason isn't infallible. It's susceptible to persuasion and open to influence from either side. It's a faithful, yet simple servant—whatever the will decides to accept, it can find ways to prove it. When we understand that our reason can be unreliable, we'll be able to detect the flawed bias of our opponent's arguments. And we'll be less likely to be confused and persuaded by every new notion that comes our way. Every mother has faced the intense logic of a child who asks very logical but difficult questions and has drawn the wrong conclusion. So we [pg 151] know they're not too young to deal with serious matters, but only as they come up. Our first priority is giving them a sense of reassurance, not boring or distressing them with the complex questions of life.

Children can drive us crazy arguing a trivial point to death just because they enjoy using their reasoning power. Yet many dislike the very school subjects that seem like they'd give an outlet for their reasoning ability, and might even strengthen it. But very few children enjoy grammar, especially English grammar, which depends so little on inflection. Arithmetic and Math don't appeal to most children, either, no matter how intelligent. Most children are baffled by math, although they may love reasoning out questions of life in literature or history. Since so many dislike those subjects, maybe we should take that as a hint and stop putting so much pressure on those subjects. It would make sense to push grammar and math if children's reason was waiting for us to develop it. But when we see that they have plenty of ability to reason in other subjects, we have to face the fact that they have plenty of reason. They have as much ability to reason as they have ability to love. They don't need us to give them subjects to develop their reason. Our job is to give them lots of material for their reason to work on. If their reason gets sharper, it will be a side effect as they learn their other subjects. At the same time, we can't let them skip grammar and math. Some day they'll delight in language, and in the beauty of the most appropriate words to express a thought. They'll see that words are the vehicle of truth, and shouldn't be carelessly thrown around, or mutilated when written. We need to prepare them for that day. We should probably wait before we have them parse sentences until they're used to analyzing whether they make sense. We should let them play with figures of speech [pg 152] before making them try to break sentences down to small parts. We should keep proper grammatical terms to a minimum. The truth is, children can't really draw conclusions about abstract things. They're good at busily collecting particulars, but they don't commit themselves to deducing anything definite, and we shouldn't rush them. And if language has its own confounding rules, imagine how much more baffling it is for children to work with abstract lines and mathematical figures! We remember how John Ruskin amazed and taught us with his thesis that two and two make four, and the universe has no way of ever making two and two equal three or five. Children should approach math from the perspective of that unalterable law. They should understand how impressive it was when Euclid said that two and two equals three or five is an absurd possibility, as absurd as a man claiming that, on his tree, apples fell upwards. It's absurd to think that apples would break the law of gravity. Figures and abstract lines work just like an apple falling. They are confined to an unchangeable law. It's a great thing to understand the nature of these kinds of laws by experiencing them in their lowest application, gravity. A child who understands how immutable the laws of math are will never divide 15 pennies between five people and give them the wrong amount. He will understand that math answers aren't arbitrary, they're logical, and even a child can use reason to come to the right answer. Math can be enjoyable for a person who loves perceiving a law of nature and figuring out the law behind why things work the way they do. But not every child can be a star wrestler, and not every boy 'takes' to math. So perhaps teachers should make it their duty to expose the child to as many interests as possible. Math is just one subject in education, and it's one that not everyone excels at. So it shouldn't monopolize too much time in the school day. And youths shouldn't be denied good jobs because the subject they're the worst at is one [pg 153] that test examiners love. They probably love it because the answers are final and easy to grade. There are no essay questions to have to make subjective judgments about.

We want to send youths out into the world with 'solid reasoning powers, stable will, endurance, preparedness, strength and skill.' [*She Was a Phantom of Delight, Wordsworth*] To those qualities we should add determination. We can hardly expect to turn out such a person of character from a steady course in only one discipline, such as mathematics.

[pg. 154]

Chapter 10 - The Curriculum

Principle 12. "Education is the science of relations" means that children have minds capable of making their own connections with knowledge and experiences, so we make sure the child learns about nature, science and art, knows how to make things, reads many living books and that they are physically fit.

Principle 13. In devising a curriculum, we provide a vast amount of ideas to ensure that the mind has enough brain food, knowledge about a variety of things to prevent boredom, and subjects are taught with high-quality literary language since that is what a child's attention responds to best. [pg 155]

Principle 14. Since one doesn't really "own" knowledge until he can express it, children are required to narrate, or tell back (or write down), what they have read or heard.

Principle 15. Children must narrate after one reading or hearing. Children naturally have good focus of attention, but allowing a second reading makes them lazy and weakens their ability to pay attention the first time. Teachers summarizing and asking comprehension questions are other ways of giving children a second chance and making the need to focus the first time less urgent. By getting it the first time, less time is wasted on repeated readings, and more time is available during school hours for more knowledge. A child educated this way learns more than children using other methods, and this is true for all children regardless of their IQ or background.

A school's curriculum should be chosen according to the principles and knowledge of those in charge of the school. But it's not, and schools are sadly lacking in a good curriculum. Most junior high schools and high schools work towards passing entrance exams to the universities. The standard and curriculum is set, then, by the university exams, and the school officials are forced to submit to them.

Elementary schools don't directly 'teach the test,' but, since their best students will be tested for entrance to the best secondary schools, they're affected by those tests, too. Secondary schools have much less freedom than elementary schools in selecting which subjects are taught and how much time to spend on each. The result is startling. An eight-year-old elementary student may show more intelligence and wider knowledge than a fourteen-year-old Preparatory school student—if the elementary student has been taught using the principles I recommend, and the Prep student has been taught to pass a standardized scholarship test. The Prep student will reach the test standard in Latin, perhaps Greek, and Math [*but that's it.*]

If we were to establish a nationwide standard that every child had to meet in [pg 156] a wide range of subjects, then average students would have a fair shot and gifted students would naturally move ahead.

We work under a mistaken notion that there is no natural law or inborn principle for planning a student's studies. Instead, we teach him those things that are proper for a person of wealth to know (as Locke said), OR we teach him enough art, reading, writing and arithmetic to prevent him from being illiterate. In both cases, the focus is on utilitarian education. The child is being indirectly educated to a profession rather than for personal growth.

But what if, in the very nature of things, we find that a complete curriculum has been suggested? Voltaire said, 'The human race has lost its title deeds.' and has been trying to get them back ever since. This applies to education. We are still lost. We haven't found our title deeds, so we have nothing to offer children with any conviction. The highest aim we can think of is to educate youth so that they're useful to society, and anyone with a novel new theory is free to teach whatever he wants because we know of no grounds to oppose him. In one sense, education does fall under the law of supply and demand [*create from students what society needs*], but instead of parents and teachers determining what society needs, the children should be the ones whose needs are met. But how will they let us know what they need? We need to consider this question carefully. Our answer will depend on our perception of human nature, which is limitless and varied. It isn't just budding geniuses from distinguished families who have impressive human natures. Every child, even a street child in the slums, is a marvel.

A nine-year-old British boy living in Japan remarked, 'Mom, isn't it fun learning all these things? [pg 157] Everything I learn seems to fit with something else!' The boy had only discovered half the secret. What he still hadn't figured out is that everything fitted into something within himself.

The days of educating as befits a person of high society, or a craftsman are over. Now we must deal with a human being who has an inborn craving to know the history of his race, the story of his country, what men used to think, and what they think nowadays. The best thoughts of mankind have been archived in literature, and, at its highest level, as poetry or art, which is poetry in a solid form. Each student is a child of God, and his supreme desire and glory is to know about and have a relationship with God. Each child is a living being with many parts and passions. He needs to learn how to make use of himself, care for himself and discipline himself in body, mind and spirit. Each child has many relationships and fills many roles. He interacts with his family, his church, his community, his country, his neighboring countries, and the world at large. He inhabits a world full of beauty and fascination. He needs to learn to recognize the features of his world and name them. His universe is governed by certain rules, and he needs some understanding of those rules.

This is a tall order, but the educational rights of humans demand a wide program. It's a lot to teach, but it's not impossible, and it's not for us to pick and choose, or to educate in one direction or another. We can't even choose between science and humanities—the child needs both. It appears that our mission is to give children a zestful grip on as much of the range of relationships as possible that are appropriate. Shelley offers us the key to education. He talks about 'understanding that gets brighter as it gazes on lots of different truths.'

Since a child's relationship to his world is so varied, the education we give him needs to be varied, too. A teacher in Cape Colony writes, 'The papers included in

A.C. Drury's pamphlet, A Liberal Education: Practice, witness a [pg 158] high standard of proficiency. The mistakes found there are the mistakes you'd expect of children, nothing more. And there are just enough mistakes to prove that these are real children. There are none of the hilarious blunders, either fact or expression, that make a teacher wonder if her teaching had any effect at all.'

When children are taught this way, their knowledge is consecutive, intelligent, and complete in the areas they study. It isn't true that the student has to work harder when more subjects are covered. In fact, the opposite is true. The variety is refreshing. A child can write thirty or forty sheets of exam essays in a week and not be bored. It isn't the total number of different subjects that counts, but the total hours that fatigue the student. With this in mind, our curriculum has short hours with no evenings required to prepare or do homework.

Section I - The Knowledge of God

Children need three kinds of knowledge: the knowledge of God, the knowledge of man, and the knowledge of the world around him. Of those, the knowledge of God is the most important, the most necessary and the one that has the potential to bring him happiness. Mothers do a better job of teaching children about God than teachers. They know their children better and don't underestimate their minds as much, so they tend not to talk down to them. But, to read educational publications, one would think that the art of education is dumbing down concepts for the 'little' minds of children! If we give up that preconception that assumes the superiority of adults, we'll be surprised at how much and how profoundly children are able to understand. We'll realize that a relationship with God is an inborn attraction and it's up to us [pg 159] to help our children attain that relationship. Mothers know how to talk about God in the same way they would talk about a beloved but absent father, drawing attention to his love and care for her and the children. She knows how to make her child feel a thrill of joy and gratefulness as he looks at a meadow full of flowers, or a huge tree, or flowing river by making him understand that God made all of it. Children aren't too simple to understand that, 'the mountains, valleys and glittering rivers belong to the one who knows their Creator and whose eyes brim with tears of holy joy.' [freely adapted from the poem The Freeman, by William Cowper] We remember how Arthur Pendennis [from Pendennis, by Thackeray] walked in the cool of the evening with his mother, reciting passages from Milton, and both of their eyes would fill 'with tears of holy joy,' and he was only eight! A teacher can never have the same kind of opportunities with an entire class, but if she makes an effort to get a true estimate of what a child's mind can comprehend, she'll be surprised with how much can be done.

The arrogant mindset of some teachers is the reason that so many students never achieve much. Students are seen as 'just kids' and not expected to understand much, and they live down to that expectation. Our PNEU begins formal lessons when children are six years old. Children are undoubtedly capable of beginning even a year or two before that, but the world of nature and home life provides so much education already. It seems best to wait until age six before requiring any direct educational efforts.

What about teaching that's told to children [*such as instructions, information, stories*]? They'll get that whether they go to school or stay home. But, since narration isn't required, it doesn't demand any deliberate effort from them. That's how we all learn—by telling back [pg 160] whatever it is, a sermon or lecture or conversation that we want to remember, even if we just tell it back to ourselves silently. People have done this since man had a mind. The tragedy is that it hasn't been harnessed as a learning tool in education! This is what Samuel Johnson said about it:

'Children should always be encouraged to tell a sibling or servant whenever they hear something remarkable. They need to tell it right away, before the impression is erased with newer incidents.' 'He remembered clearly the first time he heard of heaven and hell. His mother made sure to describe both places in such a way that she thought sure would seize his attention as he lay next to her in bed. Then she immediately got him up and dressed him, even though it was earlier than he usually got up, and sent him to visit his favorite servant in the house. She knew that he would tell him what he had heard while it was still fresh in his mind. That's exactly what she wanted. He credited that method for his ability to remember events and conversations that had happened long ago.' [*from a book about Johnson by Mrs. Hester Lynch Salusbury Thrale Piozzi*] The most important part of education is religious training, and our mission is to give children the knowledge of God. We won't go into the area of intuitive knowledge, we'll stick to the knowledge that is attainable because it's what God expressed for us. That knowledge comes from the Bible. The worst indignity we can commit on children is giving them our own rendering of scripture or a well-intentioned re-telling of the clear, beautiful language and poetic phrasing of the Bible itself.

The best literature is always direct and simple. A normal six-year-old will enjoy hearing stories from both the Old and New Testaments, passage by passage. He can narrate it, too, adding his own personal charm. There are two aspects to religion. There's the attitude of our will towards God, which is how we think of as Christianity. And there's the perception of God that comes over time as we see the way God deals with mankind. In the first regard, Goethe couldn't have been considered religious. Yet, the second aspect, the perception of God, became like a peaceful backdrop in his otherwise restless, uneasy life. It's [pg 161] worth our time to explore how he came to such a beneficial understanding of God. He tells his full story in *Aus Meinem Leben* (*From My Life?*) and what he shares about education is well worth our study. He says,

'People might go where they please and do what they want, but in the end, they have to return to that road that Dante wrote about. That's what happened to me. My efforts at learning Hebrew when I was ten by reading the scriptures made me imagine vividly the things I was reading about—the beautiful land that inspired songs, and the countries around it, and the people and events that have happened there for thousands of years. You may wonder why I'm talking about this in so much detail when everyone already knows about Israel's history. But it's the best way to show how, even with the stress of my life and my unorthodox education, I focused my mind and feelings on that part of my life. It's the only way I can account for the peace that surrounded me even when my life was disturbed and I was going through troubles. My over-active imagination may have led me here and there, and I've been obsessed with fables, histories, and myths, but I could always think about those holy lands and be at peace. I would lose myself in the first five books of the Bible and, there among those Hebrew shepherds, I would find peace and comfort.'

How did Goethe come to possess this kind of peaceful rest for his soul and fresh background for his thoughts? It seems that this inner place of sanctuary was with him his whole life, in spite of all the mistakes he made in his rebellious life. It has been said that his eyes had a peaceful tranquility, and this is the secret of that peace. In Goethe's words, we also see a principle for education that we should consider: teaching the New Testament without the grounding and accompaniment of the Old Testament won't result in that kind of thinking about God. [pg 162]

The wide, all-encompassing, completely permeating presence of God is found in David's Psalms, which are in the Old Testament. We need to have the faith and courage to give children such a complete and gradual picture of Old Testament history, that they unconsciously think of the history of mankind as being like the panorama of the history of the Jewish nation as told in the Bible. If our children are little skeptics, like Goethe, who delighted in stumping his teachers with Bible inconsistencies, then we should follow the example of wise old Dr. Albrecht. We shouldn't rush to explain away the difficulties. We shouldn't belittle or avoid their questions, or give final answers as if we were the authority. Instead, do what Albrecht did. Introduce them to a thoughtful commentator who takes care in researching and explaining difficult questions. By doing this, we won't allow difficult questions to detract from the gradual unfolding of God's design to teach the world His plan. For children aged six to twelve, the best commentator I know of is Canon Paterson Smyth, who wrote *The Bible for the Young*. He is one of the few writers who knows how children think and can help them with difficulties. He knows how to inspire their thoughts and guide their actions.

Between the ages of six and twelve, children using Paterson's book cover the narrative stories of Old Testament Biblical history, and the Prophets as they correspond to the lives of the kings. The teacher begins the lesson by reading the passage from Paterson's book that illustrates the scripture reading. For example,

'This story takes place on the battle field in the Elah Valley. The camp of the Israelites is on one side of the slope, the big tents of the Philistines are on the other slope. The Israelites aren't huge men, but they're agile and clever. The Philistines are huge brutes, stupid thick-headed giants. Samson used to play tricks on them and make fun of them long ago. Both sides are agitated,' etc.

There might be some discussion after [pg 163] reading this passage. Then the teacher will read the Scripture text and the children will narrate. The commentary merely serves as a background for their thoughts. Their narrations are usually very interesting. They don't miss even one point, and they add colorful touches of their own. Before the end of the lesson, the teacher brings out any new concepts about God or points of behavior that may have been included in the reading. She emphasizes the moral or religious lesson in a reverent, sympathetic way, and doesn't attempt to tell them how to apply it personally.

Twelve to fifteen year olds read Rev. H. Costley-White's *Old Testament History* to themselves. He has made some wise omissions that make students more able to deal with Jewish history in King James English than they would if they just used the actual Bible. Each period, such as Psalms or the various prophets, uses references from contemporary literature to illustrate. Brief historical explanations and notes of general commentary are included in the proper places. For example, as an introduction to the Gen 3 story of Cain and Abel, it says,

'The original purpose of this story was to show how sin spread throughout mankind, and where homicide started. In this case, it was actual cold-blooded murder. There are some difficult questions that we don't have enough information to answer. For instance, 'Why didn't God accept Cain's offering?' 'How did God show that He didn't accept it?' 'What was the sign put on Cain?' 'Where did Cain find a wife?' The best way to answer such questions is—to admit that we don't know! But we should add that these early stories are just selected fragments about what happened, not the whole story. The story of Cain and Abel is an obvious example of a story that's been cut down and edited.

'The lessons taught in the story of Cain and Abel include: 1. God judges motives, not actions. 2. It isn't the sin of [pg 164] murder itself that's condemned so much, but the reasons behind it, such as jealousy and hatred. Jesus talked about this in the Sermon on the Mount in Matt 6:22. 3. The doctrine that all men are brothers. Each person is responsible to those around him, and he is obligated to be concerned about the conditions they live in. 4. Sin always brings its own consequences. 5. God always tries to reason with man before sin reaches a climax.'

Commentary is done with concise, to-the-point footnotes.

This gives students detailed, extensive knowledge of the Old Testament from scripture text itself. It trains them to accept Bible difficulties comfortably, rather than feeling like such difficulties invalidate the Bible as God's oracle and our only original source of knowledge about God and how He deals with people. This will prepare them to study religion further from the Bible.

We like Dummelow's *One Volume Bible Commentary* for high school students. It's designed to provide in one convenient book:

'A brief explanation of the meaning of the Scriptures. There are introductions for the books of the Bible, and notes to explain major textual, moral or doctrinal difficulties. The beginning of the book has a prefix of articles about the larger questions that the Bible as a whole may suggest. We hope that this commentary will inspire students to read some of the books of the Bible that have literary charm and help with spiritual growth, but are often overlooked and unread. In recent years, more information has become available to answer questions about authorship of the Bible and interpretations. We have tried to incorporate the most recent scholarly information while avoiding extreme bias or speculative opinions. Sometimes this means that this commentary will offer views that aren't traditional. In those cases, we hope and believe that the authority and spiritual worth of the Scriptures is enhanced and not diminished by the change.' [pg 165]

The editor of the commentary has done such a good job explaining its aims that I'll only add that we find it to be of great practical value. The students read the general articles, and the introductions to the books of the Bible. They read the Prophets and poetic books along with the notes. So they leave school with a pretty sophisticated knowledge of the Old Testament books, and of the information that modern scholarship has added to their interpretation. We hope they also leave with more reverence for God and delight in the ways God deals with people.

The New Testament has its own category. The same commentaries are used, and we use the same methods, reverent reading of the text followed by narration, which is often curiously word perfect even after a single reading. This is even more surprising because we all know how hard it is to repeat a passage we've heard a thousand times. A single reading with concentrated focus takes care of this difficulty, and we're able to take assurance in knowing that children's minds are stocked with perfect word pictures of every fond, beautiful scene from the Gospels. Students are also able to reproduce the straightforward, sweet teaching from the object lessons of each of the miracles. Little by little, the personality of Our Lord as revealed in His words and works become real and dear to them, not through emotional appeals but through impressions left by accurate, detailed knowledge of the Savior who went around doing good. Doctrine is inferred as a side effect of Biblical text. Loyalty to their Divine Master is more likely to become a guiding principle in their lives.

I can't emphasize enough how important it is to give a poetic presentation of the life and teachings of Jesus. In their Bible lessons, students should experience a wonderfully fascinating sense of the coordinated development and how each incident progressively [pg 166] reveals more of Jesus' teachings. Narration actually encourages students to pick up on this. Each incident they narrate becomes a complete event in their minds, the teachings will unfold as they talk about it, arguments will be more convincing when they articulate them, and the characters in the Bible will seem as real as people they know in real life. It won't be helpful to pressure students with practical application. It will probably just bore them, and it may cause students to form their own counter-opinions or even opposite convictions, even while they look innocently complacent. For the most part, we should let Scripture speak for itself and point to the moral.

'Right now, Christians (and those who claim to be) are at a place in thought where a contrived, unnatural study of the life and teaching of Jesus is useless. We've analyzed and broken down scripture until our minds are weary from the fragments. We've heard so many criticisms that there's no material left for the critics. But if we could just get a fresh concept of Christ's life among people, and the philosophic method of His teaching, then His own words would be fulfilled. The Son of Man would be lifted up and would draw all men to Himself. Poetic verse provides a fresh way to present the themes of scripture. Poetry is less personal, more concise and can be treated more reverently than prose. What Wordsworth called 'authentic comment' can be included more subtly. The Gospels vividly show us scenes of many people in their moment of coming face to face with Christ, and poetry allows a more dramatic yet restrained portrayal of those moments than prose.

'Shakespeare gave us a couple of lines from Scripture's great epic, a taste of what poetic presentation might be like: [pg 167]

'Those holy fields
Over whose acres walked those blessed feet
Which fourteen hundred years ago were nailed
For our advantage to the bitter cross.' [from King Henry IV]

If only Shakespeare had written poetry about the whole Bible! Every line he wrote dealing with Christ from the unique perspective and personality of his pen is a treasure.

Trench wrote the beautiful lines,

'Of Jesus sitting by a Samarian well
Or teaching some poor fishers on the shore.'

And Keble wrote,

'Meanwhile He paces through the adoring crowd
Calm as the march of some majestic cloud.'
        [John Keble, *Advent Sunday*]

and,

'In His meek power He climbs the mountain's brow.'
        [John Keble, *Fourth Sunday After Epiphany*]

Every line of this kind of poetry is precious, but there aren't very many, probably because the subject is so overwhelmingly immense. So we'll have to wait for a great poet to wrote an epic work. In the meantime, I tried to write something to use in the interim.' [*from the preface to Charlotte Mason's six-volume poetic work, The Saviour of the World.*] A 13-year-old girl in Form IV answered this question in her Easter exam: *'The people sat in darkness . . . I am the Light of the World.* Show as far as you can the meaning of these statements.' She wasn't asked to wrote her answer in verse, yet her own instinct recognized that the quotes she was writing about were essentially poetry, and could best be expressed in poetry:

"The people sat in darkness—all was dim,
No light had yet come unto them from Him,
No hope as yet of Heaven after life,
A peaceful haven far from war and strife.
Some warriors to Valhalla's halls might go
And fight all day, and die. At evening, lo! [pg 168

"They'd wake again, and drink in the great hall.
Some men would sleep for ever at their fall;

Or with their fickle Gods for ever be:
So all was dark and dim. Poor heathens, see!
The Light ahead, the clouds that roll away,
The golden, glorious, dawning of the Day;
And in the birds, the flowers, the sunshine, see
The might of Him who calls, Come unto Me."

A 17 year old girl in Form V responded to the request to *Write an essay or poem about the Bread of Life* with the following lines:

"'How Came He here,' ev'n so the people cried,
Who found Him in the Temple: He had wrought
A miracle, and fed the multitude,
On five small loaves and fish: so now they'd have
Him king; should not they then have ev'ry good,
Food that they toiled not for and clothes and care,
And all the comfort that they could require?—
So thinking sought the king.
     Our Savior cried:
'Labor ye not for meat that perished,
But rather for the everlasting bread,
Which I will give'—Where is this bread, they cry,
They know not 'tis a heavenly bread He gives
But seek for earthly food 'I am the Bread of Life
And all who come to Me I feed with Bread.
Receive ye then the Bread. Your fathers eat
Of manna in the wilderness—and died—
But whoso eats this Bread shall have his part
In everlasting life: I am the Bread,
That cometh down from Heaven; unless ye eat
Of me ye die, but otherwise ye live.'
So Jesus taught, in Galilee, long since.

"The people murmured when they heard His Word,
How can it be? How can He be our Bread?
They hardened then their hearts against His Word,
They would not hear. and could not understand,
And so they turned back to easier ways,
And many of them walked with Him no more.
May He grant now that we may hear the Word
And harden not our hearts against the Truth [pg 169]
That Jesus came to teach: so that in vain
He may not cry to hearts that will not hear,
'I am the Bread of Life, for all that come,
I have this gift, an everlasting life,
And room within my Heavenly Father's House."

The higher forms [*high school*] in the PUS [*Parents Union School*] read *The Saviour of the World* volume by volume, along with the Scripture text arranged in chronological order. The lower forms [*grades 1-6?*] read the first three

Gospels one at a time, which provide a synopsis of Christ's life. Form IV [*8th and 9th grade*] reads the Gospel of John and Acts, supplemented with Bishop Walsham How's wonderful commentaries, available from the S.P.C.K. [*Anglican Church's Society for Promoting Christian Knowledge*] The Epistles and Revelation are saved until Forms V and VI [*grades 10-12*] The Catechism, Prayer-book, and Church History are taught in a similar manner, using appropriate texts. They provide an opportunity to sum up the church's doctrine, which is covered by preparing for Confirmation and Sunday services at the student's church.

SECTION II - The Knowledge of Man

(a) History

I've already said that history is a vital part of education. Michel de Montaigne said that teachers should learn who the worthiest minds of all time were by studying history. We especially, who live in one of the great epochs of history, need to know what's happened before our time in order to be accurate judges of what's going on today. For example, the League of Nations [pg 170] has reminded us, not only of the Congress of Vienna, but of the many Treaties of Perpetual Peace that have marked the history of Europe.

'Things done for the first time, that have never been done before, are to be feared. Do you have a precedent for this action?' (*loosely paraphrased from Shakespeare's Henry VIII*)

We applaud the candid king's wisdom, and we wish we could find precedents for WWI, and the uneasy peace and depressing uncertainty that have come after the war. We recognize that we lack sound judgment to decide upon the complex issues we face. We're aware that we would have more confidence if we had more familiarity with what's happened before, and that comes from knowing history. The more educated people in the places where England rules [*England had dominions in India, Australia, Canada, and Africa; Kipling wrote that, 'the sun never sets on the British Empire'*] complain because the young people there have no sense of history. Therefore, their driving thought is, 'we are the people.' Even if Westminster Abbey itself was destroyed, they wouldn't care. Why should they be sentimental about the places where great events happened, and where great people lived and worked? Unfortunately, this apathy about history isn't just typical of those in the dominions. Youths right here in England are just as apathetic. Their elders don't have stories to pass on and information that might inspire the young people with the idea that every country in every period of time has had important deeds to be done, and great men who have risen to the occasion. Any day, a person—maybe even themselves—might be called on to do some heroic service that will change the course of history. Patriotism that is logical and thought-out depends on a thorough knowledge of history from reading many books. Our youths need to be informed patriots, not emotional fanatics.

If we don't know enough about history, it's the fault of our schools. Teachers will blame a lack of time. They'll say that the best they can squeeze in is a sketchy overview of British history taught with lectures where [pg 171] students take notes and write reports. We all know how unsatisfying that method is, even when the teacher is an entertaining lecturer. Not even a great writer like Thackeray himself could give real knowledge in his lectures titled *The Four Georges*. We need to get more from history lessons than impressions and opinions, but it does take time.

The method I advocate can multiply time. Every hour spent in school can be quadrupled and we can cover a surprising amount of world history in a thorough way in the same amount of time that most schools are only able to work in the barest sketch of English history. We know that students are very interested in history and will put their whole attention into it if they have the right books. Our own rambling lectures are usually a waste of time and strain students' attention. Our PNEU teachers only provide two things: knowledge, and a keen sympathy to student interest inspired by that knowledge. It's our job to make sure that every student knows, and is able to tell back in either oral narration or written essay. Using this method, we can cover so much material so well that students won't need to review before their exam. We insist on a single reading, because we are all naturally careless, and our tendency is to put off the effort at paying close attention as long as we think we'll have a second or third chance to get the information. But it doesn't take any extra work to pay attention. Complete and entire attention is a natural function of the mind. It takes no effort and causes no fatigue. In fact, the stress of mental labor we're sometimes aware of is when our attention wanders and we have to make ourselves bring it back. But the kind of attention that most teachers want is already in each of their students. They're born with it, and it's a tool to be used to educate them. It isn't something that school trains into them. Our business [pg 172] is to give students material written with good literary style, and make them certain that they won't have a second chance to go over a lesson.

A teacher's personality can be useful, but from an intellectual standpoint, not an emotional one. The teacher should look very interested. It's motivating for the students to think that their minds and their teacher's mind are working in harmony. But a sympathetic teacher who thinks that paying attention is hard work will overlook a student's wandering focus and distractedness a hundred times. And then the teacher has to finally draw in that child's attention, which is tiring for both him and the student. The teacher thinks he's being understanding, but he's actually doing a disservice to the student.

A six year old child in Form IB doesn't have stories from English history. He has a certain number of pages of consecutive reading, perhaps forty pages per term. His book is chosen carefully. It's a well-written, large volume [*i.e., not a typical first grade book?*] with nice pictures. Children won't be able to read it themselves since it isn't written down to a six-year-old's level. So the teacher reads it aloud, and the student tell it back, paragraph by paragraph, passage by passage. The teacher doesn't talk much, and never interrupts a child who is narrating. The first attempts at narrating may be stumbling, but soon the children get a feel for it and are able to narrate back long passages accurately. The teacher might let other children correct narrations. The hardest part for the teacher is looking receptive and interested, perhaps commenting on a passage that's been narrated, or showing a picture, that sort of thing. She'll keep in mind that the child as young as six has begun the serious business of getting an education. It doesn't matter whether he understands every word, the important thing is that he's learning that knowledge comes from books. We know that if a person, whether a child or adult, can tell something, they really know it. But if he can't put it into [pg 173] words, then he doesn't really know it. The practice of 'telling back' was probably used more often in the 1500's and 1600's than it is now. In Shakespeare's play *Henry VIII*, three men meet together. One of them has just come from the Abbey after witnessing the coronation of Anne Boleyn. The others ask him about it, and he tells them all about it with the detailed vividness and accuracy that we usually expect from children. For Shakespeare, this 'narration' was a stage device, but he probably wouldn't have used it if it seemed strange, so people in his day must have been used to narrating. Even today, we appreciate someone who's good at telling stories with flair. Only a generation or two ago, men studied the art of telling a good story, because it was expected of a gentleman. But someone may ask, isn't that kind of skill just rote memorization? When someone has to memorize a passage, they use some tricks and lots of repetition, but their mind isn't thinking about the passage, they're usually thinking about something else. Their mind isn't really actively involved in the act of memorizing. But reading a passage with the whole mind focused on that passage so it can be told back is a totally different thing and has a drastically different effect. French philosopher M. Henri Bergson (1859–1941) made a distinction between word memory and mind memory. Once we understand the significance of that difference, it will inspire major changes in our educational methods.

With mind memory, as we read, we visualize a scene in our mind, or we become convinced by an argument, or we take pleasure in the style of sentences and try to think up some sentences of our own in the same style. And that bit of text is assimilated into our mind and becomes part of us every bit as much as the dinner we had the night before. In fact, more so! Because yesterday's dinner doesn't matter tomorrow, but even several months from now, we'll still be able to tell about that passage we read. It's as if we literally consumed it with all the detail and sharpness it had the first time we told it. All the powers of the mind (sometimes called faculties) are actively involved in dealing with the intellectual food [pg 174] that's treated this way. We must not interfere with the assimilation process by asking questions to get the child to reason, or show elaborate pictures to help his imagination, or point out moral lessons to sharpen his conscience. These things happen naturally, as unconsciously as the body digests food.

Seven-year-olds are promoted to form IA where they remain for a couple of years. They use the same wonderful book, Mrs. H.E. Marshall's *Our Island Story*, reading about the same number of pages in a term. In form IB they read the first third of the book, which contains simpler and more direct stories. Students in 1A read the second two thirds of the book. All the children learn to love English history. 'I'd rather have history than my dinner,' said a healthy boy of seven who obviously rarely missed his dinner.

In 1A, history is expanded and illustrated using short biographies of people from the historical period being studied, such as Lord Clive, Nelson, etc. They also read Mrs. Frewen Lord's delightful *Tales from Westminster Abbey* and from *St.*

Paul's to help personalize historical heroes. It's refreshing to hear them narrate with interest about Franklin, Nelson, Howard, Shaftesbury. They love visiting the monuments. One wouldn't think that children would be very interested in John Donne, but many onlookers were surprised to see a small group of children noticing tell-tale marks from the Great Fire that could still be seen on his monument.

There is probably no better method of imparting a reasonable and dutiful patriotism than making children familiar with the monuments of great heroes, even if they never get to see those monuments in person. In Form II (ages 9-12), students have a more challenging history curriculum, but they cover it easily and they enjoy it. The book they use is more difficult than the one used in Form IA. It's an interesting, well-written history of England, from which they read [pg 175] about fifty pages per term. Form IIA students also read a book about the social life in England to parallel the chapters they're reading in their history text. Children are introduced as early as possible to the contemporary history of other countries, since studying only English history tends to lead to insular and arrogant thinking.

Of course, we start with French history. Both forms read from the very well-written *First History of France*, reading the chapters that go along with the period they're studying in English history. The enthusiasm with which children write or tell about Richelieu, Colbert, and Bayard tells us that they are quite capable of handling this early introduction of foreign history. Because the books tell the stories sharply and clearly, the children gain so much knowledge about the history of France that it illuminates the history of their own country, and gives them a sense that history was progressing in other places, just as it was in England during the time period they're studying.

Ancient British history can't always be studied alongside French history. Instead, we use a book about a British museum [*The British Museum for Young People*] that is arranged chronologically. It was written for P.U.S. (Parent's Union School) students by the late Mrs. W. Epps. She had a wonderful gift for understanding how the ages progress and how that is represented in our great British museum. I have already mentioned one child's visit to the Parthenon Room and her excitement in recognizing something she had read about. This shows how valuable this kind of book is for opening ancient history to children. Ms. G. M. Bernau has made these studies even more valuable by producing a 'Book of Centuries.' Children draw pictures in it as they come across household objects, art, and other things from the century they're reading about. Touching on the British museum in this way is very valuable. Whether the children [pg 176] actually have the opportunity to visit the museum or not, this inspires an interest in going. Also, they are made aware of what kinds of treasures there are in their own local museums.

In Form III children continue with the same history of England as they were doing in Form II, as well as the same French history, and the same British museum book. They continue adding to their 'Book of Centuries.' In addition, they read about 20-30 pages per term from a short book about the history of India, a subject that they are very interested in.

Their geography studies touch on the history of other parts of the British Empire.

In Form IV, students move up to Gardiner's *Student's History of England*. It is clear and sufficient, but somewhat stiffer than what they've been used to. At the same time, they read Mr. and Mrs. Quennell's *History of Everyday Things in England*. This book is also used in Form III. Form IV students begin an outline of European history. They continue the British museum book and their 'Book of Centuries.'

All teachers know how difficult it is to find just the right book in each subject. For a few years we regretted that Lord's delightful book *Modern Europe* was out of print, but it's back in print again.

In Forms V and VI (ages 15-18) history is more advanced and there is more of it. They are illustrated with the literature of the period being studied. For instance, their English history text, Green's *Shorter History of the English People*, might be amplified with Macaulay's *Essays on Frederick the Great* and the *Austrian Succession*, on *Pitt*, and *Clive*. For the same period they read from an American book about Western Europe and a well-written book about French History by M. Duruy, translated into English. They might read Madame de Stael's *L'Allemagne* or another equally well-written [pg 177] book as part of their French lesson. It's not possible to study Greek and Roman history in this kind of detail, but a well-written, enthusiastic overview is provided with Professor de Burgh's *The Legacy of the Ancient World*. Students make history charts marking every hundred years, using the plan of the late Ms. Beale of Cheltenham. It uses a square divided into one hundred blocks of ten in each direction. Each block has a symbol in it depicting an event to illustrate that particular ten years. For instance, crossed battle-axes might represent a war.

The geographical aspects of history are studied under geography. The reading plan I've just described is very valuable because it gives youths a knowledge of the past that relates to and illuminates the present. I remember meeting some brilliant Oxford undergraduates, sharp and interested, but sadly ignorant. They said, 'We want to know something about history. What can you suggest for us to read? We know nothing.' No youth should go to college without a basic course of English, European, and especially French, history, such as our P.U.S program provides. This kind of general knowledge of history should be learned before taking any advanced course, and should be required before students take academic studies to prepare them for research work.

You will note that the studies throughout the school years are always chronologically progressive. Children rarely cover the same material twice. But if it should happen that the whole school has studied up to the current time period, and there is nothing else to do but begin again, the books they use will shed new light and bring them up to date with the latest discoveries.

But any period of history studied in Forms V and VI depends on the supplement of [pg 178] literature. Plays, novels, essays, biographies, and poems are all used. Whenever possible, the architecture, painting, and art produced in the historical period are also studied. Thus students are able to answer the following kinds of questions to test and record the term's reading,—'Describe the condition of (a) the clergy, (b) the army, (c) the navy, (d) the general public in about 1685.' 'Trace the rise of Prussia before Frederick the Great.' 'What theories of government did Louis XIV hold? Tell about some of his most important ministers.' 'Describe the rise of Russia and it's condition at the beginning of the 18th century.' 'Suppose Evelyn (in Form VI) or Pepys (in Form V) is in counsel at the League of Nations. Write three day's worth of their journal entries.' 'Write about the character and habits of Addison. How does he appear in *Esmond*?'

It's a wonderful thing to have a pageant of history as a backdrop to one's thoughts. We might not be able to remember this or that detail, but the imagination has been inspired. We will know that there are many good arguments on both sides of every issue, and we will be saved from having crude opinions and acting rashly. Our own current time will be enriched with the wealth of all that has gone before.

Perhaps the most serious flaw in school curricula is that they don't give a comprehensive, intelligent and interesting introduction to history. To end with, or even to begin with, the history of our own country is fatal. We can't live sanely unless we understand that other people are the same as we are, but their individual circumstanes are different. They have a history like we do, but with different particulars, they have been immortalized by their own poets and artists, they have their own literature and their own patriotism. It's as if we've been asleep and our awakening is a shock. The people that we have failed to teach rise up against us in their ignorance, and 'the rabble,' [pg 179] '...make decisions as if the world has just begun, history didn't exist, and there were no traditions.' **(loosely translated from Hamlet)**

Unfortunately the decision does rest with them, and they'll need all the luck they can get. They know nothing of Antiquity and Custom, which approve and help support every present word or action. It's never too late to learn, but we must not hesitate in offering a rich and generous diet of history to every child in the country in order to make his decisions count, make his actions well-reasoned and his conduct reliable. The lack of stability has plunged us into many stormy seas of unrest.

Stability distinguishes the educated classes. When we think about how our times are disturbed by labor unrest, and when we reflect on the fact that political and social power is shifting to the majority (the working class), we can't help feeling that it is right to educate people of all classes. Right now, an emotional, ignorant working class is a danger to our nation. I'm not sure that education that provides everyone the same opportunity to climb the ladder of success is the best motive for national tranquility. It's right for everyone to have the same opportunity to reach the top, but that's no revelation. Our history tells about many men who have risen to leadership. The Roman Church and the Chinese Empire are largely founded on the doctrine of equal opportunity. However, let's not forget that men who climb to the top tend to be unstable members of society. On the other hand, the desire for knowledge for its own sake is satisfied with knowledge for its own sake, rather than using education to gain a competitive edge.

With education, our young people will be inspired with vision. The hardships of their daily lives will seem less burdensome. An alert and informed mind will lead to decent, honest living rather than a restless desire to subvert society for the sake of [pg 180] opportunities that might be gained by upheaval of the entire system. Wordsworth is right:

'Men are humble if they are trained and bred correctly.'

These times are critical for everybody, but especially for teachers. It depends on them to decide whether to aim for personal good, or for the good of the general public. They must decide whether education should be merely a means of earning a living, or a means of progressing towards high thinking and decent living, and therefore an instrument of the greatest good for society. (*Exam results will give some idea of the range of our P.U.S history study, and may be seen at the P.N.E.U. office.*)

(b) Literature

After Form I (grades 1-3), literature readings are coordinated with the history period being studied. Fairy tales such as those by Hans Christian Anderson or the Brothers Grimm are read in Form IB (first grade). The children narrate these tales enthusiastically, vividly, and with the kind of exactness that they demonstrate when they notice something left out while their favorite book is being read to them. Aesop's *Fables* are used successfully. After being read aloud concisely just once, children are able to figure out the moral themselves. Mrs. Gatty's *Parables from Nature* serve another purpose. They feed a child's sense of wonder and lend themselves well to narration. No attempt is made to dumb down work to a juvenile level. Form IA (grades 2 and 3) students listen to *Pilgrim's Progress* a chapter at a time and narrate it. Their narrations are delightful. No beautiful thought or memorable character escapes their notice. Andrew Lang's [pg 181] *Tales of Troy and Greece*, a big, thick book, is used as a spine for a number of terms.

Ancient tales from the heroic age appeal to children. They can imagine every detail and narrate enthusiastically. The unusual foreign names aren't an obstacle, rather, they enjoy them because, as one schoolteacher says,

'Children are instinctively able to sense the meaning of whole passages, and even some of the difficult words, from context.'

This next quote from the same teacher illustrates how children love the beautiful sound of these classical names:

'A seven-year-old in my school the other day asked his mother why she hadn't given him one of the nice names he had heard in the stories at school. He thought Ulysses was a much better name than Kenneth, and that his friend's mother should have named him Achilles instead of Allen.'

In these days when we fear that London itself is in danger of losing the rich historical associations which its streets are named after, we desperately need to cultivate an appreciation for beautiful names. We don't want to be like New York, with street names like X500. It would be as bad as identifying people with social security numbers instead of names. What a sad time we live in when we honor the discovery of a new peak in the Himalayas by naming it D2! Children at this age are naturally drawn to beautiful names, and this affinity should be cultivated. The Hindu who announced that his name was going to be 'Telephone' showed that he had an ear for pleasing sounds. Kingsley's *Water Babies*, Lewis's *Alice in Wonderland*, Kipling's *Just So Stories*, and scores of other classics written *for* children, but not **down to** them, are appropriate for this stage.

Form IIB (fourth grade) has a challenging reading schedule. It isn't that they have so many *more* books, it's the *quality* of their books that's important. Therefore [pg 182] children should spend two years in Form IA (grades 2 and 3). In the second year (third grade) they should be reading a lot of their scheduled books for themselves. In IIB (fourth grade) they read their own geography, history, and poetry. Shakespeare's *Twelfth Night* and books like Scott's *Rob Roy* and Swift's *Gulliver's Travels* should be read to them and narrated by them until they are ten years old (fifth grade). They are surprisingly able to understand, imagine, and tell back a Shakespeare play from the time they're nine years old. They don't add anything to their narrations that wasn't in the play, and they don't miss a thing. They can present a passage or scene by contrasting characters in an interesting way. One or two books of high quality such as *The Heroes of Asgard* are also included in the term's schedule.

In Form IIA (grades 5 and 6), students are expected to do more individual reading, as well as take on a few more books. They begin reading Shakespeare plays for themselves, each student taking a part. We heard of some boys from the Council School who insisted on taking parts with a book by Sir Walter Scott to read this way. They read Bulfinch's *Age of Fable* to introduce them to the imaginations of people who lived without knowledge of the truth. They might also read Stevenson's *Kidnapped* and poems by Oliver Goldsmith during a term. In all of these books, students show the same evidence of their power to know, proved by the one sure test: they're able to narrate (tell) each book accurately, and with enthusiasm and their own individual added touches. One might wonder how 'individuality' can be shown in a narration. Let's ask Scott, Shakespeare and Homer, who only wrote what they had heard somewhere else (and that, after all, is what narration is!), but with the continual sparkle of their own personal genius added to the text. In a similar way, children tell their narrations. They imagine it all so vividly in their own minds, that, as they tell it or write it, the theme gleams as we read or listen to them.

Students stay in Form II until they are twelve years old. Here, I'll add a comment about the steadfast progress children make [pg 183] in their ability to deal with books. All we do is present the scheduled books as if we're laying out an abundant, delicious feast, and each young guest digests what's right for him. The bright, advanced child gets a lot more than a slower peer, but they all sit down to the same meal and each one gets just what he needs and can handle.

The surprising effect this kind of education has on slow or even mentally handicapped students is encouraging and enlightening. We claim to understand that humans are educable. But when we open the floodgates and allow children to learn everything they want, we see how limited our views really were, how poor and restricted the knowledge we offered them actually was. Yet we see that, even in challenged or learning disabled children,

'What a piece of work man is! When it comes to learning, he's like a god!' (*loosely translated from Hamlet*)

In Forms III and IV (grades 7-9), students begin a *History of English Literature*, which was carefully chosen because it gives students a kind-hearted interest and enjoyment of literature without giving stereotyped opinions and outdated information. They read about fifty pages per term, and the portion they read corresponds with the historical period they're studying. That book is a special favorite with the students. They love Shakespeare, whether the term's assignment is *King Lear, Twelfth Night, Henry V*, or another play. The *Waverley* Novels provide a story from the time period. There was some discussion in our Elementary Schools about whether abridged editions of Scott might make it easier to finish the book in a term, but teachers at a meeting in Glouster presented strong reasons for using the unabridged version. Students enjoy the dry parts, the descriptions and such. This is proved by how beautifully they narrate those parts. Students in Form IV (grade8/9) have a varied booklist. For instance, if they're learning about the part of history that includes the Commonwealth, they might read *L'Allegro, Il Penseroso*, Milton's *Lycidas*, and an anthology of various poets from that time period. If they're studying [pg 184] a later period, they might read Pope's *Rape of the Lock*, or Gray's poems. Form III (grades 7 and 8) might read poems of Goldsmith and Burns. The purpose of the literature selections isn't so they'll know who wrote what during which king's reign, but to instill a sense of the vastness of the era, not just the Elizabethan era, but all the historical periods that poets, journallers and storytellers have left living pictures of. This way, children get more than the kind of facts that have no cultural value. They gain wide spaces in their minds where their imaginations can go for vacation journeys that prevent life from becoming dreary. Also, as they make judgments, their minds will go over these memory files they have stored and they'll have a broader base of knowledge to draw from when considering decisions about a particular strike, or issues of country rights, or political unrest. Every individual is called on to be a statesman since each person has a say in how the government is run. But being a good statesman requires a mind alive with the kind of imaginative impressions that come from wide reading and some familiarity with historic precedents.

The reading for Forms V and VI (ages 15-18, grades 10-12) is more comprehensive and challenging. It also corresponds with the historical period they're studying, which may be current history supplemented with occassional modern literature. Even in making selections among modern books, we have found that students who have been brought up with this kind of curriculum can be trusted to continue selecting the best books that are being written as time goes on. Depending on the historical period being covered, a term might include Pope's *Essay on Man*, Carlyle's *Essay on Burns*, Frankfort Moore's *Jessamy*

Bride, an edited version of Goldsmith's *Citizen of the World*, Thackeray's *The Virginians*, and an anthology of poets from the same time period. Form VI would read Boswell, Swift's *The Battle of the Books*, Macaulay's *Essays on Goldsmith*, Johnson, Pitt and that era's poets from *The Oxford Book of Verse*. Both Forms read Goldsmith's *She Stoops to Conquer*. Their booklist isn't exhaustive, but [pg 185] will lead the student to read more about that time period in later years. As far as how much reading there is in each term, it's probably the same amount that any of us would read in a term, but we read and forget because we don't put in the effort to know as we read. These young students will have the power of perfect recollection, and they'll be able to apply their knowledge wisely because they've read with full attention and concentration, and in every case, they've reproduced what they read by narrating aloud or, in some cases, in writing.

Students' answers in their exams show that literature has become a living, vital power in their minds. Their exam papers can be viewed at the PNEU office.

(c) Morals and Economics: Citizenship

Like literature, this subject is treated like a supplement to history. In Form I (grades 1-3), children begin to form impressions about the way the world works from tales, fables and stories about famous heroes. In Form II (grades 4-6), they actually begin to learn Citizenship as a subject, gathering inspiring impressions about what makes a good citizen while continuing to learn the things that every citizen should know. Plutarch's *Lives* is especially inspiring. The teacher reads these aloud, leaving out what may not be suitable, and the students narrate them enthusiastically. They learn to answer questions like, 'In what ways did Pericles make Athens beautiful? How did he persuade people to help him?' And we hope that children will catch the idea of preserving beauty and making their [pg 186] community more beautiful. This is a fresher way of instilling this idea than constant lessons and reminding, which will only bore them. They will also be able to answer, 'How did Pericles handle the people during war so that they wouldn't force him to take an action he knew was wrong?' And from these kinds of questions, we believe that students will gain some understanding of the delicate issues of leadership. Then, when they learn about their own current time period, they'll be able to answer, 'What do you know about (a) Local City Councils, (b) State Councils, (c) Church Councils?' And this should help children realize that they too are learning and preparing to become worthy citizens, and that each person has several duties, even if he doesn't lead in government. Mrs. Beesley's *Stories from the History of Rome* is better for Form II (grades 4-6) than Plutarch. Macauley's *Lays of Rome* helps to make it even clearer. When we teach children about men and events that deal with citizenship, we'll be faced with the problem of exposing children to good and evil. Many sincere teachers share the concerns of this teacher who said,

'Why are we giving children the story of Circe, with its offensive display of greed? Why not just give them heroic tales that present noble examples to live up to? Time is so short, why waste it on bad examples instead of making the most of every opportunity to give examples of living a good life and having good manners?'

Or,

'Why should students read *Childe Harold*, and become so familiar with a poet whose works are so unedifying?'

Plutarch is like the Bible in this respect: he doesn't label the things his characters do as good or bad. He leaves it up to the reader's conscience and judgment to make that distinction. What to avoid and how to avoid it is as important for a citizen to know as what's good and how to do it, whether he's a citizen of heaven or of his local community. Children recognize [pg 187] an artificially doctored story as soon as it starts, and they begin to get bored with it. But true stories about real people with all their good and bad qualities never get old. Even though Jacob was chosen by God, we don't get bored hearing about him because we know he was a real person. We recognize the truth in his own words, 'the days of my life have been few and evil.' We recognize that the foreign kings he came in contact with had more integrity than he did, just like in the New Testament, the Roman Centurion had a finer character than most of the Jews who were religious in name only. Perhaps we've been made so that heroes who are perfect, and goodness that's totally virtuous, bore us. But when we read about great figures who had failings and weaknesses, we preach little sermons to ourselves. Children are no different than us. They need to see life in its entirety to learn from it. Yet, at the same time, they need to be protected from obscenity and rudeness that might be in their reading material. A newspaper might tell about real people and events, but it's in no way on the same level as Plutarch's *Lives* or Lang's *Tales of Troy and Greece*. A 10-12 year old who is familiar enough with a dozen or so of Plutarch's Lives that they influence what he thinks and how he acts, has learned to put his country first, and to see individuals from the perspective of whether they serve their society, or do a disservice to it. And those are his first lessons about the science of proportion. Children who understand that society isn't the government but the people, will be glad to learn about the laws, customs and government about their own country. They'll also come to understand something about themselves, their mind and body, heart and soul. They'll want to know how to govern themselves so that they can be of service to their society.

We have a challenge in choosing books, the same challenge that has concerned all great thinkers from Plato to Erasmus to concerned school officials in our own day. [pg 188]

I'm referring to the vulgar and raunchy things that come up in so many books that would be otherwise useful for teaching sound judgment. Milton assures us that to the pure, all things are pure. But we're still uneasy. When older students read the *Areopagitica*, they learn that seeing impurity makes you impure. Younger children learn from reading *Ourselves*. Properly taught children will learn to keep watch even over their thoughts because they know that God's angels are watching them. When possible, we use expurgated editions of books (books that have had objectionable content removed). When that's not possible, the teacher reads the book aloud and leaves out unsuitable content. We try to be careful when teaching about the natural processes of plants and animals [*presumably referring specifically to reproduction*] not to awaken impure thoughts in students. One word about this—the strict rules that school officials have about games isn't just for the sake of the games themselves. St. Paul exhorted us to keep our bodies always under subjection. Games that exhaust the physical body need some understood boundaries to keep students decent. And they do, although some incidents of indiscretion have occurred even in the best schools. A fact not always recognized is that these kinds of incidents that distress teachers and parents have their root in the mind, and especially in an empty mind. And that's why parents who take their children away from the corruption of public schools to teach them at home so often miss the mark. The increased free time that homeschooling provides is like sweeping the room in the mind free, and can be an invitation to secret sins of the mind that thrive in solitude. And schools also make the mistake of not providing students with enough work that's interesting and absorbing enough to cause students to think and reflect on it so that students' minds are always wholesomely occupied. A child needs [pg 189] plenty of mental food, and I don't mean from haphazard reading of this and that, which causes idleness that leads to mischief, but with a definite plan of teaching to know. If a child has enough healthy mental food on which to imagine, speculate, and aspire to, then he'll be a pure-minded youth who doesn't mind hard work and enjoys the fun of games. This may look like a detour from the subject of citizenship, but all children need to know that they owe their society the contribution of a sound, pure mind and body.

Ourselves, our Souls and Bodies [*Volume 4 of the CM Series*] is used extensively in our PUS [*Parents Union Schools*]. I don't know of any other book that tries to present a basic diagram of human nature that will enable students to know how they can be effective in their efforts to be good. The book tries to instill the concept that all people have within themselves the possibilities to be beautiful and noble, but each person is also subject to attacks and obstacles of various kinds. Students need to be aware of them so that they can watch and pray. Lectures that try to appeal to children to behave are boring (to children as well as adults!) But a systematic teaching that presents all the possibilities and powers that we all have in our human nature, as well as the risks and pitfalls that go along with them, will enlighten students and stimulate them to use the abilities they have to control themselves.

But the goals we have in mind in teaching everyday morals and citizenship are best illustrated with a few essays written by students of different ages. They deal with managing oneself and they exemplify the virtues that make a person useful to his society. Their exam papers can be viewed at the PNEU office. One little girl, as she came out of her bath, said, 'Oh no, I'm just like Julius Caesar! I don't even want to do a thing if I'm not the best at it!' This shows that children gather the principles that will guide their lives from unlikely sources, and in the most unlikely ways.

[pg 190]

(d) Composition

In Form I (grades 1-3), composition is almost all oral and is so intertwined with history, geography and science that it hardly even comes up as a special subject, except as it relates to Tales. Teachers waste a lot of effort implementing careful, methodical programs to teach composition. They go through drills and exercises to teach young children how to form a sentence, but their work is unnecessary, or even damaging. It makes as much sense as putting a child through a curriculum of detailed exercises to teach him the steps in chewing food or extracting nutrition from bread! Their effort is well-intentioned—they want to do everything they can to help children. But, too often, they take on themselves what children can do very efficiently for themselves. One of these things is composition: expressing their thoughts, the art of 'telling' that is best exemplified by great writers like Sir Walter Scott or Homer. It begins with toddlers as young as two or three who babble constantly to each other, and have lots to say, although adults, including their own mother, can't understand. But by age six, they can express themselves fluently. The mother who attempts to write down their re-telling of 'Hansel and Gretel' or 'The Little Match Girl' or a Bible story will fill lots of pages before the story ends! And the story's details will be accurate, with surprisingly lively expression, compelling and confident. There aren't many adults who could tell one of Aesop's Fables with the crisp clarity that children are capable of. Children's narrations aren't disjointed, either. They narrate in the same order as their text assignments, continuing to tell back each chapter week by week from whatever book they're reading, whether it's Mrs. Gatty's Parables From Nature, fairy tales by Grimm or Andersen [pg 191] or Pilgrim's Progress, starting at the same point where they left off. Their knowledge is never sketchy. They know the answers to questions like, 'What happened at the meeting of Ulysses and Telemachus?' or 'What happened at the meeting of Jason and Hera?' or 'Tell about Christian and Hopeful meeting with Giant Despair,' or, "Tell about the Shining Ones.'

Children are in Form IA (about grades 2 and 3) at ages 7-9. They read about more varied things, and they have more composition [*referring to oral narration*]. In their exams [which are oral], they tell about Jesus feeding the Four Thousand, about building the Tabernacle, How Doubting Castle was destroyed, about how St. Paul's cathedral burned down, why we know that the world is round, and lots of other things. All of the reading they do lends itself well to narration, and the ability to narrate like this is something they're born with, not something they learned from school. There are a couple of things to keep in mind. Children in Form IB (first grade) need a lot of material read aloud, increasing incrementally in difficulty. They don't need to have their faculties developed from scratch, since they were born with the power they need. But they do need a little time to learn how to use their power of concentrating their attention and narrating. So young children should probably be allowed to narrate a paragraph at a time. By age seven or eight, they'll be able to tell a whole chapter at a time. Corrections shouldn't be made during narration [*but can be made afterwards!*] and narrations shouldn't be interrupted.

Children shouldn't be hassled or pressured about using proper punctuation and capital letters when they write their narrations. Those things will take care of themselves if the child reads a lot, and too many coaxings to use correct punctuation usually results in the over-use of commas. While children don't need to be forbidden from reading well-intentioned second-rate books, such books should never be used for school lessons. Right from the start, children should get into the habit of reading good literature, and they should absorb what they will from it themselves, in their own way, whether it's a lot or a little. Since every writer's goal is to explain himself in his own [pg 192] book, the child and the author need to be trusted alone together, without a middle-man telling the child what the book said or what to think about it. Whatever the author chose not to say must be left out for the time being. Explanations won't really help the child. Defining words and phrases will spoil the story and shouldn't be done unless the child asks, 'What does that mean?' and then another student [*if it's a classroom*] will probably tell him.

In Form II (grades 4-6), students have more variety in their reading, more new ideas to think about, and lots more subjects for composition. They can write short essays themselves, and with accurate knowledge and clear expression that makes one stand in wonder. They can describe their favorite scene from The Tempest or Woodstock. They can write or tell stories based on Plutarch or Shakespeare, or current events. They narrate from history, the Bible, *Stories from the History of Rome*, from Bulfinch's *Age of Fable*, poetry like that of Oliver Goldsmith or Wordsworth, or *The Heroes of Asgard*. In fact, composition isn't a separate subject in addition to everything else, it's an integral part of every other subject. Narrating is something the children enjoy. I guess we all like to tell what we know. Their narrations are artless in the sense of being totally sincere. In fact, the more artless their narrations are, the more artistic the results are. Any child can produce his own style that's enviable for its liveliness and polish. But, I repeat, there must not be any effort to 'teach' composition. Our mistake as teachers is that we underestimate the intellectual ability of our students. And, since children are so humble, they will sit back and let their teacher do for them what they think they can't do for themselves if she volunteers. But give them the opportunity, and do them no favors, and they'll have no problem describing their favorite scene from a play they've read, or anything else. [pg 193]

In Forms III and IV (grades 7-9), composition is still the natural narrations of a free use of carefully scheduled books and still requires no specific attention until the student is old enough to become interested on his own in analyzing and using words. Children enjoy the cadence of poetry as much as adults, and many can write poetry as easily as prose. The exercise of making their narration concise and weighty enough for verse is a great mental challenge. But keep in mind that, although rhythm and accent can be learned by merely reading poetry, knowledge of metrical patterns needs to be learned if one is going to write poetry. At this age, the term's reading, current events, and the passing of the seasons provide lots of subjects for short essays, or for poems, which can be more abstract in Form IV (grade 8 or 9). Just remember that whatever subject the child writes about should be, as Jane Austen put it, something that has 'warmed' his imagination. They should only be asked to write about subjects that have keenly interested them. Then, during term exams, they can answer questions like, 'write twelve lines about Sir Henry Lee, or Cordelia, or Pericles, or Livingstone,' or perhaps a question about the early days of the current war [*WWI*], such as, 'Discuss Lord Derby's Scheme. How is it working?' Students in Form IV (grade 8/9) might write an essay about, 'the new army still developing, showing what some of the challenges have been and what it has accomplished.'

Forms V and VI (grades 10-12) should have a little teaching about writing compositions, but not too much. Too much teaching might encourage a pretentious, artificial style that might encumber them for the rest of their lives. Maybe the methods that University tutors use is the best one. What they do is, [pg 194] they take one or two points from a composition and talk about corrections or suggestions. Since students have read so much great literature from skilled authors, they will have picked up a certain amount of style. Since they've been exposed to so many great minds in books, they'll be less likely to copy a single author. Instead, they'll be more likely to find their own individual style from the wealth of voices they've been reading. And since they've received all kinds of interesting ideas from their lessons, they'll have important things to write about and won't be unnecessarily wordy without having something to say. Here's an example of a term's assignments for Form V: A concise summary of a book, a letter to the editor about some current event, subject taken from the term's reading, notes from a picture study, dialogs between characters from the term's reading, poetic ballads about current events. Form VI's assignments might also include essays on current events and issues, and a patriotic play. Here are some assignments from another term: A praise song, either rhyming or blank verse, about the Prince of Wales' tour of British-occupied regions, an essay dated 10 years in the future about the League of Nation's accomplishments. Form V might write a sad poetic ballad about conditions in Ireland, a poem about the King's garden party with his Vice Chancellors, an essay about the current condition of England, or US President Wilson.

The students' response to these assignments is very encouraging and fun to read. Their work has literary, or even poetic value, but the fact that they can write well isn't the most important accomplishment. Even more importantly, they can read, appreciating every nuance of the author's thoughts. They can consider current events and political concerns with educated minds. In other words, their education is relevant to the issues and interests of the real world they live in, and they are making real progress in becoming broad-minded citizens [pg 195] and future leaders. Here are some samples of student work from various aged children. These are from exam papers and have not been corrected.

Form IIA (grade 5 or 6)

Armistice Day

Soldiers dying, soldiers dead,
Bullets whizzing overhead.
British soldiers stand nearby
Waiting for their time to die.
Soon the lull of gunfire comes
No sound but the roll of drums.

Now the last shell crashes down,
A soldier reels in pain.
Too late the good news comes for him,
He never moves again.
He's the Unknown Soldier,

A man without a name.

Two years later, home he comes
To those who loved him well.
Who is the Unknown Soldier?
No lips the tale can tell.
His tomb is in the Abbey,
Where the souls of heroes dwell.

A nation's sorrow and its tears
Go with the nameless man.
Who can know this soldier's name?
We know that no one can.
So let our sorrow turn to joy
On the grave of the unknown man. [pg 196]

Form III (grade 7)

The student was asked to write a poem in blank verse about one of the following:
(a), Scylla and Charybdis; (b), The White Lady of Avenel; (c), The Prince of
Wales' trip to India.

The White Lady of Avenel

The sun had set and it would soon be night
The hills looked black against the sky at twilight.
A sliver of a crescent moon shone dimly
On a group of pine trees on the hill,
Making the river look silver.
Now everything was quiet. Not one sound disturbed
The summer night, and not even a whisper of wind
Stirred the pine trees. Everything in nature slept peacefully.
But what is that, standing in the shade?
It's a woman, tall and thin, wearing all white,
With a misty crown on her long hair,
And every now and then, she sighed,
Leaning against the rugged mountain rock,
As vague as a moonbeam or a wisp of smoke.
Over her shimmering, moonlit robe she wore
A gold girdle intervowen with
The fortune of the Avenel family.
A cloud crossed and covered the moon. The woman, ghostlike,
Faded and disappeared into thin air.
A breeze began blowing the tall pine trees;
And then a river, murmuring as it flowed on its way
Whispered a sad lament in the night.

Form III (grade 7)

Write a poem in Ballad Metre about Armistice Day or Echo.

Armistice Day, or, This Unknown Warrior

Within the ancient Abbey's sacred pyle,
Which proudly guards the noblest of our dead.
Where kings and statesmen lie in every aisle,
And honoured poets, soldiers, priests are laid; [pg 197]

Behold a stranger comes. From whence is he?
Is he of noble birth? Of rank or fame?
Was he as great as any whom we see
Around, who worked to make themselves a name?

Surely he is a prince. Nay, e'en a king?
For see the waiting thousands gathered here;
And hear the streets of ancient London ring
To the slow tramp of men who guard his bier!

And, surely it's the King himself who comes
As chiefest mourner on this solemn day,
And these who walk behind him are his sons—
All here to mourn this man. Who is he? Say!

How long the ranks of men who follow him
To his last resting-place—the House of God.
Our bishops, soldiers, statemen all are here,
Gathered to lay him in his native sod.

You ask 'Is he a prince?' I answer, 'No.'
Though none could be interred with greater state!
This man went forth to guard us from a foe,
Which threatened this our land—He did his work!

He raised the flag of Liberty on high
And challenging the powers of Wrong and Might
He gave up all he had without a sigh
And died for the good cause of God and Right.

The students also show some sense of humor:

Form III (grade 7)

Write a poem in Ballad Metre about Echo.

Echo

Jupiter once left his wife alone
To fiirt with some nymphs in the wood
But Juno his wife suspected him
And followed as fast as she could. [pg 198]

Now, Echo, a nymph, knew that Juno was there
And the nymphs would soon be found out,
And so she kept Juno away from the wood
For if they had gone she did doubt.

But Juno knew all, and her anger was great
And Echo this dreadful thing heard:
'Since you are so fond of talking so much,
You always shall have the last word!'

Now Echo went far from the dwellings of men
And spent her sad days all alone
 And often she'd weep and think of the past
And her sad fate would make her moan.

Echo loved a Greek youth, but he did not love her.
And she watched him all day from her bower
Till she pined away, all but her voice, which lives still,
And the youth was turned into a flower.

Form III (grade 7)

Write some verses about (a) Dandie Dinmont, or, (b) Atalanta, or, (c) Allenby.

Atlanta was a huntress,
Who really loved to race,
She outran deer in swiftness
And had a lovely face.

Lots of suitors sought her,
But they wooed in vain,
For she vowed to stay single
And all her beaus were slained.

For she had heard the warning
From a witch who knew her art
Who told her if she married
All joy would leave her heart.

But a youth favored by Venus
Came one day to run to run the race,
and by throwing golden apples,
He beat her in the chase. [pg 199]

But while they shared their gladness
Venus they failed to thank.
She, being so offended,
lowered them to animal rank.

Form III (grade 7)

Phaëton was a stubborn youth who always got his way.
He asked to drive his father's horse upon a fateful day.
But Phoebus knew quite well what danger lurked up in the sky;
He begged of him to wish again for something else to try,
But Phaëton had decided he was going to have his way,
He leaped into the chariot despite his father's sway.
The horses started forward at a dashing breakneck pace,
Phaëton tried to hold them back and make them slow their race.
With dreadful swiftness on he flew, and lost his proper road,
The earth and sky began to smoke in an alarming mode.
At last when all had burst in flames, Jupiter cried aloud,
Phaëton who had lost his wits was killed beneath a cloud.

Form IV (grade 8 or 9)

Write thirty lines of blank verse about (a), 'A Spring Morning' (following 'A
Winter Morning Walk'), or, (b), Pegasus, or, (c), Allenby.

A Spring Morning

It's Spring; and now the birds with merry song
Sing with full-throated voice to the blue sky
On which small clouds float, soft as a dove's wing.
Against the blue the pale-green leaflet gleams.
The darker green of elder, further down,
Sets off the brilliance of the hawthorn-hedge.
Close to the ground, the purple violet peeps
From out its nest of overhanging leaves.
On yonder bank the daffodils toss their heads
Under the shady lichen trees so tall.
Close by a chestnut, bursting into leaf,
Drops down its sticky calyx on the ground;
An early bumble-bee dives headlong in
To a half-opened flower of early pear.
O'erhead, in the tail beech trees, busy rooks, [pg 200]

With great caw-caws and many angry squawks
Build their great clumsy nests with bits of twig
And little sticks just laid upon a bough.
And by the long, straight, path tall fir trees wave
Their graceful heads in the soft whisp'ring breeze
And pressed against one ruddy trunk, an owl
In vain tries to avoid the light of day,
But blinks his wise old eyes, and shakes himself,
And nestles close amid the sheltering leaves.
Now on the rhubarb-bed we see, glad sight,
Large red buttons, which promise fruit quite soon
And further down the lettuce shoots up pale

Next to a row of parsley, getting old.
But see the peas, their curly tendrils green
Clinging to their stout pea-sticks for support.

Form IV (grade 8 or 9)

A Spring Morning

Soft on the brown woods
A pale light gleams,
And slowly spreading seems
To change the brown wood to a land of dreams,
Where beneath the trees
The great god Pan,
Does pipe, half goat, half man,
To satyrs dancing in the dawning wan.
And then comes Phoebus,
The visions fade
And down the dewy glade
The rabbits scuttle o'er the rings they made.
In the fields near-by
The cattle rise
And where the river lies
A white mist rises to the welcoming skies.
Where the downs arise
And blue sky crowns
Their heads, fast o'er the mounds
The mist is driv'n to where the ocean sounds. [pg 201]

White wings against blue sky,
Gulls from the cliffs rise,
Watching, with eyes
That see from shore to where the sky line lies,
Where blue sea fades in bluer skies
Soft, doth the tide creep
O'er the golden sands
With sea-weed strands
Which, maybe, knew the dawn of other lands.

Form IV (grade 8 or 9)

Write thirty lines of blank verse on 'Pegasus.'

The sky was blue and flecked with tiny clouds
Like sheep they ran before the driving wind
The sun was setting like a big red rose
The clouds that flew by him like rose-buds were
And as I gazed I saw a little cloud
White as the flower that rises in the spring
Come nearer, nearer, nearer as I looked

And as it came it took a different shape
It seemed to turn into a fairy steed.
White as the foam that rides the roaring waves
Still it flew on until it reached the earth
And galloping full lightly came to me
And then I saw it was a wondrous thing
It leapt about the grass and gently neighed
I heard its voice sound like a crystal flute
'Oh come' he said 'with me ascend the sky
Above the trees, above the hills we'll soar
Until we reach the home of all the gods
There will we stay and feast awhile with them
And dance with Juno and her maidens fair
And hear dear Orpheus and the pipes of Pan
And wander, wander, wander up above.'
'Oh fairy steed, oh angel steed,' I said,
'Horse fit for Jupiter himself to ride,
What is your name? I pray thee, tell me this.'
Then came the magic voice of him again,
'If you will know my name then come with me.'
'Yet tell me first,' I hesitating said.
He told me, and when I had heard the name
I leapt upon his back and flew with him. [pg 202]

Form V (grade 10)

Write a poem in the same metre as Pope's 'Essay on Man,' on the meeting of the
League of Nations.

From each proud kingdom and each petty state
The statesmen meet together to debate
Upon the happy time when wars shall cease
And joy shall reign, and universal peace.
No more shall day with radiance cruelly bright
Glare down upon the carnage of the fight.
No more shall night's dark cloak be rent aside
By flashing shells and searchlight's stealthy glide
No more shall weary watchers wait at home
With straining eyes for those that cannot come
The nations shall forget their strife and greed
The strong shall help the weak in time of need
May they succeed in every peaceful plan
If war can cease as long as man is man.

Form V (grade 10)

Gather up the impressions you have received from reading Tennyson's poems,
and write a poem in blank verse.

Take up a volume of the poet's works,

Read on, lay it aside, and take your pen,
Endeavour in a few, poor, worthless lines
To give expression of your sentiments. . . .
Surely this man loved all the joys of life,
Saw beauty in the smallest and the least,
Put plainer things that hitherto were dim,
And lit a candle in the darkest room.
His thoughts, now sad, now gay, may surely be
The solace sweet for many a weary hour,
His words, drunk deeply, seem to live and burn
Clear, radiant, gleaming from the printed page,
Nature to him was dear and so has made
Her wiles for other men a treasure vast.
Old Books, his master mind could comprehend
Are shown to us as pictures to a child,
Read on and when the volume's put away,
Muse on the learnings thou hast found therein;
The time thus spent thou never will repent,
For love of good things all should seek and find. [pg 203]

Form V (grade 10)

A Lullaby Song

The little waves are sighing on the shore,
And the little breezes sobbing in the trees;
But the little stars are shining,
In the sky's blue velvet lining,
And Lady Sleep is tapping at the door.

The little gulls are flying home to shore,
And the little lights are flashing from the ships,
But close your eyes, my sweet,
And be ready then to greet
Dear Lady Sleep who's tapping at the door.

The wind is rising all around the shore,
And the fishing boats speed home before the gale;
But hark not to the rain
That is lashing on the pane,
For Lady Sleep has entered by the door.

The storm has sunk the ships and swept the shore,
But there's weeping in the town and on the quay,
But, sweet, you're dreaming fast
Even though the dawn be past,
And Lady Sleep has gone, and closed the door.

Form VI (grade 11 or 12)

Write a letter in the style of Gray about any modern subject.

Mr. Gray to Mr. ___
At Torquay.

My dear friend —

'Savez vous que je vous hais, que je vous detestevolci des termes un peu forts,' still, I think that they are justified. Imagine leaving a friend for two months in this place without even once picking up a pen to write him a letter. If this neglect is due only to your low spirits, I will for once pardon you but only on condition that you come down here to visit me, which will at the same time strengthen your constitution. I don't have much in the way of entertainment, but I think that the scenery will make the journey worthwhile, not to speak of getting to see me. You will also be able to study [pg 204] many 'venerable vegetables' which are not usually found in England. But, I'm wasting your time and my paper with these 'betises' and I know very well what subject your mind is presently dwelling on: which of us is not thinking of Ireland? I would love to hear your views on the subject. For my part it seems to me that there can be only one true view, and it surprises me mightily to hear so much discussion on the subject. Are we not truly a peculiar nation who pass bills of Home Rule etc. with so much discussion and debate, when neither of the two parties concerned will accept the conditions that we offer them? They give one side too little freedom, and the other too much. Accursed be the man who invented a bill which was and will be the cause of so much trouble 'in saecula saeculorum.' Surely we need not have any doubt as to what line of action we should adopt, surely it has not been the habit of England to let her subjects revolt without an attempt to quell them, surely the government will not stand by and see its servants murdered, and the one loyal province oppressed. But, alas, many things are possible with such a government. Here it is said by people who have been driven from that country by incendiaries that the Government will let things take their course till everything is in such a condition that the Premier will rise in the house and say, 'You see how things stand—it is no use trying to control Ireland, let us leave it to the Seinn Feiners, and live happily ever afterwards, free from such unprofitable cares,'

Such is the talk, but I don't believe it. We have as a nation always muddled things, but we have muddled through and been triumphant in the end. It is so obvious that our interests and those of Ireland coincide, that even to contemplate separation seems incredible to me,

Thus I remain your harassed friend, etc,

Form IV (grade 11 or 12)

Gather up the impressions you have received from reading Tennyson's poems, and write a poem in blank verse.

On Reading Tennyson's Poems.

Oh! Prophet of an era yet to come,

When men shall sing where men were wont to speak
In words which even Englishmen knew not
And when I read your songs, at once I felt
The breath of Nature that was lurking there, [pg 205]
And then I knew that all your life you dwelt
Amid the changing scenes of Nature's play,
And knew the very language of the birds,
And drank the essence of the honeysuckle.
And when you were but young, I knew your thoughts,
Thy Doubts and struggles, for you gave them me;
And yet, had I been you, my thoughts would still
Have rested deep within my heart; but still
T'would be relief to pour out all my woes
In the sweet flow of sympathetic verse.
Your epithets produce a vivid scene
Of knights in armour or of maiden fair,
And yet, I think, the fairness of her face
Does sometimes cover many a fault below.
But to your genius and your work for ever
Is owed a debt of thankfulness that we
No longer tread the paths of level Pope
Or read those words that are not English-born.

Form V (grade 10)

The Clouds

Among the spirits of the nearer air
There are three children of the sun and sea—
The genie of the clouds; it is their care
To give the ocean's bounty to the earth:
Oft they retain it in a time of dearth,
But they give all, however much it be.

The youngest of the three is very fair;
She is a maiden beautiful and sweet,
Of ever varying mood, changeful as air.
Now, plunged in merriment, she takes delight
In all she sees, now tears obscure her sight;
A breeze-swept lake shows not a change more fleet.

The fleecy clouds of April own her sway—
They, golden, lie against the golden sun,
Or sport across the blue when she is gay;
But when, anon, her girlish passions rise,
She marshalls them across the sunny skies
To flood the earth, then stops ere half begun. [pg 206]

Her elder brother is of different mien.
The clouds he governs are of different mould;

When the earth pants for moisture he is seen
To spread his clouds across the filmy blue.
When his rain falls, it steady is and true;
Persistent, gentle, ceaseless, yet not cold.

From the grey bowl with which he caps the earth,
It sweetly falls with earth-renewing force.
Not April's rapid change from grief to mirth
Excites its fall, but calm, determined thought
Of middle age, of deeds from judgment wrought;
He recks not blame, but still pursues his course,

Aged, yet of awesome beauty is the third,
Of flashing eye and sullen, scornful brow—
With an imperious hand she guides her herd
Of wild, tempestuous mood; quick roused to ire
Is she, slow to forgive, of vengeance dire;
Before her awful glance the tree-tops bow.

And when enraged, she stretches forth a hand—
A long, thin hand to North, South, East and West,
And draws from thence clouds num'rous as the sand;
They crowd on the horizon, and blot out
The sun's fair light; then, like a giant's shout,
The thunder booms at her dread spear's behest.

(No age given)

Write a scene between Mr. Woodhouse, if he lived in our times, and his neighbor.

Scene: Mr. Woodhouse's private study.

People in the study: Owner of study (Mr. Woodhouse), and Miss Syms, a very modern young lady.

Mr. Woodhouse—'Oh, good afternoon Miss Syms, I am delighted to see you. My, how dark it is. One might almost think it were evening, if the clock on the opposite wall did not directly oppose the fact.'

Miss S.—'Oh, I don't know, it's not so bad out. I'm awfully sorry to drop in like this, but I came to ask about Miss Woodhouse's cold. Is she better?' [pg 207]

Mr. W.—'How thoughtful of you! No, I am afraid dear Emma is still sick. It is so challenging to have an invalid in the house, it makes me miserable when I think of my poor daughter having to stay home all alone, in bed. But really, that is just about the best place to be in this dreadful weather. Have you really been out taking a walk?'

Miss S.—'Yes, why shouldn't I? It's the best way to get warm.'

Mr. W.—'If the liberty might be allowed me, (dryly) I should say, that it was the best way to get a feverish cold, besides making oneself thoroughly miserable; and the ground is so damp under foot!'

Miss S.—'Oh. it hasn't been raining much lately. I only got caught in a little shower, (visible start from Mr. W.). (coyly,) Excuse me, but is that a box of cigarettes up there on the mantlepiece?'

Mr. W.—'Cigarettes? Oh, no! I couldn't think of keeping them near the house. I never smoke. It irritates my throat, which is naturally weak.'

Miss S.—'But don't your visitors ever take the liberty of enjoying something of the sort? And what about Miss Woodhouse?'

Mr. W.—(horrified,) 'Dear Emma, smoke a cigarette!! Why, I never heard of such a thing. What would she say if I told her? Dear Emma smoke? No, no, certainly not'.

Miss S.—(laughing,) 'Oh, I'm very sorry. I didn't mean to offend you. How do you think the old Johnnies in Ireland are behaving themselves?'

Mr. W.—(coldly.) 'I beg your pardon?'

Miss S.—(sweetly,) 'I said, how do you think matters are looking in Ireland?'

Mr. W.—'I am sorry, I think I could not have heard aright before.—Matters in Ireland, yes. Oh, I think the Irish rebels are positively awful. To think of them breaking into houses, and turning the poor inhabitants out into the cold streets, (where they will probably nearly die of cold), it is too dreadful!'

Miss S.—'Oh, I know they are rather brutes sometimes. But in a way I almost sympathize with them. I wouldn't like to have to knuckle under to the English (catching sight of Mr. W.'s expression of horror and pained surprise.) I really think I'd better get a move on. Please don't look at me like that! I really don't mean half of what I say. I must be running!' [pg 208]

Mr. W.—'Good afternoon Miss Syms, it was so kind of you to come. (aside) Oh, how insensitive of dear Emma to have a cold, if it means visitors like this every hour. (aloud) Good afternoon, can you find your way out? I really shall catch cold if I move out of this room.'

Form V (grade 10)

Write a poem about 'Spring' in the same metre as 'Allegro.'

Spring

Begone! for a short space
You whistling winds, and fogs, and snowy clouds,

And frosts that with fair lace
Each window-pane in dainty pattern shrouds,
Offsprings of Winter, ye!
Begone! find out some icy arctic land.
Upon that cheerless strand
Amongst piercing ice, and chilling glaciers dwell
Such regions suit you well,
Go, cold Winter, well are we rid of thee!
Come Spring, you fairest season, come!
With the bee's enchanting hum,
And the dainty blossoms swinging
On the tree, while birds are singing.
See how they clothe the branches gray
In dress of freshest pink, all day,
Then when the dewy evening falls
They close their flowers till morning calls.
Sweet Morn! Spring leads you by the hand
And bids thee shine o'er all the land;
You send forth beams of purest gold,
To bid the daffodils unfold,
While Spring bends down with her fresh lips
To kiss the daisy's petal tips.
And as she walks o'er the green sward
A cheerful mavis, perfect bard
Breaks into song; his thrilling notes
Are echoed from a hundred throats
Of eager birds, who love to sing
To their sweet mistress, fairest Spring. [pg 209]
Then as she sits on mossy throne
A scarlet ladybug, alone,
Bids her good welcome; and above
Is heard the cooing of the dove.
Two butterflies in russet clad
Fly round her head with flutt'rings glad;
While at her side a giddy fly
Buzzes his joy that she is nigh,
Oh! Spring my heart's desire shall be
That you'll forever dwell with me!

(e) Languages

English is a study of logic, dealing with sentence structure and where words are positioned, and the nature of those words themselves. So it's best for a child to start by learning about what makes a sentence before he learns the individual parts of speech. In other words, he should learn to analyze the whole before he begins to parse the separate parts. It takes some abstract thought for a child to grasp the concept that when we talk, we use sentences that speak of a *thing* and say something *about* that thing (i.e., the rule that a sentence must contain a subject and verb). All he needs to know at the beginning is that languages is composed of sentences, and that a sentence has to make sense. It's possible to string words together haphazardly, such as—'Tyler immediately light switch hilarious and'—a string of words that makes absolutely no sense. In fact, it makes *nonsense* and, therefore, isn't a sentence. If we put words together in such a way that they make sense, such as 'John goes to school,' it's a sentence. Every sentence has two main parts: (1) the thing we're talking about, and, (2) what we say about it. In our example, we were taking about *John* and what we said about him is that he *goes to school*. At this early stage, children need lots of practice to find those two ingredients [pg 210] in simple sentences. Later, when they're familiar and comfortable with the concept of the first part of a sentence being the thing we're talking about, they'll be ready to learn a name for it: the *subject*. For example, we might say that the subject of a conversation was parsley. That's just another way of saying that the thing we were talking about was parsley. To sum up this kind of lesson, a class should learn that: Words that are put together in such a way that they make sense, form a sentence. A sentence has two parts: the thing we're talking about, and what we're saying about it. The thing we're talking about is called the subject.

It won't be easy for children to grasp this kind of information because it's so abstract, and we need to remember that this kind of knowledge is difficult and not very user-friendly. Children's minds are accustomed to dealing with concrete things—they have no trouble imagining concrete details when they hear the sketchiest details of a fairy tale. A seven year old can sing,

'I can't see fairies, but I can dream them.
No fairy can hide from me;
I won't stop dreaming until I find him.
Ah, there you are, Primrose Fairy!
I see you, Blackwing Fairy!'

But a child can't imagine and dream about parts of speech. Any silly grown-up attempts to personify such abstract concepts offends the little child, who, in spite of his love for play and nonsense, actually has a serious mind. Most children can eventually grasp the concept of a sentence consisting of words that make sense, especially if they are allowed to spend some time playing with silly, nonsensical strings of words that make gibberish. And, with lots of practice exercises in which the concept of *the subject* is kept at the forefront, they can come to grasp that concept.

One more initial concept is needed before children will be ready to deal with the abstract world of grammar in its proper [pg 211] form, as written rather than in colloquial speech. That is, they need to be familiar with the concept of verbs. The simplest way to introduce this is to have them create two-word sentences containing the thing they're talking about, and what they're saying about it— sentences such as 'Megan sings,' or 'Grandma bowls,' or 'Hayden runs.' In all of these sentences, the child can easily spot the thing being talked about, and what's being said about it.

But teachers already know these things and I don't have anything new or innovative to share about teaching grammar. Still, my method benefits grammar because the habit of paying full attention helps with grammar as well as in every other subject. We hope that someday, grammar will be unified so that students will no longer have the confusion of learning separate grammars for English, Latin, and French, each with its own terms.

Students in Form IIB (grade 4) have easy French lessons with pictures for them to describe. Later, in Form IIA (grades 5/6), while they continue using the Primary French Course, children start using narration, which is as beneficial with foreign languages as it is in English. They narrate a sentence or paragraph that's read to them. Young children don't have any problem making their mouths form French sounds. At this stage, the teacher should have the children help her translate the passage that they'll be narrating. Then she should read them the passage in French and have them narrate it. With some practice, they become surprising good at this. The very act of having to narrate helps them develop better proficiency with French phrases than they'd get from memorizing those phrases by rote. Forms IIA and IIB also learn some French songs. Students in Form IIA (grades 5/6) act out *French Fables* by Violet Partington. The use of careful reading followed by narration is continued in each of the Forms. So Form II (grades 4-6) might have to 'describe, in French, Picture number 20,' or 'Narrate the story Esope et le Voyageur.' In Form III (grade 7), students might also 'Read and narrate [pg 212] Nouveaux Contes Francais by Marc Ceppi.' Form V and VI have to 'write a resume of Le Misanthrope or L'Avare' and 'translate 'Leisure,' on page 50 of 'Modern Verse,' into French.'

We don't have enough space to thorough describe in detail the PUS's work in French. Of course, French grammar is studied, and what House of Education students are able to accomplish in their narrations is remarkable. The French teacher might give a lecture about French history or literature for perhaps thirty minutes, and then the students are able to narrate the content without leaving much out or making many mistakes. Mr. Household writes about what he saw in some French classes during a short visit to the House of Education:

A French lesson was given to the second-year students by the French teacher. She was from Tournal, and had come to Ambleside in 1915 (probably about seven years earlier) She had been teaching in England before that, but wasn't familiar with Charlotte Mason's methods. What I observed in her class was that she followed Miss Mason's methods exactly. She used a high-quality literary book, one single reading, and narration (in French, of course) immediately after the reading. The book used was Alphonse Daudet's Lettres de Mon Moulin. The class read the chapter about 'Le Chevre de M. Seguin.' Before the reading started, a few (very few) words of explanation were given in French. Then nine pages from the book were read through without stopping by the teacher. She didn't slow her reading because of the language; she read at the same speed one would read English. The students didn't have their own books, so all they could do was listen. As soon as the reading was done, without hesitating, students began narrating in French. Different students took turns telling part of the story until they got to the end. The narrations were all surprisingly good. All the students were able to think and speak French with ease, yet students only spend 2 hours and 45 minutes on French every week. These kinds of results surely warrant further investigation. I might add that last year, [pg 213] I heard a history lecture about the reign of

Louis XI given by this same teacher to a class of seniors. The lecture was narrated in the same way, and had the same great results.'

This tool of harnessing the power to concentrate and use it in modern and ancient languages hasn't been used before. It seems that if we start using children's ability to focus their attention, we will soon have a nation of children who are fluent in two or more languages. We've had good results with Italian and German by using this same method, both in the teaching of languages to our teachers at the House of Education, and the training school where students teach local children. We expect to have the same results in Latin. A classical teacher writes,

'At the House of Education, Latin is taught by thoroughly studying grammar, syntax and style, and then narrating. The literature selected is easy to begin with, but increases in difficulty as the students get more advanced. Only correct Latin is used, so the students gain a sense of style as well as grammatical structure. When students narrate, they often use the same phrases and style as the text being narrated. This way, students learn what Latin really is. They experience it as it was intended, as a living, spoken language, rather than the dry grammar of a dead language.'

In this way, the structural grammar of foreign languages is learned in the same way as English grammar—by hearing it spoken by people who know what it's supposed to sound like. The enthusiasm with which students learn new words means that we might expect that they'll have as large a vocabulary in a second language as they do in English. This is something that had been sadly lacking in this country.

(f) Art

Art appreciation is regarded with a lot of respect, but teachers tend to be intimidated about how to teach it. We all agree that children should cultivate their ability to discern and appreciate beauty, especially those who already have that ability. The question is *how* to do that. The novel solution suggested by South [pg 214] Kensington in the 1860's—freehand drawing, perspective, drawing from the round (from life?) has been rejected, but nothing has arrived to fill its place. We still see schools with models of cones, cubes, etc. placed so that the student's eye can take them in freely and perhaps inspire the hand to reproduce it on paper. But now we understand that art can't be experienced through mechanical exercises. Art is a thing of the spirit, and we need to teach it in ways that affect the spirit. We realize that the ability to appreciate art and interpret it is as universal to all people as intelligence, or imagination, or the ability to form words to communicate. But that ability needs to be educated. Teaching the technical skill of producing pictures isn't the same as appreciating art. To appreciate, children need to have a reverent recognition of what's been created. Children need to learn about pictures: they need to learn about them a line at a time, and as groups, by studying pictures for themselves rather than by reading about them. In our schools, we have a friendly art dealer who provides six nice copies of the pictures of one artist each term. The children hear a short story about the artist's life, and a few words to draw their attention to the artist's best features, perhaps his trees or skies, or rivers or figures of people. The six reproductions are studied one at a time so that the students learn to not just see a picture, but to look carefully at it, absorbing every detail. After looking at the picture, it's turned over and the children narrate, telling what they saw, perhaps, 'a dog driving a flock of sheep along a road all by himself. No, wait, there's a boy, too. He's lying at the river, getting a drink. You can tell by the light that it's morning, so the sheep must be going out to graze in the pasture,' and so on. The children don't miss any details—the discarded plow, the crooked birch tree, the beautifully formed clouds that look like it might rain. There's enough to talk about to keep the children busy for half an hour, and afterwards, the picture will have formed such a memory that the children will recognize it wherever they see it, whether it's a signed proof, an oil reproduction, or the original itself in a museum. I [pg 215] heard of a small boy who went to the National Gallery with his parents. He had wandered off on his own, and came running back, saying, 'Mommy! They have one of our Constables on that wall!' With this plan, children get to know a hundred or more great artists during the years they're in school. And they learn with the kind of intimacy that will stay with them all their lives. A group of children were in London on an excursion. When asked what they'd like to see in the city, the answer was, 'Oh, Mommy, let's go to the National Gallery so we can see the Rembrandts!' Another group of young children went for tea to a place they'd never been before, and they were excited to see two or three De Hootch pictures on the walls During the course of their school years, children have many opportunities to visit galleries. In art, they have the opportunity to see glimpses of life illustrated. As Robert Browning said,

'Keep in mind, we're designed so that we only come to appreciate and love something we've passed by a hundred times, only after we see its beauty in a painting.'

Here's an example of how beautiful but familiar and common things can grab our attention when an artist brings them to our notice in a picture. A lady writes:

'I was invited to a small village to talk about the Parents Union School. Even though it was raining heavily, twelve very interested ladies came to listen. I suggested that I introduce them to some friends their children had made at school—some great artists they had been learning about. We had a nice 'picture talk' with the works of artist Jean B. Corot. I enjoyed it even more because of one of the women's narrations. She narrated as if she'd been liberated for the first time in months. We were looking at his 'Evening' picture. It has a canal on the right and a great group of trees in the middle. Most of the ladies talked about individual parts of the picture, but this woman talked about everything. It refreshed her like a green pasture.'

These women were all familiar with the kinds of details that are in Corot's paintings—he paints the kind of natural beauty that is common in the area where they live. But Browning is right, we tend to overlook what's common to us until we're clued in to its beauty by seeing it in a painting. Only then do we learn to truly see and appreciate it.

Remember that the talks that are recorded, (they can be seen at the PNEU office) [pg 216] are from the children themselves. They don't mention 'schools of painting,' or art style. These are things they'll consider later, when they're older. In the beginning, it's more important for them to simply know the paintings. In the same way we do with worthy books, we let the artist tell his own story without our interference telling the child what to think about it. We trust a picture to say what the artist wanted via the medium the artist chose. In art, just like in everything else, we eliminate the middleman and let the work speak for itself.

Students in Forms V and VI are asked to 'describe, by doing a study in sepia colors, Corot's Evening.' Students never do more than this kind of a rough sketch from memory. Their picture studies aren't for the purpose of providing them with drawing material. In fact, they are never asked to copy the picture, because attempting to copy might diminish the student's reverence for the picture as a great work of art. I am hesitant about sharing how we teach drawing now that Herr Cizek has shown us what great things children are capable of with very little discernible teaching and a little bit of suggestion. But that kind of training probably only works under the inspiration of an unusually gifted artist. The people I'm writing for are mostly teachers who will need to depend on their students rather than rely on their own inherent talent. We have students illustrate their favorite episodes from books they've read during the term, and the spirit their pictures show and the appropriate details they include make it apparent that they've picked up more from the passages than even the teacher! They aren't afraid to try to tackle techniques they've never learned about, which shows us something about children. They attempt to draw a crowd with wonderful ingenuity, such as including a crowd of people listening to Mark Antony's speech, or a crowd cheering for the Prince of Wales in India. Whenever they try to show a crowd, they seem to do it in the same way that most real artists do: by just showing the heads. Like the children in Vienna, they use all the space on their paper, whether they're drawing a landscape or the details in a room. They add horses leaping brooks, dogs chasing cats, sheep wandering on the road, always giving a sense of motion. Their drawings show that they've studied the things [pg 217] they see with some attention. When they draw people, they show them doing something appropriate: a gardener sharpening his clippers, their mother scrapbooking, a man steering a boat or driving or mowing. Their chairs always stand on four legs, their people always stand on two legs with surprising regularity. They're always quick to correct their mistakes when they see that their drawing doesn't match what they see in the real world. They're not afraid to use bold colors. Almost all children will try to convince you that they have what it takes to be an artist. Their nature notebooks give them a perfect opportunity to practice. The first buttercup in a child's nature notebook is crude enough to scandalize someone who teaches brush-drawing, but later, he'll paint another buttercup, and this one will be much improved, capturing the delicate poise and radiance of a real buttercup.

Drawing is pretty much well-taught enough these days. All we need to do is to emphasize a couple of points about the specific kind of drawing our students will be doing—studying the work of great artists and illustrating their nature notebooks.

We try to do what we can to introduce students to architecture. We also do a little modeling with clay, and other various handicrafts, but nothing extraordinary.

You can see more details by taking a look at our Parents Union School Program schedules.

We do more with music appreciation. The best way to explain what we do is to share a quote from Mrs. Howard Glover from the talk she gave at the Ambleside Conference in 1922:

'Music appreciation is focused on so much these days. We began it in our PNEU schools about 25 years ago, when I was playing a lot of the best music that I was interested in for my own young child. Charlotte Mason heard about what I was doing. She realized that music just might provide much joy and interest to everyone's life. Since students in her PNEU schools were getting the best of everything—the greatest literature and art, she thought they should have the greatest music, too. She asked me to write an article in the Parents Review about the results of what I was doing, and to plan a schedule of music for each term that could be played for the students. Since then, [pg 218] music has been included in the Programme schedule each term. And that's how the movement began, and it's spread far and wide.

Of course, music appreciation has nothing to do with playing the piano. It's often been thought that 'learning music' can only mean that. So it was assumed that children who showed no special talent for playing the piano were simply not musically inclined and wouldn't like concerts. But music appreciation is different from playing an instrument in the same way that being a natural actor is different from enjoying a Shakespeare play, or being able to paint is different from enjoying a painted picture. I think that all children, not just the musically inclined ones, should learn to appreciate music. It's been proven that only three percent of children are actually tone-deaf. If children are started early, it's amazing how even those who seem to have no musical 'ear' can develop one, and can learn to listen to music with understanding and enjoyment.

SECTION III - The Knowledge of the Universe

(a) Science

Huxley liked to say that science education in the schools should be concerned with common information rather than being overwhelming by trying to teach everything. But we have found that children's minds are not designed to be limited to a body of knowledge that has been deemed as common knowledge. Their young minds are eager and want to know more. In science, just like history, books should be literary (i.e., told in story form). We'd probably all benefit and be more scientific people if we got rid of all science text-books and used less chalk outlining and summarizing. French people already know that science needs to be taught with literary books, the same as with all other subjects. They also understand that foundational scientific principles are [pg 219] so simple and so profound at the same time, and affect so many other things, that the way scientific principles are taught can elicit emotional reactions in people. So these principles are perfect opportunities to use a literary approach. But the technical details of how those principles are applied are so specialized that they aren't really general knowledge and, therefore, aren't necessary to be learned in school, unless they help to illustrate the principle. We don't have a lot of scientific literature in our English language, but we have enough for school. There's an American book called *The Sciences*. Its author (Edward Holden) seems to be a fairly good writer. This book does a good job of relating general universal principles with common incidents from daily life in a way that's interesting enough to hold a child's attention. This book can help any child learn the scientific principles that make an electric bell ring, where sound comes from, how a steam engine works, and many other matters that are explained very clearly. It has experiments to do that are easy to follow because of his wonderful diagrams and descriptions. With this book, children get their first notions of science without the confusing fog of too many complex words. Form IIA (grades 5/6) reads Life and Her Children by Arabella Buckley. Her book gives them a surprising amount of knowledge about earlier and lower life forms. Form IIB (grade 4) enjoys Charles Kingsley's Madame How and Lady Why. They also do some outdoor work every month as a way of observing the changing seasons during the year. They record their findings by adding notes and drawings to their Nature Notebooks, and they do special studies on their own every season, drawing and making notes in their Nature Notebooks.

In Form III (grade 7), a term's work helps children to—'Make a rough sketch of part of a ditch or hedge or seashore and include the names of the plants you would find there.' 'Write about the special study you did this term and include drawings.' 'What are calyx, corolla, stamen, pistil? In what different ways are flowers fertilized?' 'How would you find [pg 220] the North Star? Name six other stars and tell which constellations they're part of.' 'What's the difference between Early, Decorated and Perpendicular Gothic? Use drawings to explain.' These kinds of questions reveal a lot of field study as well as reading from a half dozen carefully selected books on nature, botany, architecture, and astronomy. The main idea to keep in mind is that children need to observe and to record their observations, but their observations should have some guidance.

Studying nature and botany with field guides continues through all their school years, but other fields of science are done term by term.

The exam questions for Form IV (grade 8/9) show how varied the science subjects are in nature, general science, hygiene and anatomy. In fact, the subjects are so diverse that it's difficult to figure out what to call them on the Programme schedules, as these samples show:

Geography
1. Write a little about Asia, including a roughly sketched map
2. Compare the Middle East's geography with the moors of Yorkshire. Describe the valleys of Jordan.
3. What does Isabella Bird say in Eothen about the Church of the Holy Sepulcher?

Nature
1. What do you know about
   a. manatees

b. whale-bone whales (include a sketch of its skeleton)

OR

1. Describe
    a. quartz rock crystals
    b. felspar
    c. mica
    d. horneblend
       In what rock do these occur?
2. What do you know about insectivorous plants? Name some you know about.
3. What do you notice about a walk in the summer?

General Science
1. What do these mean?
    a. electrical attraction
    b. electrical repulsion
    c. conductors
    d. insulators [pg 221]

2. How might you prove that we never see matter itself? How does sight give us knowledge?

Physiology (anatomy)
1. Describe the human ear.

Of the half-dozen books that our Form IV (grade 9) students are using now, Bishop Mercer's Some Wonders of Matter is probably the most inspiring. The following exam questions show how varied students' subjects are, and their answers demonstrate how wide and thorough their knowledge is. All of our PNEU students are usually ready to answer any of the questions about what they learned during the term.

In the same way, Forms V and VI (grades 10-12) cover a wide variety of subjects, as these term exam questions indicate:

Geography
Form VI. (grade 12)
1. Show how the discovery of the New World affected England as far as finances and war.
2. Life forms are distributed on the earth according to a general law. What is that law?
3. Describe Cortez's siege of Mexico, and its surrender.
Forms VI and V (grades 10-12)
4. How has WWI affected:
(a) Luxembourg
(b) eastern Belgium
(c) Antwerp and the Scheldt?
Form V (grades 10/11)
1. How did the Restoration affect the American colonies?
2. Explain how longitude is determined.
3. Give a sketch of the life and character of Montezuma.

Geology and Science
Form VI (grades 11/12)
1. Give a thorough explanation of
(a) what causes radioactivity
(b) what causes gravity
2. What can you tell about the scenery of the English Trias? Name a dozen fossils, sketching pictures of half of them
Form V (grades 10/11)
1. Explain color as fully as you can.
2. Describe what igneous rocks are composed of. Where are they found?

Biology and Botany
Form VI (grades 11/12)
1. What are the characteristics of animals without backbones? [spineless?] Describe six examples. [pg 222]

2. Describe the plant life and explain what conditions make it suited for its environment in the following locations:
(a) woods
(b) low desert
(c) swamp
(d) meadow
Form V (grades 10/11)
1. How can you classify animals by what they do? Give some examples.
2. Describe what kinds of plants grow along the seashore.
Forms VI and V (grades 10-12)
3. Describe and include drawings of the special study you did this term.

Astronomy
Form VI (grades 11/12)
1. What does 'precession' mean? Describe the precession and mutation of the earth's axis.
Form V (grades 10/11)
1. Write an essay about the planet Mercury.

If we need an excuse for giving children a wide, varied curriculum that introduces them to at least the areas of science that every common person should know something about, we might find it in these critical words of Sir Richard Gregory in his Presidential Address given in the Education Science Section of the British Association. He said that,

'Education might be defined as a deliberate attempt to manipulate a growing human being to make him adapt to his environment. How much and what he learns should be determined by how well it meets that criteria of adapting him to his environment. What was best for one culture in the past may not be best for another. The most basic mission of science education has been to prepare students for living in a civilized society. This has been done by revealing to them some of the beauty and power of the world they lived in, and introducing them to the methods used to increase our knowledge of the universe. Science education in schools was never intended to prepare students for science careers. It was intended to equip students for living in their culture. General science should be a part of general education. It should not be specialized and connected to college classes that a student might take later. Less than three percent of public school students went on to college, yet most public school science classes were based on university entrance exam curriculums! The needs of the many were sacrificed for the needs of a few.

'There was too much focus on what the child should have been finding out for himself by doing his own experiments and observations. The final test for graduation was testing students for things that were common sense to anyone with experience in a particular field of science, but nothing [pg 223] that would give students a broad knowledge of general principles to add to laboratory work.

'The number of students wanting to take entrance exams [*for college science classes?*] was evidence that general science education was almost nonexistent. The range of subjects taught was limited to what could only be taught in a laboratory. There was no attention given to learning all the different ways in which physical science was broadening man's ability to deal with his world, and no reading or learning for the sake of interest because those things didn't count on exams! Students desperately needed to be reminded that science wasn't all just about taking measurements, and taking measurements isn't always science.'

It's reassuring that the methods we've been advocating for over thirty years are confirmed by such an authority in science. The only rational way to teach science is with personal observation (field study) combined with lab work with a little bit of reading to add comments and clarification when possible. For example, John Ruskin's Ethics of the Dust gives children an enthusiasm for crystals that simple observation might not. In fact, much of our science education has suffered because of the unnecessary and harmful division between science and humanities.

Nature notebooks, which started with our P.U.S. (Parents Union Schools) have become like travel records and journals for students. They keep notes about all their finds: birds, flowers, fungus, mosses are described and sketched every season in the same way that Gilbert White did. A nature notebook can be kept by anyone anywhere. It can be used to record stars on their course in the heavens, or a fossil of an anemone on the beach at Whitby. These notebooks help to make science come alive and relate to the common man. Science should not be taught merely as a utilitarian means of preparing students for a career!

[pg 224]

(a) Geography

The teaching of geography has suffered a lot from our utilitarian mindset. The focus seems to be on stripping the planet we live on of every trace of its beauty and mystery. There's nothing left to admire or wonder about in our beloved world. We can't agree anymore with Jasper Petulengro, who wrote, 'The sun, moon and stars are sweet things, and so is the wind on the plain.' Instead, geography is confined to the question of how and under what conditions the earth's surface can turn a profit and be made comfortable for man to live on. Students are no longer indulged in imagining themselves climbing Mt. Rainier or Mount Everest, or skating on the fiords of Norway, or riding a gondola in Venice. In the world of corporate profit, these things don't count—all that matters is how and where and why money can be made in any region's conditions anywhere on the surface of the planet. Yet it's doubtful whether such teaching is effective, whether it even makes any impression at all on students. The minds ruminates on great ideas. Given great ideas, the mind can work to great ends. But if education doesn't teach a child to wonder and admire, it probably doesn't teach him anything at all.

Probably the most enjoyable knowledge is when one has such a familiarity with the earth's surface region by region, that a map of any area unfolds a panorama of delight. A map of every part of this beautiful earth not only brings to mind the great geographical features like mountains and rivers, but associations, images of people busy at different things both in history and in the present. In our schools, we focus a lot of attention on map work. Before reading a lesson, children find the places mentioned in the text on a map. They learn where they are, their relativity to other places, and to specific parallels and meridians. Since children don't think in generalities but in [pg 225] particulars, they read and picture in their minds places like the Yorkshire Downs, the Sussex Downs, the mysteries of a coal mine. They envision 'pigs' of iron flowing from a furnace, the bustle of the great towns, the occupations of the villages. Students in Form II (both A and B, grades 4-6) are busy working with a map of the counties of England. They study one county at a time. The counties are so different in geography, history and what the people do, that knowing England well will provide children with a reference point to the geography of every part of the world by either comparing or contrasting. For instance, even now as I write this book, the students in Form IIA (grades 5/6) are learning about the counties that touch the Thames basin. Part of their work for the term is to 'write poetic verses about The Thames.' H. W. Household's book Our Sea Power is very helpful in linking England with the world using an enthusiastic account of our navy's glorious history. The late Sir George Parkin, a highly qualified authority, writes books that help transport students around the British Empire. Students are left to their own devices to learn the facts that are usually considered geography. For instance, students might be asked to 'learn what you can about the political map of Europe after WWI.'

In Form III (grade 7), students still focus on their region, forming an acquaintance with the countries of Europe. In this way, a map of any country will make the child think of wonderful images in his mind's eye of the variety in another place, and the people who live there—their history and what they do. The only way to gain this kind of mental picture is by taking the countries one at a time. Students begin with an overview of the sea and shoreline of a continent, then they learn about the country and its people—the language they speak, the history of its people, its plains, mountains, rivers and basins. After [pg 226] such an overview, they should be able to answer questions like, 'Name three rivers that flow into the Baltic Sea.' 'Which countries form the southern and eastern shores of the Mediterranean Sea?' 'Between what parallels does Europe lie? What other continents lie partly within the same parallels?' In this way, the young students become familiar with the map of Europe before they begin to focus on the individual countries.

The image we want to present of the individual countries in these lessons should be, above all, interesting. At the same time, it should give an intelligent and fairly thorough knowledge of the specific country. Whatever else the child learns about the country will be learned alongside this scheme. For example, they might also read *'The Rhone Valley and the Border lands'* (the fourth book of Charlotte Mason's *Ambleside Geography* series):

'The warm, fertile Rhone Valley has a climate like the southern region where grapes are grown, but even more plantations grow olives and mulberries. We tend to think of southern France as the sunny south, but a writer we quoted earlier says that it's 'bleak, grim and somber.' The mulberry bushes are for feeding the silkworms that make the threads that are made into silk in the factories of France. Lyons, the second most important city in France, is the main place where silk is manufactured, including velvets and satins. Lyons is situated on a tongue of land where the rapid Rhone River meets the sluggish Saone River. There are piers along the banks of both rivers.'

You can see from that portion of text how geographical facts are casually worked in, similarly to the way someone actually traveling through the country might come across them. In one term, students might learn about Belgium, Holland, Spain and Portugal. There are many ways in which these countries are interconnected. For example,

'Katwyck is on the seashore near Leyden, where the Rhine River is nearing its end. A wide man-made channel provides no less than thirteen pairs of enormous floodgates to help the river empty itself into the sea. These floodgates are closed to keep the sea out when [pg 227] the tide is coming in, and opened to let the streams pass on their way out to sea at low tide. Even with these impressive gates, the Rhine River that was once so glorious makes a humble exit. The river's delta might be said to be wide enough to cover the whole width of Holland.' (*Ambleside Geography*, Book IV)

Notice that an attempt is made to give an exciting idea of the country's natural features, its history, and its industries. In this way, no country is merely a set of names on a map, or an outline of contour shapes. Those kinds of generalizations aren't geography. They're the kind of information that someone should draw a slow conclusion about as they become intimate with a region. The geography lessons need to have some literary character. What's new about these lessons is the addition of map study, which should be very thorough. For the other part of geography lessons, a single reading followed by narration is enough, the same as with every other subject we've discussed. Children can't tell about what they haven't seen in their own minds with their imaginations. And they can't imagine what's in their books unless their books are written with some vividness and some grasp of the subject. You can see how thorough their map study is from the questions on their term exam: 'Where in Belgium does the Scheldt drain? Name any of the waterways that feed into it. Name ten famous places in its basin. What port is at the head of its estuary?' The little yet very literary book, *Fighting for*

Sea Power in the Days of Sail, is a very enlightening book about the English Empire's geography.

There are two rational ways to teach geography. The first is the *inferential method*, and it's popular right now. The student learns specific geographical principles, which he will supposedly apply universally. But this seems defective to me for two reasons. First, it can be misleading because every principle has to be modified to fit specific places. Also, the regional color, local historical and personal interest are [pg 228] missing, and the student doesn't form any kind of mental image or personal associations about the place he's learning about. The second way to teach geography is the *panoramic method*. The landscape of the whole world is unrolled region by region, right before the child's eyes. Every region is presented with its own climate, its specific products, its people, what they do, and their history. Geography is a fascinating subject, and this way of teaching it seems to bring the area to life with brilliant color and a wealth of detail along with a sense of proportion and familiarity with general geographical principles. I don't think that pictures are very useful in geography study. After all, as we all know, the images that stay with us are the ones we construct in our own imaginations from written descriptions.

The geography book (*The Ambleside Geography*, Book V by Charlotte Mason) used in Form IV (grade 9) covers Asia, Africa, America and Australia. The same principle is followed: vivid descriptions, geographical information, historical details, and facts about the area's industry. These are presented for the purpose of making an impression so that the child feels like he 'owns' that region, like it's a possession in his imagination. It also adds to the collective store of knowledge in the mind from which to make future judgments. Students begin with a survey of Asia, and then Asia is broken down into separate countries, regions and geographical areas. So the part about Siberia says,

'All travelers admire the free peasants of Siberia. As soon as you cross the Urals, you're surprised by the extreme friendliness and cheerfulness of the people, and by the rich vegetation of the carefully tended fields and the roads that are kept in such good condition in southern Tobolsk.'

or,

'The shiny black soft thick fur of the otter is the most valuable of the Russian skins. Next is the black fox. But even though the otter's skin is a thousand times more valuable, [pg 229] the little gray squirrel is the most important fur to Siberian fur traders. Millions of them are exported to other countries.'

Here's what it says about Further India:

'Pigou, the middle division, is really the huge delta of the Irrawaddy, which is a low-lying land where huge quantities of rice are grown. On the higher ground that walls in the great river, are forests where the finest teak wood in the world grows.'

Africa comes after Asia, and students learn about David Livingston, John Hanning Speke, Richard Burton, James Augustus Grant, etc. They read about African village life. Chapters in that part of the book are titled Abyssinia, Egypt, Up the Nile, The Sudan, The Sahara, The Barbary Coast, South Africa, Cape Colony, The Islands. America is studied next. Students learn about the discovery of the continent, the geographical area of South America, the Andes and Mountain states of Peru, Chili, and Bolivia. They learn about South America's Pampas (great plains), Central America, North America, and Canada. They get a historical sketch of the United States, the eastern states, the Mississippi valley, the prairies, and the West. The section about the eastern states says,

'Stretching the Allegheny mountain chain is the great Appalachian coalfield. It extends through Pennsylvania, Virginia and Ohio for 720 miles. They say that there's enough coal there to supply the whole world for 4000 years! There's an abundance of iron mixed with the coal. Most of the coal is the kind called Anthracite. It burns very lowly with no smoke, but it can dry out the humidity of a room. Sir Charles Lyall visited the Pottsville coal field and said, 'I was pleasantly surprised to find a flourishing manufacturing town here, with tall smokestacks from a hundred furnaces burning continually, yet emitting no smoke. And when we left this clean, clear atmosphere to go down into one the mines, we were just as pleased to discover that we could pick up and handle the coal without getting our fingers dirty.'

That should be enough to indicate the kind of familiar intimacy that Form IV (grade 9) students get in all the regions [pg 230] of the world and their terrain, landscape, history, industry and all the things that affect climate and industry. Geikie's Physical Geography does a good job introducing students to the principles of physical geography.

Forms V and VI (grades 10-12) also have to keep up with current events by reading the newspaper and finding out what's happening in the country they're studying. Also, correlating to the period being studied in history, readings are included like these books from one term: Seeley's Expansion of England, The Peoples and Problems of India, Geikie's Elementary Lessons in Physical Geography, Mort's Practical Geography, and Kipling's Letters of Travel. In these Forms, students are expected to apply their knowledge to both practical and theoretical geography, and to be able to use an atlas without the leading questions that guide younger students.

(b) Mathematics

The subject of math is usually very important to educators. As long as the idea still prevailed that children's faculties needed to be developed, it seemed good to focus a lot of attention on a subject that could help develop the faculty of reasoning. But now we know that children come with reasoning powers already born in them, and those powers don't wait for training from us. They are there with or without us. So if we want to make math the main focus and priority of education, we'll have to find some other excuse to justify it. One strong case for giving math a central place in our curriculum is because of its truth and beauty. As John Ruskin points out, two and two always make four and couldn't possibly make five. That's a truth, an inevitable law. It's a [pg 231] great thing to come face to face with a law, with a whole natural law system that exists and is true whether we agree with it or not. Two straight lines can never enclose a space. That's a true fact that we can grasp, say, and act upon—but there's nothing we can do to change or alter it. This kind of truth helps children have a healthy sense of living with limitations, and inspires a reverent respect for natural law.

Being persons of integrity in all our dealings depends on Mr Micawber's [*David Copperfield*] golden rule about living within limits *["Annual income 20 pounds, annual expenditure nineteen nineteen and six, result happiness. Annual income 20 pounds, annual expenditure 20 pounds ought and six, result misery."*] But Harold Skimpole's [*Bleak House*] disregard for these things is a moral offense against society. The mental challenge of math is good for us. Although it's true the body needs more than strenuous aerobic exercise, some exercise is invigorating and healthy. This is as true for the mind as it is for the body.

But education needs balance. No single subject should assume greatest importance at the expense of other subjects that a child needs to know about. Math is easy to test, and as long as education is ruled by test scores, we'll have teaching focused on training exactness and solving problems efficiently, instead of teaching to awaken a sense of awe in contemplating a field of knowledge where perfection lives with or without us.

Some will ask what's wrong with training exactness and problem-solving. But these qualities developed in math lessons don't carry over into other departments of our lives. If they did, then math would be the best way to get a total education. But that's not the case. The habits and powers trained for one specific educational subject will only work for that subject. The anecdote about Sir Isaac Newton making a large opening in his door for his large cat, and a small one for his small cat illustrates this. It isn't that his mind had a mental lapse, but his greatness was in a specialized area and didn't carry over to everything else he thought about. Specialized training only makes a person qualified to work [pg 232] in that specialized field. It's not uncommon to hear about a challenged student who takes to Bradshaw [*railroad schedules and routes*], or an accountant who's gifted at numbers but unable to function at anything else.

A boy can get straight A's in math, and yet not do well in history because the accuracy and problem-solving skills developed while doing his sums will only apply to working on his math worksheets. How valuable is math to everyday life? Those of us who never excelled in math will heartily agree with the respected military staff officer who said,

'I've never found that math, beyond simple addition, made any difference to my life except when taking my staff entrance exam. As far as the claim that math provides the challenge of mental exercise and training in accuracy, I don't agree that math is the most effective to develop that.'

Most of us have always believed that understanding the theory and practice of battle strategy depends on math. So it's worth considering the officer's words above. Our basic point is that math should be studied for its own sake, not for the purpose of making the mind smarter or quicker. Math is profoundly worthy of study for its own sake, and because it's connected to other equally noble subjects. We should strive for balance when putting together a curriculum, remembering that a brilliant mathematician who knows nothing about the history of his own country or any other isn't very well educated.

Yet we can't overlook the fact that genius has rights of its own. A mathematical genius should be allowed to pursue nothing but math, even if it means sacrificing other subjects that any person should learn. He will be naturally driven to solve math problems, and he should be indulged. He won't even need very much laborious teaching, a lot will come easily to him. But not very many students are math whizzes. Why should they be pressured to focus on math as if they were? And why should a person's success depend on his skill at one thing—the drudgery of math? [pg 233]

The tendency of our universities is to deny students entrance if they aren't strong in math., which means denying them the opportunity to get some jobs. So students who aren't gifted in math have to expend extra time and effort trying to excel at something they have no natural talent for—all the while neglecting the humanities that they're better equipped for. That hardly makes for the balanced, liberal education we hope for.

As a case in point, the bold claims of the London Matriculation exam [this must be like our SAT's] are acknowledged by many teachers to be out of step with the concept of a broad education.

Math, more than any other subject, depends on the teacher rather than on the textbook [*because it's easier to grasp a math concept when you see it being explained and used, rather than trying to grasp it from reading a book?*] Yet few subjects are taught worse, mostly because teachers don't usually have time to give the inspiring ideas that quicken the student's imagination. Coleridge calls those inspiring ideas the 'Captain' ideas.

Imagine how interesting and alive geometry would seem if students also knew about Euclid and his trials and challenges in discovering geometric principles!

To summarize, math is a necessary part of any education. It needs to be taught by someone who knows math. But math shouldn't take up so much time and attention that other subjects have to be squeezed out. Knowing about those other subjects is every student's natural right.

It's not necessary to exhibit any student math work, since it's the same kind of work that other schools are doing, and reaches the same standard. Having the habit of paying attention undoubtedly gives our PUS students an advantage.

(c) Physical Development and Handicrafts

It's not necessary to say anything about games, [pg 234] dancing, physical exercise, needlework or any other handicrafts since our schools aren't doing anything unusually extraordinary in those subjects. [To see what our schools are doing, look at some Parents Union School Programme schedules.]

[pg 235]

Book II - Applying the Theory

Chapter I - A Liberal Education in Elementary Schools

I don't need to convince my readers that a generous, liberal education is the natural birthright of every child, like justice, freedom of religion, liberty, or fresh air. We all already know that. And we don't need to discuss how much that education should cover. We know that a good life should include a mind that's been guided to learn the proper things. As Plato said, knowledge is virtue, although that isn't true in every case. Educated teachers are quick to understand that Humanities must play a role in any educational plan worth anything. But teachers are faced with so many challenges, which Miss M. L. V. Hughes sums up nicely in her book, *Citizens to Be*:

'It's a tragedy that, for so long, Humanities has failed to maintain the kind of conditions suitable for realizing its goal for the general population.'

But we of the Parents Union Schools have succeeded in teaching Humanities under those conditions, and we think we've solved the great problem of education. We're able to offer Humanities in our own language to large classes of children from illiterate homes in such a way that the students enjoy it and assimilate it. I realize that one single swallow doesn't make a summer, but one school's experience [pg 236] demonstrates that it can be done. It's possible to teach a fairly literary curriculum enjoyably and easily, while still including all the other usual school subjects. The electric currents that make wireless telegraphy possible were always there, but it wasn't until Marconi sent his historic first message that wireless telegraphy was a reality, and any passenger on board a ship in the English Channel could send a message. In the same way, the experiment done in the Drighlinton School in Yorkshire showed how a humanities education could be done by any teacher. I'm impressed by how much of this kind of work is already being accomplished in our PNEU schools. The other day I heard of a man whose entire life had been uplifted by a single poetic sentence that he'd heard as a child. And I heard someone else remark that the average person can't resist a shelf of books. People are also saying that the war has made us a nation of readers, both those who remained at home and the soldiers on the frontlines. And not just readers of dime-store novels, but mostly readers of the best books in poetry and history. Isn't the school system to be credited with this change? But teachers are still not satisfied. Their reach goes beyond that, and they are more aware than ever of those around them living sordid lives, and the apathetic ignorance that prevails, casting a cloud over any successes they've attained. So they worry about having so little time that it's impossible to do a thorough job teaching vast subjects like history and literature.

I wonder if this uneasiness is caused by something we're too slow to recognize: that the mind's requirements aren't that different from the body's. They both need certain things to be happy—exercise, variety, rest, and, most of all, food. But we have offered intellectual or physical gymnastics instead of knowledge, which makes no more sense than expecting a child to be physically fit because you fed him a good meal. And our understanding of education is partly to blame. [pg 237]

The mind is usually defined by what it can do, not how much stuff it holds. A child is born with the ability to absorb and appropriate knowledge—but he doesn't have any knowledge in him yet. But we seem determined to work on him to make him more fit to absorb and assimilate, instead of using the time to get him the knowledge he wants and needs, but doesn't have. We train his reason. We cultivate his judgment. We develop his creativity/imagination. We exercise this or that faculty. But we can't develop those things in a healthy child any more than we could develop his digestive system. In fact, the more we meddle, the worse it is for the child. We notice that our youth seem apathetic. They get excited about football games, but don't care about things of the mind. What if these things are the result of the very methods we use in our schools—the simplified, pleasant ways in which we explain, coax, demonstrate, illustrate, summarize, and do all the helpful things we do for children that they're quite capable of doing for themselves? In fact, they were *born* able to do those things. Undoubtedly, some of what we give them is intellectually nourishing, but we don't give them as much as they need. Let's take courage, and we'll be surprised, as we've all seen from time to time, at how much challenging intellectual mind food almost any child will take at a 'meal.' Then he'll ruminate and digest it in his own time.

Maybe the first thing we need to do is to get a real picture of how the mind and knowledge work together, something I call 'the relativity of knowledge and the mind.' The mind takes in knowledge, not to *know*, but to *grow*. The mind grows wider in its variety of interests, more profound in depth, better able to make sound judgments, and more noble. But it can't grow without the food of knowledge.

The truth is, we're handicapped. It isn't so much the three or four difficulties I've already mentioned that are the problem. It's certain errors of judgment, ways we unwittingly under-value things, that we all fall into because that kind of attitude is universal. As teachers, we under-value ourselves and our role as teachers. We don't realize that it's the nature of the world for teachers to have a prophetic charisma and inspiration. His job mustn't be seen as a wearisome routine of spoon-feeding cereal to babies. His job should be the delightful interaction of equal minds. His role is that of a guide, philosopher and friend. The conflict [pg 238] of wills between teacher and student that makes school work so stressful almost ceases to be a factor when we deal with students as mind-to-mind equals, sharing and discussing knowledge.

Not only do we under-value ourselves, but we unwittingly under-value the very children that we would lay down our lives for with passionate devotion. For so long, we've been taught to think of children as the end product of *education* +

environment. So we forget that, from the first, they are total little persons. As Carlysle has well said,

'To the person who has a sense for the godlike, the mystery of a person is always divine.'

We can either reverence children, or we can despise them. We can't do both. We can't reverence them if we continue to think of them as incomplete, undeveloped beings who need our input to arrive at completeness of human-ness. We should see them as complete persons who are weak and ignorant. Their ignorance only needs to be informed, and their weakness only needs our support, but their potential is as great as ours. No matter how kindly we treat children, we are despising them as long as we see them as incomplete persons.

As soon as a child can form words to communicate with us, he lets us know that he can think with surprising clearness and directness. He sees with the kind of intent observation that we've long lost. He enjoys and sorrows with an intensity we no longer experience. He loves with a wild abandon, trust and confidence that we, unfortunately, can't share. He imagines with a creative power that no artist can match. He acquires intellectual knowledge and mechanical skill at such an amazing rate that, if an infant could continue to progress at the same rate into adulthood, he could learn the entire field of knowledge in his lifetime! (It might be helpful to re-read the early chapters of David Copperfield in relation to this.)

I'm defining the child as he truly is. I'm not making him out to be as divine as the heavens above, like Wordsworth does. And I'm not making him out to be as low as the depths, like evolutionists do. A person [pg 239] is a mystery. We can't explain him, or account for him. We can only accept him as he is. The wondrous individuality of personality doesn't disappear or cease to be when a child begins school. He's still 'all there,' to use a slang term in a different way. But we begin to lose access to his mind from the day he enters the classroom. The reason for this is because we've embraced the belief that knowledge only comes from what we get through our five senses. We think that a child can only know about what he sees and handles—we forget that he can *conceive in his mind* and *figure out in his thoughts*. I'm belaboring this point because our faith in a child's spiritual/intellectual ability to learn is one of our chief assets. Once we realize what a wonder a child's mind is, we begin to see how important it is to nurture it, and we see that knowledge is the food of the mind in the same way that meals are the food of the body. In the days before WWI, which seem like a lifetime ago, our narrow-minded contempt for knowledge was well-known. Nobody other than teachers or a few thinkers here and there took knowledge seriously. We boldly proclaimed that the content a child learned wasn't important; what mattered was *the way he learned it*. We had a bold contempt for mere 'book-learning.' But that's changing. We are beginning to suspect that ignorance is a national problem, one of the main reasons for our difficulties at home that hinder our efforts in other countries. There's only one cure for ignorance, and that's knowledge. School is the place where children get knowledge. Whatever else teachers do for children, their first priority should be giving them knowledge—not in carefully measured dosages like a pharmacist counting out antibiotics, but in regular, generous servings. If we ask, 'What is knowledge?' we find that there's no clear, concise answer at hand. We know that Matthew Arnold had three classifications of knowledge: knowledge about God and divine things, knowledge about man, which is humanities, and knowledge about the physical world, which is science. That's enough to start with. But I'd like [pg 240] to challenge his classifications. I'd like to classify *all* knowledge under the heading of humanities when it makes a direct appeal to the mind through a literary means [*books*]. Divine knowledge is contained in one of the three greatest books of the world [*presumably the Bible; I wonder what the other two are?*]. Science is written about in beautifully poetic literature that's clear, precise and graceful, at least in France, if not always in England. So, doesn't it seem allowable to include all knowledge under 'humanities' when literature is a proper medium from which to learn it? One thing we know, at any rate. No teaching, and no information, is processed as knowledge in anyone's mind until his own brain has actively assimilated it, translated it, rearranged it, and absorbed it so that it becomes a part of the person and shows up, like food that the body takes in, as part of the living organism. Therefore, teaching, lecturing, dramatizing, no matter how brilliant or coherent, does no good until the student becomes an active participant and goes to work on it in his mind. In other words, *self-education is the only possible education*. Anything else is like mere paint that's spread on the outside surface of the student's nature and has no effect on who he is.

I've tried to draw your attention to the way our current twentieth century educational ideal undervalues children and undervalues knowledge. The mind and knowledge are like a ball and socket, or two halves of a pair of scissors. They're made for each other, necessary to each other, and can only act as a team. When we understand that, we'll realize that our task as teachers is to provide students with the supply of knowledge that they need. If we do that, then everything else—character, behavior, efficiency, ability, and large-mindedness, which is the finest quality that a person can have, will take care of itself. 'But how?' asks the frenzied teacher, who has been working with the unending toil of Sisyphus. I think we've discovered the answer. At least, it seems to work admirably. I'm anxious to share the principles with you and tell you how it works. [pg 241]

Let me first repeat some results that I've had with thousands of children, which I mentioned in the introduction. In the last few years, in fact, many Council Schools have seen the same results:

— The students, not the teachers, are responsible for what they learn. They do the work by their own effort.

— The teachers give encouragement and support. If necessary, they clarify, summarize, or explain. But the actual work of learning belongs to the students.

— The student, depending on the age and grade/year, reads between 1000 to 2-3000 pages from a large variety of scheduled books. The sheer amount of work scheduled for each term doesn't allow for more than a single reading.

— Reading comprehension is tested with oral narration

— No review is attempted to prepare before term exams because too much material has been covered to allow going back to look things up.

— Whatever the students have read, they know. They can write about any part of it easily and fluently in lively English. They can usually spell well.

— During term exams, which last a week, students fill 20-60 sheets of Cambridge paper [*probably sheets of lined paper like notebook paper, or possibly pages in a composition notebook*] depending on their age/grade. If they had ten times the number of questions, they'd most likely fill ten times as much paper!

— It's rare that all the students in a class can't answer all the questions in all the subjects, like history, literature, citizenship, geography, science. But children do have individual differences, and some do better in a specific subject. Again, some write long answers, and a few don't write as much. But, no matter how they answer, practically all of them know the answers to the questions.

— During a term exam, students freely use [pg 242] a lot of substantives [*specific detailed nouns*], including many proper names. One time, I had a ten-year-old's paper counted to see how many substantives he used, and there were well over a hundred! Here are the ones he used beginning with the letter A:

Africa, Alsace-Lorraine, Abdomen, Antigonons, Antennae, Aphis, Antwerp, Alder, America, Amsterdam, Austria-Hungary, Ann Boleyn, Antarctic, Atlantic—

and here are the M's:

Megalopolis, Maximilian, Milan, Martin Luther, Mary of the Netherlands, Messina, Macedonia, Magna Charta, Magnet, Malta, Metz, Mediterranean, Mary Queen of Scots, Treaty of Madrid—

and, on all these subjects, students wrote as easily and thoroughly as if they were writing to a sister who was away, and telling her about a new litter of kittens!

— Students write with perfect understanding that's appropriate for their age, and there is hardly ever a blooper even in hundreds of sets of papers. They have an admirable ability at getting to the gist of a book or subject. Sometimes they're asked to write their answer about a person or event in verse, and the result is remarkable. Not that it's great poetry, but it sums up a lot of thoughtful reading in an imaginative way. For example, one student summed up Cordelia from King Lear in twelve lines:

Cordelia

Nobliest lady, doomed to slaughter,
An unloved, unpitied daughter,
Though Cordelia thou may'st be,
"Love's" the fittest name for thee;

If love doth not, maid, bestow
Scorn for scorn, and "no" for "no,"
If love loves through scorn and spite,
If love clings to truth and right,
If love's pure, maid, as thou art,
If love has a faithful heart,
Thou art then the same as love;
Come from God's own realms above!

M.K.C. age 10, Form II (grade 4-6) [pg 243]

David Livingstone's life (read for its geography of Africa) is summarized like this:

Livingstone

"The whole of Africa is desert bare,
Except around the coast." So people said,
And thought of that great continent no more.
"The smoke of thousand villages I've seen!"
So cried a man. He knew no more. His words
Sank down into one heart there to remain.
The man who heard rose up and gave his all:
Into the dark unknown he went alone.
What terrors did he face? The native's hate,
The fever, tsetse-fly and loneliness.
But to the people there he brought great Light.
Who was this man, the son of some great lord?
Not so. He was a simple Scottish lad
Who learnt to follow duty's path. His name
Was Livingstone, he will not be forgot.

E. P. age 15, Form IV (grade 9)

And here is how a 14 year old girl in Form IV (grade 9) rendered Plutarch's Life of Pericles:

Oh! land, whose beauty and unrivalled fame;
Lies dead, obscure in Time's great dusty vault.
Not so in memory, for truly here,
Each and alike look up and do revere
Those heroes of the hidden past. Plato,
Who's understanding reached the wide world's end;
Aristides, that just and noble man.
And last, not least, the great wise Pericles
Who's socialistic views and clever ways
For governing the rich and poor alike
Were to be envied. In his eyes must Greece
Live for ever as the home of beauty.
So to the Gods great marble shrines he made,

Temples and theatres did he erect;
So that the beauty of his beloved Greece
Might live for ever. And now when seeing
What is left of all those wondrous sights
We think not of the works themselves
But rather of the man who had them built

J.F. [pg 244]

It's possible that she used 'socialistic' when she meant 'democratic.' At any rate, her notion is original! Her poetry technique isn't anything extraordinary, but I think you'll agree that each poem shows thoughtful appreciation for some part of the term's reading. The verses are uncorrected.

A lot of time is spent between ages 6-8 learning to read and write. But the students still get a good deal of consecutive knowledge in history, geography, tale and fable. At the end of the term, they dictate their answers to the term exam questions. Their answers form well-expressed little essays on whatever subject they're dealing with.

The time scheduled for teaching a half-dozen or more less literary subjects like Scripture and the subjects I've already indicated, is mostly spent with the teacher reading maybe two or three paragraphs at a time from one of the scheduled books. Then the children, from here and there in the classroom, narrate. The teacher reads, expecting that the children will listen and know. Therefore, she reads with distinctness, force and careful enunciation. It is merely a way of giving the children help and support in understanding. She is being careful to convey the meaning of the author and not her own interpretation. This procedure of the teacher reading aloud and the class narrating is continued throughout elementary school by necessity because some of the books are rather expensive, so only one copy is purchased for the class. I wonder if the habit of listening carefully with full attention might equalize children from uneducated homes, and children from privileged homes? At any rate, the work they turn in seems surprisingly equal. By the way, no subjects, passages or episodes are selected because the children have a special interest in them. The best available book is chosen and read through during the course of possibly two or three years. [pg 245]

Let me add that these principles and this method don't just appeal to the clever child, but to the average child and even the challenged child. Just as we all come to a feast of Shakespeare and get out of it whatever we need or want, students do the same thing at the intellectual feast we set before them in their lessons. There's enough to satisfy the sharpest mind, yet the slowest child is able to keep up with his own willing effort. This fairly varied and successful intellectual program is done in the same time, or even less, as it takes other schools to do their normal schedule. There's no review, no preparing the night before (because more work is accomplished during the normal school hours than other schools where students are often just passively hearing lectures), no note-taking because it isn't necessary, since students have the material in their books and know where to find it, and, since there's no cramming for exams, there's more time to spare for vocational training or other work.

This kind of education should act as a social lever, too. Everyone is so concerned about improving the conditions and lives of the poorer class. But have we considered that, by giving them a better education, the problems of decent living will take care of themselves, as most people will be able to solve them on their own?

Like all great ventures of life, this method that I propose is a venture of faith—faith in the power of knowledge, and faith in the power of children to absorb it. It will succeed because of the nature of two things: the nature of knowledge, and the nature of children. If the two are brought together in ways the mind can handle, a chemical combination takes place and something totally new appears: a person of character and intelligence, an admirable citizen whose own life is so full and [pg 246] so rich that he won't become a useless drain on society.

Education is closely connected with religion. Every passionate teacher knows that he's obeying the precept to 'feed My lambs'—to feed them with all good, healthy things for man's spirit—most importantly, the knowledge of God.

I've spoken about the laws of mind or spirit, but, really, we can only guess here and there and hesitantly follow whatever light we get from the teachings of the wise and from general experience. We have to look for general experience because individual experience can be misleading. I learned that principles and methods that had been tried for a long time could be used in classrooms of forty children in a mining village. Therefore, I felt sure that we were following laws that would result in a satisfying kind of education.

The mind needs sustenance as much as the body does in order to grow and be strong. Everybody knows that. Long ago, people realized that the kind of mental gruel used in schools was the wrong kind of diet. Grammar rules, lists of names, dates and places—all the things the old schoolmasters used to use—were found to be just the kind of material that children's mind reject. Because we were wise enough to see that the mind actively seeks what it needs, we changed our tactics. We thought we were following the children's lead. It worked well, and we were ready to improve even more, if necessary. But what if all of our educational tools, our illustrations, our clarifying, our leading questions, our tireless patience in driving a point home with the students, were all based on false assumptions? What if we made a mistake in our assessment of the immature mind of the child by assuming that immature meant imperfect and incapable? 'I think I could get it, Mama, if you didn't explain quite so much.' Is this the silent thought-cry of school children today? Children really [pg 247] are capable of so much more than we give them credit for. But we get their capable minds into action the wrong way.

We make a mistake when we let our own well-intended teaching get between children and the knowledge their minds need. The desire for knowledge (curiosity) is the main component in education. But a child's natural curiosity can be rendered as useless as a crippled arm by encouraging other desires in its place.

Other desires might be emulation (the desire to be the best), prizes (greed), power (ambition), or praise (vanity). I'm told that grades, first place standing and prizes aren't really a part of elementary education (except prizes for attendance). So, the love of learning for its own sake is more likely to have free reign in elementary schools than in other schools.

Children are already persons from the time they're born. This is the first article of the educational creed that I want to advance. Being born persons implies that they come pre-wired with the ability to pay attention, hunger for knowledge, ability to think clearly, discriminating tastes in books even before they can read, and the ability to handle many subjects [*and keep them all straight*].

The practical-minded teacher might say, 'if you can guarantee that our students will pay attention, we can guarantee that they'll make good progress in reading what Colet calls good literature.' I explained on pages 13-15 how I found the solution to this dilemma—the problem of how to get students to pay attention.

Let me say again that these principles and methods are especially good for large classrooms. The number of other children stimulates the class [to conform], and the lessons go on with more momentum. Each child is eager to participate in narrations, or do a good job on written narrations. By the way, only short answers are required when writing, so there's less work making corrections.

Let me make two more points about the [pg 248] choice of books and what term exams are like. The best way I can think of to describe the sort of books that children will agree to deal with, is to say that they have to be literary. A seven or eight year old will narrate a difficult passage of a book like Pilgrim's Progress with unusual interest and insight. Yet I doubt many adults would retain anything from Dr. Smile's excellent book called *Self-Help*. The fact that children across the board will reject a wrong book makes one wonder, and should teach us something. And it's equally fascinating how children given the right book will drain it to the dregs. The thing they need from books seems to be quantity, quality and variety: the best books about a variety of subjects—and lots of them! But the question of which books to choose is a delicate, difficult issue. After twenty five years experience (the Parents Union School was started in 1891), selecting lesson books for children of all ages, even we still make mistakes. The next term exam reveals the error! Children can't answer questions based on the wrong book. The difficulty in selecting books is further complicated by the fact that we can't rely on children's tastes any more than we can let their preferences dictate their meals.

The moment has come for the case of *Education vs. Civilization* to come to court. Hopefully, Civilization will retire to her area of improving life and stop intruding on the higher functions of inspiration and direction, which are within the jurisdiction of Education. Both Education and Civilization are subservient to Religion, each in its own place. One may not overstep the boundary of the other. At any rate, it's encouraging that we're within sight of giving stability of mind and nobleness of character to people of all socio-economic classes. That's the proper outcome and the unfailing test of a LIBERAL EDUCATION. Also, [pg 249] it's good for the great basic principle of fun to be discovered in unexpected places—like the schoolroom, which is all too often a place associated with drudgery.

Milton's ideal of 'a complete and generous education' is sufficient for any occasion—'it prepares a person to do everything he needs to do in his private and public life, in peace or in war, and to do it with justice, skill and nobility.' Our generation will have to prove whether this ideal works with all kinds of people in various conditions, and whether this ideal is necessary. It has been well said by Rudolf Eucken that,

'Just as there's only one kind of truth, and it's true for everyone, so there's only one education that works for everyone. Regarding the education of the people, the only question that matters is, How is this common education going to work under the most meager conditions, and with large masses of people? Real education should be able to accomplish that.'

Eucken didn't make any suggestions as to what kind of education could accomplish that. It's up to the reader to determine in his own mind whether the method I've outlined in this book might be worth a try.

[pg 250]

Chapter 2 - A Liberal Education in Secondary Schools

[*Some notes about the British school system are included in the front of this book.*]

A persistent message can be very powerful. The author of *The Pagan* may not be criticizing Pelmanism [*a system of training the mind to improve the memory*], but Pelmanism certainly is criticizing secondary education. Half a million people are criticizing the education they received—judges, generals, admirals, lawyers. Perhaps the spirit that whispers in the ear of critics is a lying spirit, but when so many credible people are saying the same thing, we have to suspect there's some truth to what they're saying. And it makes those of us involved in secondary education a little bit nervous. Also, the Board of Education wants accountability from schools who aren't already communicating with the State. This will help in various ways to ensure that citizens get a broad education. One popular saying is, 'If you pay the teachers more, education will improve.' So, in one neighborhood, a village teacher gets a salary of $600 and housing, and another teacher, an Oxford graduate, just as qualified who has a wife and family to support, gets no housing and is expected to live on $250 a year! But work is more important than wages, and this exclusive focus on salaries demeans teachers. Most of us know of some enthusiastic educational project making progress without any financial reward, or even praise. So what's the real hindrance to a teacher's work, and the stumbling block in the way of a broad, generous [pg 251] education? It's the continuous drudgery of having to teach what no one wants to learn. Before the war (WWI), the President of the British Association complained that school was boring for students, teachers and parents. That's why we're always in the learning process, yet never knowing. That's why teachers expend so much effort to create learning games, and why crafts and 'Eurhythmics' [*rhythmic movement training*] and similar things are offered, not to supplement education, but instead of education! That's why our Public Schools are under pressure to change, and smaller private schools are facing extinction.

All of the creative, zealous effort of teachers shows how enthusiastic and devoted they are. They understand that education isn't just an interest, it's a passion. This isn't just true of those working in major schools, but little private schools scattered all over England, too.

We've all heard of 'the two Miss Prettymans who kept a girls school at Silverbridge [*from The Last Chronicle of Barset by Anthony Trollope*]. Two kindlier ladies never presided over a school as they.' As for the elder sister, Annabella Prettyman, 'it was assumed that she did all the thinking. She knew more than any woman in Barsetshire. All of the Prettyman educational ideas came from her mind. Those who knew them best also said that she was more good-natured than her kind sister, and the most generous, loving and conscientious teacher.' The younger sister, Ann, may have known more about Roman history and Roman law than current events and English law, but which would you rather have as your teacher?

This was the kind of school that Anthony Trollope was familiar with many years ago. And maybe it wouldn't be too hard to find another school like it in a similar town of [pg 252] today. But these days, we're uneasy. In our anxiety, we create a 'Joan and Peter' kind of education—where small schools protect and encourage freaks, and even great schools with a lot going for them suspect that something's not quite right. They fail to turn out students who have broad intellectual interests, or who have a flexible mind that can, like Matthew Arnold said, be of benefit to our neighboring countries. And there is that ongoing problem of Pelmanism, which accuses current methods of being inadequate. There always seems to be some new book by an author bringing railing accusations against the school he went to. Here is one of the more restrained protests by Colonel Repington, which is revealing:

'When I remember my Eton school, I have mixed feelings. I loved the five years I spent there. I gloried in its beauty and traditions, and I graduated at the top of my class. Yet, at the same time, I was conscious that Eton wasn't teaching me the things I wanted to know. Instead, I was being taught things that revolted me, especially math and classics. What I wanted to learn was history, geography, modern languages, literature, science and political economy. At Eton, I didn't have much chance of learning more than a smattering of any of those things. I disagree with those who say that we didn't learn anything, or that we were lazy— we worked very hard. But the things we were putting forth so much effort to learn were, as far as I was concerned, useless things. So, with my feet planted firmly in the ground, I stubbornly resisted any attempts to teach me dead languages and higher math. I believed I was right. Classics have left me with no more than a few ideas that I could have learned better in kindergarten.'

The author is probably wrong about what he owes to Eton. Without those five years, he might not have become a Colonel with expertise on war theory and tactics. Who knows how much those classics like Caesar may have influenced him as a little boy! Public schools undoubtedly have many faults, but they still do a worthy job of turning out the men who do the world's work. We know about the 'playing fields,' [?] but maybe, when all is said and done, it's the influence of the classics [pg 253] that children learn in school that makes them different. Yet the accusation that, 'Eton wasn't teaching me the things I wanted to know,' is something worth considering.

It's easy to criticize and condemn schools. But, the fact is, a human being is born with a desire to know a lot about all kinds of things. How is a school going to get them all in adequately in twelve years? And, children can be excessively resistant and stubborn. Every child resists attempts to teach him, not only dead languages and higher math, but literature, science—in fact, every subject that the teacher works at. With the average child, a gallon of teaching results in just a half cup of learning. What's a teacher to do? Yet, behind that stubborn resistance, there's a hunger for knowledge—not just the right kind of knowledge, since *every* kind of knowledge is the right kind—but taught in the right way. I can't say that every way of teaching is the right way.

I'll explain what the PNEU (Parents National Education Union) has done to solve this problem. I'll explain with tentative modesty, yet with confidence, because I know that no one is more open to conviction than many distinguished Headmasters and Headmistresses if they can be shown reasonable cause. If they are convinced, may they have the courage to follow through on their convictions!

There's so little known about how the mind works that's it's open to anyone to make discoveries in this mysterious territory. I'm not talking about psychology. We hear a lot about that, although we actually know very little. I'm talking about the mind itself. Its ways are subtle and hidden. Nevertheless, the only valid education is education that focuses on the mind. The main challenge is the huge amount of subjects to introduce children to. They have a right to them as human beings, and they need to find out about the things that they're drawn to as people and that [pg 254] they'll spend the rest of their lives pursuing further. The first and the most important is the knowledge of God. This is to be learned most directly from the Bible. Then comes the knowledge of man. He learns this from history, literature, art, civics, ethics, biography, drama, and languages. And last, enough knowledge of the universe as he needs to help him understand the phenomena we're all familiar with, and to give him at least the names of birds, flowers, stars and stones. And the knowledge of the universe can't go very far in any direction without some knowledge of math. The proposed curriculum is immense, but the hours of school are limited. The 'Academic' solution to this dilemma is to teach one thing thoroughly—perhaps Greek, or Chemistry or Math, and then he'll have the key to all knowledge. Therefore, proponents say, it isn't the detail of what you know that matters, it's how you learn it. A grueling course of Grammar, a class in higher math, or some lab with a few other things thrown in, is supposed to be all the education a person needs. This plan is fine for the few top students in a school who are so smart that they'll do their own learning in various extracurricular subjects on their own. But it isn't enough for the average student who has just as much right to a decent education. Soon I hope we'll have a new guiding rule: every school will have to teach all students about the three kinds of knowledge that are due to every human being. Some will ask, 'what is knowledge?' There's no clear-cut answer to that, but we do know this—Knowledge is that which we know, but a person can only know what he expends the effort to learn. Nobody can learn for him, it's something he has to do for himself. But an appalling apathy is in the way. Children don't care to know, so they don't learn. And, when they grow up, their intellectual diet will consist of nothing more than evening poker games and golf on weekends.

We of the PUS (Parents Union School) have discovered [pg 255] a great thirst for knowledge in children of every age and class. Children also have a remarkable ability to focus their attention, retain, and respond intellectually on the mental diet they consume. The first step is paying attention, and every child of any age, even mentally challenged children, seem to have an unlimited ability to pay attention. And they don't need grades, prizes, first place standing, praise, threats or blame to do it, either. When a teacher realizes this, great things will be possible, although at first, he may find it hard to believe, or even ludicrous. But education of the future will probably result in intellectual progress as surprising as the moral ethics we saw demonstrated in WWI.

We haven't attained it yet, but I think we're well on our way. After 25 years of experience on a wide scale, and after consequently doing some research, we've discovered what children are capable of learning, and what they want to know. We know what their minds will act on when it comes to judgment and imagination. We know what they aren't able to learn. And we know what conditions have to be met for them to learn. We don't need to make learning a game, or spend school time doing arts and crafts or physical movements. We don't need to fill school time with sports on the false assumption that boys will take to it better than learning. Physical and vocational training are necessary for upbringing the young, but training shouldn't be confused with education. Training is for the physical body; education is concerned with the things of the mind. Current educational methods are good for 'developing the faculties,' but what if there aren't any faculties in need of developing? If all there is to develop is a mind that's already alert, active on its own, discriminating, logical, capable of both great imaginings and the tiniest processes—then we'll need to change our educational tactics. Occasional gymnastics benefit the mind as much as the physical body, but the mind can't live [pg 256] on that any more than the physical body can live on calisthenics.

Like I said, knowledge is the food that the mind needs. Knowledge is, roughly, ideas clothed with facts. This is the kind of mental diet a child needs—in large quantities and about varied subjects. The wide curriculum I have in mind is designed so that, in every detail, it meets some specific need of the mind. What's interesting is that when a curriculum has lots of subjects, students aren't at all confused trying to keep them all straight. They don't make comical blunders, or mix things up, like mixing a bit of English trivia with a fact from French history.

We've made another discovery—the mind refuses to learn anything that isn't presented in a literary [*usually story*] form. It's no surprise that this should be the case with privileged children who are used to a literary atmosphere. But it's surprising that it's just as true of uneducated inner-city children. People can expend the effort to commit facts from the driest compilation of data in a textbook to short-term memory for a public exam, but that information doesn't seem to reach the real mind. Yet, for someone like young Paschal, who enthusiastically pursued math on his own, the knowledge is handled directly by the region of higher thinking. The knowledge seemed to him like poetry itself. Geniuses like that will learn no matter what, they can't be held back. But they have a gift, it's not a result of their own laborious efforts to plod along against their will. But for the majority of students, the general consensus of teachers is probably right—a lower, less exacting standard should be used for standardized tests.

In teaching science, too, we need to realize that the way to the wonder of nature isn't through the confusion of science the way it's usually taught, but through field study or other personal observation, supplemented with literary reading.

The French Academy was able to advance science and art, probably due to the use of the charmingly lucid and exquisite prose of the many French books [pg 257] about science subjects. The mind is like a container that can use its own ability to work on whatever is put into it. But the one power that it lacks is the ability to sift through the sand and sawdust and filter out the pure essence of ideas from it. That should help us to understand the kind of diet that the living organism called 'the mind' needs for its daily subsistence. I've already mentioned that the mental diet needs a lot of variety, and we remember Dr. Arnold urgently insisted that students have 'very varied reading' in all three fields of knowledge: knowledge of God, knowledge of man, and knowledge of the world around him.

But the mind is always deceiving us. Every teacher knows how a class will work away quietly for a whole hour—yet accomplish nothing, even when the students think they've been reading. [*If asked for details about what they just read, they won't be able to give any.*] We all know how miserably we fail when we try to share about the daily newspaper we've spent the morning poring over. Details escape us. We're able to say, 'Did you see the article about such and such?' But we're unable to explain what the article said. We try to help our children avoid the vagueness that we fall prey to by making them take notes of their lessons, but it doesn't do much good. The mind seems to have an 'outer court' where information comes in, and then goes out, without ever making any kind of impression on the inner place where the personality is. And this is the dark secret of learning by rote. It's a purely mechanical process that can't be explained, yet it's a process that leaves the student entirely unaffected. What teacher hasn't experienced the dreariness of grading a stack of papers that lack even a shred of evidence of student personality? But now we have discovered a natural solution to the problem of merely skimming the surface of the ground with our educational plow. Give students the kind of knowledge they were made to digest, served in a literary medium, and they'll pay great attention. What's our next step? Clever comprehension questions? No. As Dr. Johnson told us, questions are an intrusion, and they're boring. We have an ancient word of wisdom to guide us: 'The mind doesn't really know anything that it can't express [pg 258] by asking itself a question and coming up with an answer on its own.' Notice—not a question asked by someone else, but a question *the mind asks itself*. We all know the trick we use when we want to remember a conversation or sermon or lecture well enough to repeat it to someone later. We go over it in our mind first. Then our mind quizzes itself by asking itself one question, the same question again and again: 'What comes next?' And, before we know it, we have it, the whole thing! We've heard the story of how a young man once recited a complete pamphlet by Burke at a college supper. And those pamphlets aren't light reading! We admire that kind of feat, and think that such an accomplishment is out of our reach. But any fifteen-year old could do it if they were allowed to look at the pamphlet only once. Allowing a second look would be fatal, because nobody gives their full attention to something they expect to see or hear again. If we get used to the crutch of being able to go back to something, we lose the ability to pay attention—forever. We teachers commit a serious offense with this mistake. We think that if we just talk more, repeat ourselves, reinforce the point, explain it one more way, add an illustration, then students will eventually hear us. We don't do this because we love the sound of our own voices, but because we don't fully appreciate and have faith in knowledge and in our students. We don't really understand that the mind and knowledge are like a ball and socket joint. Each of them is useless without the other. Education will have started off on the right foot when we finally realize that knowledge is to the mind what food is to the physical body. Without knowledge, the mind will faint and starve and finally die as surely as the body will without food.

The cure for this is very simple. Let the child (elementary age) tell back what's been read to him, all of it or even just part of it, right away. Then ask again a few months later during exam time. One might object, 'That's mere verbal memory.' All I can say is, try it yourself. Read an essay of Charles Lamb's, or maybe Matthew Arnold's. Or read *Lycidas* or the [pg 259] raven scene from *Barnaby Rudge*. Then put yourself to sleep, or wile away an anxious or boring hour by repeating to yourself what you read. The result will be disappointing. You'll find that you forgot a certain point, or a link in the chain of an argument. But you'll know the gist of the whole thing surprisingly well—the events, the characters, the subtle line of reasoning will stand out in your mind like figures on a relief sculpture cut in stone. You'll find that you've taken in 'mind stuff' that will be used in a thousand ways, perhaps for the rest of your life.

And here we see the powers of the mind that need to be continually at work in education: attention, assimilation, narration, retention, and reproduction. But what about reason, judgment, imagination, discrimination, and those other 'faculties' that teachers have been working so hard to develop? They take care of themselves and work on the knowledge that's been received with attention, and cemented with narration. They take care of themselves as naturally and involuntarily as the digestive organs work on food that's been thoroughly chewed. We need to feed the mind in the same way we feed the body—with food that's suitable, and in generous portions. The less we meddle with the digestive processes, the more healthy the person will be, whether it's the digestive organs of the body, or the mind. The human mind is an infinitely amazing thing, and it's present in completeness and power even in the slowest student. Even of the dullest child, it can be said,

'Darkness may bind up his eyes, but not his imagination. Lying in his bed, he might, like Pompey and his sons in all parts of the earth, speculate on the universe and enjoy the whole world within his own mind.'

We are paying the price today for the wave of materialism that swept over the country a hundred years ago. People don't set out specifically to be materialistic today, but our educational thought is in the midst of a trend that's carrying us where we don't want to go. Anybody espousing a new method is welcome to us. We've [pg 260] stopped believing in the mind. Although we might not say out loud, 'the brain secretes thought in the same way that the liver secretes bile,' yet we still have a strictly physical concept of the mind. Therefore, the spiritual mind isn't the objective in our educational methods. One might say that, 'mankind is like a horse, and things are in the saddle riding mankind.' We've come to believe that ideas or knowledge can't reach children.

The message for our generation is, *Believe in the ability of the mind. Let education go directly to the student's mind.* Of course, you'll need books, since nobody is arrogant enough to think that they can teach every subject of a broad curriculum thoroughly on their own, using the same original thoughts and identical facts of the expert who's made the subject his life's work and wrote a book about it. Yet we realize that teachers aren't trying to teach everything because they're arrogant. They're just trying to be helpful. They honestly believe that students can't understand well-written books, and they want to be a bridge between the student and the real instructor, which is the man who wrote the book.

But now we've proved that students, even inner-city students, are fully capable of understanding any book suited for their age. Children of age eight or nine are able to grasp a chapter of *Pilgrim's Progress* after a single reading. Students of age fourteen can read one of Lamb's essays, or a chapter of *Eothen*. Seventeen-year-olds can narrate after reading *Lycidas*. If you give children a well-written literary book suitable for their age, they'll have no problem dealing with it—they don't need us to spell it out for them. Of course, they won't be able to answer leading questions about it, because questions are an annoyance that all of us resent. But they will be able to tell back the whole thing with their own little individual touches. This might be the key to overcoming the huge difficulty of teaching humanities in English. We don't have to be overwhelmed with the thought of trying to cover such a large body of material at a snail's pace to try to make sure the student gets something out of the author he's reading. The slow process is our own invention. [pg 261] Instead, just let the student read it and tell it back, and he'll know it.

This practice of telling back sounds simplistic, but it's really a magical creative process where the person narrating 'sees' what he's talking about in his mind, clear and vivid—after reading the material just once. I keep repeating the stipulation about only one reading because—let me say it again—it's impossible to give our full attention to something we've heard before, and know we'll hear again.

Students should be treated in this reasonable way—mind to mind. I don't mean their young minds with the teacher's mind, that would exert too much of the teacher's influence. I'm talking about the minds of various thinkers meeting students, mind to mind, by way of books. The teacher performs the gracious task of introducing one enthusiastic mind to the other. With this method, students can cover an incredible amount of material in the limited time they have.

One of the best indicators of how well-educated a person is, is how many substantives [*specific people, places, events they can name*] they know well enough to use with confidence. We remember Sir Walter Scott telling how he tried various subjects to start a conversation with a stranger on his coach. Nothing worked until he brought up 'bent leather.' Then they chatted on and on, because the man happened to be a saddle-maker! We've all had such experiences, and we have to admit that we ourselves have proven to be difficult for someone else to find something in common with until the person trying to strike up a conversation with us found our own topic of expertise. And this is something that teachers should consider. There are a thousand different things we could know about thoroughly enough to be able to speak intelligently. Yet we focus on vague 'general knowledge' so that students exert their efforts trying to get scrappy information, and then make bloopers on their essay papers because they can't keep them straight. The only solution is a lot of consecutive reading from various literary books. We have no trouble making time for all these books because one [pg 262] single reading is enough, and there shouldn't be any reviewing for an upcoming exam. Look at this list of 200 names (*substantives*) that an 11-year old used easily and confidently on a term exam in Form II (grades 4-6):

Abinadab, Athenian, Anne Boleyn, Act of Uniformity, Act of Supremacy, America, Austria, Alcibiades, Athens, Auckland, Australia, Alexandria, Alhambra.

Bible, Bishop of Rochester, Baron, Bean-shoots, Bluff, Bowen Falls, Bishoprics, Blind Bay, Burano.

Currants, Cupid, Catholic, Court of High Commission, Cranmer, Charles V, Colonies, Convent, Claude, Calais, Cook Strait, Canterbury Plain, Christchurch, Cathedral, Canals, Caliph of Egypt, Court of the Myrtles, Columbus, Cordova.

David, Defender of the Faith, Duke of Guise, Dunedin, Doge's Palace.

England, Emperor, Empire, Egmont (Count), English Settlement

Flour, Fruits, French, Francis I, Francis of Guise, Ferdinand, Foveau Strait, Fuchsias, Fiords, Ferns.

Greek, Germany, Gondolas, "Gates of the Damsels," Gondoliers, Granada, Gate of Justice, Gypsies.

Henry VIII, History, Hooper, Henry II, Hungary, Haeckel.

Israel, Italian (language), Italy, Infusoria.

Jesse, Jonathan, Joseph, John, Jerusalem, James, Jane Seymour.

King of Denmark, King of Scotland, Kiwi.

"Love-in-Idleness," Lord Chancellor, Lord Burleigh, Lord Robert Dudley, Lime, Lyttleton, N.Z., Lake Tango.

Mary (The Virgin), More (Sir Thomas), Music, Martyr's Memorial, Milan, Metz, Monastery, Mary, Queen of Scots, Mediterranean, Microscope, Messina, Middle Island, Mount Egmont, Mount Cook, Milford Sound, Museum, Moa, Maoris, Mussulman, Moorish King.

Naomi, Netherlands, Nice, New Zealand, North Island, Napier, Nelson.

Oberon, Oxford, Orion.

Pharisees, Plants, Parliament, Puck, Pope, Protestant, Poetry,

Philosophy, "Paix des Dames ," Philip II, Paris, Planets, "Pink Terraces,"
Piazetta, Philip of Burgundy.
Queen Catherine, Queen Elizabeth, Queen Mary, Queen Isabella, Queen Juana.
[pg 263]
Ruth, Robin Goodfellow, Ridley, Reformation, Radiolaria, Rotomaliana (Lake),
Rea.
Saul, Samuel, Simeon, Simon Peter, Sunshine, Sugar-cane, Spices, Sultan, Spain,
St. Quentin, Socrates, Stars, Sycamore, Seed-ball, Stewart Island, Seaports,
Southern Alps, Scotch Settlement, St. Mark, St. Theodore, St. Maria Formosa
(Church), Sierra Navada.
Temple, Titania, Testament, Treaty, Turks, Toul, Thread Slime, Tree Ferns,
Timber Trees, Trieste, Toledo.
Verdure, Venus (Planet), Volcano, Volcanic Action, Venice.
Whieat, Wiltshire, William Cecil, Walsingham, Winged Seed, Wellington,
Waikato.
Zaccharias, Zebedee.

These nouns were all used appropriately and matter-of-factly. You can see the
exam among the papers included later in this book.

What if we change the perspective of a conscientious, intelligent teacher so that
he perceives that the mind is complete and already has all the ability it needs
except its suitable mental diet, so that the teacher gives up the erroneous concept
of developing faculties? And what if he yields his role as 'the fountainhead of all
knowledge,' and lets his students get at knowledge first-hand from the best books,
because he knows that students are fully capable of dealing with it themselves?
What if he abandons the use of text-books and abridged summaries he's been
using, since he realizes that the mind will never be interested in such dry
compilations, and only the short-term memory will touch such stuff? What if he
admits that students need a wide base of knowledge in many different areas, so
that a broad curriculum is needed to help them become intelligent, noble-minded
citizens? What if he becomes convinced that any student can face such a
curriculum because he knows that all children have an immense ability to focus
their attention and know their lesson after just one single reading? Doesn't he still
have one or two fallacies that we haven't attacked yet? He'll tell you that his goal
isn't to expose students to a general look at all the [pg 264] subjects that
intelligent people should know something about. No, his aim is to pick two or
three topics and give a thorough understanding of them, so that he turns out well-
bred young Englishmen. More specifically, he sees the school as a place to form
character, not a place to acquire information. And, about his choice of two
subjects—classics [*in dead languages*] and higher math—I have no real
objections, since I recognize the value of them and I realize that, under our
current system, students need to do well in them to get the opportunity for a good
career. But perhaps if students get into the habit of covering more material
quickly [*as a result of focused attention and getting it the first time*], then they'll
have more time left to pursue the additional subjects that give him a more broad,
balanced education. One of the country's major grammar schools is trying this as
an experiment. I don't need to show how valuable these kinds of experiments are
to us as a democracy. It looks like it will be possible for the masses to learn to
read at school in such a way that they'll be able to use as many substantives on a

term exam as the list I showed earlier. If the mainstream public learns about 'Sancho Panza,' Elsinore, 'Excalibur,' 'Rosinante,' 'Mrs. Jellaby,' redstart, 'Bevis,' and bogbean, then the privileged classes should be familiar with them, too. If one social class learns about the art of the Van Eycks, with 'Comus,' 'Duessa,' 'Baron of Bradwardine,' then the other classes should know about them, too. And they should all be able to use that knowledge with as much effect as a political leader does when he quotes something familiar from Horace. Such a quote should touch some sentiment in all of our hearts, because things we're familiar with seem like old friends to us. What we need is some common ground, a bond of common thought that comes when everybody reads the same books and is familiar with the same art, the same music, the same interests. When we have this solid ground of shared knowledge, we'll be able to relate to each other in both [pg 265] public speeches and personal conversations. We'll all hear about 'the wonderful works of God in our own language' [*Acts 2:11*] because we've all learned the same things, we'll all be familiar with the same great conversation that's been recorded in the books of the ages by those who lived before us, and whose purpose was to teach us. And we'll be able to speak persuasively with those who have received the same education and will listen to logic, rather than belligerently opposing reason in their ignorance.

Education for those living in a democracy needs to have certain features. We all need to be able to speak well, representing the concerns of groups of people and relating their sentiments and joys. Then we'll stop being motivated by self-interest and personal advantage in our political activism. We'll be able to touch sentiments of poetry and heroism, which most hearts will rise to. And, as a result, we'll be able to build 'a new Jerusalem right here in England's green, pleasant land.' To accomplish this, we all need to read the same books—in English, not in Latin or Greek. Most people, including the average student at a classical school, will never have the time to become fluent in Latin or Greek. Perhaps we'll still want an exclusive class of ivy-league students, and this seems like a good idea to me, since the one thing we've always done well at is instilling character and proper behavior in the top-notch schools. But we should broaden its base at the bottom, and narrow it as it gets to the top. In the earlier years, there should be a whole lot of books that *everybody* has to read. In the high school years, we need to cover less dead language classics and less higher math, to make room for more history and literature in our own language. I know I'm not an authority, but it seems to me that there's a lot of overlap from prep school to public boarding school, and from one Form (grade) to another, and from high school to the university [*eliminating redundant overlaps and review could free up some time for more learning.*] We could probably find a way to instill the same high-quality, character-building education, but we could make it inclusive rather than exclusive. [pg 266]

We could use more of the kinds of books that everyone should know. We could include enough history and geography to make everyone feel at home wherever they travel. And everyone could become familiar with the natural phenomena that affects us in the world around us. If we give up the false concept that the mind has faculties to be developed by the teacher, and accept that education needs to get a large body of knowledge to the student for him to assimilate on his own, there is a fear that traditional exclusive education will be lost. But that would be a tragedy. We need to keep what's good about it, and add a wider variety of reading to it. H.G. Wells' characters in 'Joan and Peter' should teach us a lesson. Peter isn't enrolled at a respected boarding school because his guardian doesn't like them. He prefers games [sports?] Later, Joan and Peter are at college. 'No religion has convinced Joan that she has any specific purpose in her life. Neither Highmorton nor Cambridge has taught her simple devotion, or given her any career guidance. The only future suggested by girls schools was career student, or teaching.' Wells' accusation against the schools was that each, in its own way, tried to find a substitute for knowledge for the sake of learning. Academic success isn't the same as really learning. Many good schools fail to pass on the joy of learning for its own sake, or to teach the kinds of things that influence a person's character and actions. A good school should get high ideals to sink in and affect its students slowly, even imperceptibly.

And there's another standard, possibly an even higher consideration. At our PNEU schools, we offer knowledge for its own sake. Our students discover that lessons can be something enjoyable. We don't limit our focus to the top students. We don't need to. The top students work [pg 267] well on their own. In fact, so do the average and challenged students. Historical people become real to them, and they get familiar with a pretty wide range of history. They don't grow up in woeful ignorance of other countries' histories. For example, they understand that life in India is better today than it used to be because they know something about Akbar, and they know that he lived at the same time as Queen Elizabeth. They take to heart the lesson learned from young Phaeton's presumption. Midas, Circe, Xerxes and Pericles enrich their thoughts in the background. The different Forms (grades) cover a lot of reading because we've learned that a single reading is all that's needed to get a pretty clear knowledge of a subject, if the right book is used. That means that many books are needed, and every book is read through from beginning to end so that the student's knowledge isn't just vague bits here and there. Our teachers enjoy the work scheduled for each term as much as the students do. There's no monotony or dullness in the classroom. There's hardly any idleness or wandering attention, so there's no need to disguise learning as a game, as is sadly necessary in most schools. Games should be used for fun outside of lessons, there's no need to create games to get students to do their lessons.

Using my methods can have an interesting effect on the whole family as the child shares what he just read from Waverley with the caregiver and the lawn maintenance man. I recently heard from a teacher, 'A.J. correctly identified a moss that her father picked from the very top of Ben Lawers mountain. It's very rare and only grows there and on one other mountain. She is so pleased!' And her father must be, too! The whole household thinks about and reflects on great thoughts, because nothing is as contagious as knowledge and the fine attitude of mind that it brings. Children taught this way are fun to be around because they're interested in so many things, and they have worthy thoughts. They have a lot to talk about, and this kind of talk can't help but have a beneficial effect on those around them—and on society. That pleasant sense [pg 268] of knowing about things worth knowing, and things that make life worth living, is like a delightful atmosphere. It's what makes people noble-minded. We agree with Milton that a noble mind is the most appropriate result of education.

Students taught along these lines are familiar with a large number of books, many historical and literary persons, and quite a range of natural phenomena. Compare that with what a normal school student can claim—a sterile curriculum that isn't mastered very well. This should give us cause for reflection. Perhaps the students' moral and intellectual progress reflects the teachers themselves, since they're the ones who put together the curriculum. Every head school official knows how to put together the best possible curriculum and make the students do it if they stick to just a few basic subjects. But we PNEU workers have an advantage because we recognize a couple of natural laws.

I'm sure that some of you are interested in the work we're doing in elementary schools. The work is even more impressive because it begins with children who have a narrow vocabulary and no experience with literature. Yet these children show themselves capable of hearing or reading a well-written book, and, after just one single reading, narrating passages with enthusiasm and accuracy. They don't balk at even the longest names, and they don't muddle complicated statements. This was a revelation to us. It proves that a literary education isn't out of reach for anyone, and it doesn't have to take tedious and difficult preparation, but it can work immediately. All children need is the right books, and the right methods.

I'll say it again—we live in times that are critical for everybody, but especially for teachers. The world is depending on them. Will education aim at what's best for the individual, or what's best for everyone? Will it just prepare students to get a job, or will it try to work towards [pg 269] higher thinking and contentment for everyone, which would be best for society as a whole?

I beg school officials who understand what I'm saying to realize that we're at a parting of ways, and to please consider a method that will bring some promise of educational improvement.

For example, we're able to answer the question that the Departmental Committee on English is considering:

'Can history and literature be made more a part of the school curriculum than it is now? How much grammar is necessary? Can oral composition, drama and debate help to turn around our country's loss of verbal skills? How can prep schools teach English better? How can we get more substance into school essays? How can exams test English without destroying students' love for literature?'

One couldn't have planned better questions to provide a chance for the PNEU to list its advantages. History—European as well as English—is taught consecutively with literature. Some knowledge of syntax is necessary, as well as a lot of what we call grammar. But that's not to teach the art of correct writing and speaking. Those skills come naturally, and the beautifully eloquent, consecutive articulating of our student narrations is a thing to be heard with some envy. As far as our national loss of verbal skill, I'll quote a Director of Education: 'Being ready and willing to speak becomes normal. If all children in England are schooled using this method, then, in twenty five years, a strong silent Englishman will be a rarity!' One teacher said that his older students are now eager to speak for long time periods—something he's never seen before. Imagine how valuable this will be in the future as our country's safety depends more and more on the ability of the common people to communicate clearly and with confidence. Oral composition [narration] is routine for our schools in all [pg 270] grades—students narrate from age six to eighteen. One reporter from a local newspaper was sent out to investigate the PNEU method after reading an article that a teacher wrote for the magazine *The Nineteenth Century and After*. The article the reporter wrote after investigating was called, 'Ten Year Olds Who Read Shakespeare.' As far as prep schools, the best we can offer is a method that has some surprising results in the teaching of English. The final concern about how exams can help students' minds can be answered by looking at some PUS [Parents Union School] exam papers.

School officials shouldn't take on any project without some thought. This method requires a solid understanding of certain principles, and practicing them faithfully. Some people smile politely and say that all things have something good in them, and one educational method is as good as another. In fact, they say, taking a little from each of them should work just fine. But this kind of casual attitude doesn't provide enough conviction in any one method to try very hard—so the resulting progress is disappointing. I feel strongly that trying to use my method without following its few principles will be worse than useless—it will be disastrous. One teacher said, "If we had your booklist, we could accomplish anything!' So he used the booklist—but utterly failed because he ignored the principles [*CM's 20 Principles*]. We teachers don't like to brag by coming right out and saying that we're better at handling a subject than a carefully selected author who specializes in writing books about that subject. One bright young teacher said, 'Yes, but we know more about reaching the minds of children than any writer, no matter how eloquent, who speaks through the pages of some dull book.' But this is the misconception that we're finally getting rid of. We've shown that the bulk of knowledge, taught in a way that leaves a vivid impression and encourages sound judgment, gotten from the right books, is far superior and visualized much more sharply by [pg 271] students than hearing lectures from even the most enthusiastic and effective teacher. That's why we insist on the use of books. It isn't because teachers are incompetent. It's because a student can't really know something unless his mind actively processes and assimilates it by itself, without someone else's influence.

School officials and teachers can be very generous and they might be justified in thinking that parents can be stingy about providing the necessary books for their children. It's our job to make sure that books have an important place in the hearts of our students. It's the parent's job to be sure that a variety of books is available. We need to make parents understand that it's impossible for children to have a broad education without lots of books. It's also impossible to teach students to spell well if they don't read for themselves. We hear how difficult spelling is, and how we should butcher our beloved language to make words phonetic so everyone can spell them. But we've seen with thousands of our students that children who spend more time reading books on their own can spell well because they tend to visualize words as they read. Those who always listen to read-alouds don't receive an English guide to help them visualize the words they're hearing. That's why oral lessons and lectures should only be used occasionally, as an introduction or review. But for actual education, students need to do their own work by reading their own books with the moral support and guidance of an intelligent teacher. I think we'll find that, once parents realize how important it is to have a good supply of books, they'll be only too willing to provide the books scheduled every term. Mr. Fisher says, 'There are real books, and there are textbooks.' The day is soon coming when everyone will realize that textbooks have no educational value. We hardly ever use textbooks in our Parents Union Schools. Whenever possible, we use books that spark the imagination and have a touch of originality. These are the differences between [pg 272] a real book and a text book. Maybe we should apologize for not providing books, just booklists. Any school official can come up with a booklist. But, since there are changes made to their lists every term, trying to keep up with 170 different titles can become a job in itself! We think we can provide some help to over-burdened teachers. Some people say that teachers should have the complete freedom to select their own texts, but that makes about as much sense as advocating the freedom for everyone to make their own shoes! Instead, it should be a question of how we'll divide up the tasks that need doing. If it's a question of freedom, why not take it a step further and say that students ought to have the freedom to choose their own books? But we know that 'freedom' is an elusive gold ring, and it's not always convenient or best to do all the things that we have the freedom to do.

Term exams are very important. They aren't just fleeting measures of what a child learned, but they're evidence of his progress that will probably be part of his permanent records. There are specific things that every student must know—and I mean every child, not just the privileged elite who are being groomed to be prestigious British 'gentlemen.'

The knowledge of God is the most important thing to know. Any Bible teaching that doesn't work towards that purpose is of no religious value. To that end, students read a passage of scripture that covers an incident or specific teaching. If they're too young to be able to read, the teacher reads it to them. If students need to know the geography of the place that comes up in the episode, or a local custom, the teacher goes over that and briefly but reverently emphasizes any spiritual or moral truth before the reading. After the reading, the students narrate. They're able to narrate with striking accuracy, adding their own originality, yet conveying the truth that the teacher indicated. This isn't a case [pg 273] of rote memory. It's the result of assimilating the passage so well that it's become a part of them. If you try this method yourself, perhaps by reading and then narrating the story of Nicodemus, or Jesus' talk with the woman at the well, you'll see how clear each incident becomes to you, and how every phrase has a fullness of meaning as a result of your own personal effort. This method works especially well with the gospels, but those of us who read the Bible during WWI couldn't help but notice that the books of Moses and the prophets still show us what God is like. We must not regard the Old Testament as too outdated to use as a guide in our lives.

After religious knowledge, the most important thing to know is history. In fact, our curriculum is built around history. History is like a beautiful, green countryside in the mind. It becomes richer and fuller when we add knowledge of historical people and events, and when we can include national pride. Nationhood is the only way to combat the intolerable individualism that our modern education breeds. As James Amyat wrote in his preface to Plutarch's *Lives*,

'Reading history is very valuable. History can give us more examples in a day than all the experiences of a long life. Those who read history when they're young, as they should, will gain the same wisdom of understanding world affairs that old, experienced men have. Yes, even if they never leave the comfort of their house, yet they'll be cautioned and informed about everything in the world.'

And that's why the Old Testament is so valuable. It has history, poetry, the law and the prophets. Perhaps nobody understood the educational value of scripture more than Goethe, although he never did realize their spiritual worth. We try to use first-hand accounts from the same time period when studying the Bible. [pg 274]

We use what's in some of the rooms in the British Museum as a basis. Events from Greek and Roman history come up, not just for their historical significance, but for their distinctly ethical value, too. And we use Plutarch as our foremost authority.

Thomas North wrote, 'Plutarch has written the most profitable story of all authors. Other authors wrote about things that came to no consequence. But Plutarch was sharp, educated and experienced. He chose the notable actions of the best people from the most famous nations of the world for his subject.'

We study English history in every grade. But in the earliest years, it's studied alone. We know from experience that it's not always possible to get the perfect book, so we use the best one we can find and supplement it with the best literary essays from the historical period. Literature hardly even seems like a separate subject because it's so closely associated with the term's world or English history. It might be a first-hand document or a story to teach a little about the time period. It's amazing how much actual knowledge children get when the thoughts and ideas from a time period are meshed with their study of the same time period's political and social developments. I'd like to make a point about the way poetry helps us to understand the thoughts and ideas of a time period—including our own. Every age, every era, has its own poetry that captures the soul and spirit of the time. It's a wonderful thing for a generation to have someone like Shakespeare, Dante, Milton or Burns to collect and preserve its essence as a gift for generations to come.

Let me say it again—what people think of as 'composition' is a natural result of the free but exacting use of carefully planned books. Composition doesn't require any special lessons or exercises until the student is old enough to naturally start becoming interested in the critical use of words. Civics [*political philosophy*] is a separate subject, but it's so closely tied in with literature and history on the one hand, and ethics (everyday morality) on the other hand, that it hardly seems like a separate subject. [pg 275]

We already discussed (in chapter ten) what we do for students as dwellers of a universe bound by natural laws. And here we have to disagree with some science teachers who think that students can only learn what they discover themselves by first-hand experience. The concept sounds good in theory, but in practice, it's disappointingly narrow and limited. The teacher got much of what he knows from books, so why shouldn't the student use books? Maybe because science textbooks are so dehydrated and empty that that the teacher hopes to make up for their lack of vitality with casual talks, such as Hydra being a creature able to make close friends, or a sea-anemone as a grandmotherly figure who lives a long time. In other words, side issues are used to create an interest in the subject. French scientists know better. They understand that, just as history has a beautiful essence that's like poetry, science also has a beauty that can be expressed in exquisite prose. There are a few of these kinds of books in English, and we use them along with field study and drawing. Drawing is great for promoting an enthusiasm for nature.

I've already explained how we help to make children acquainted with great music and great art. One leading art dealer paid us a nice compliment by saying, 'God help the children!' if our work ceased. He had good reason. He had just sold thousands of beautiful little reproductions by Velasquez to PUS students for their term's picture study. It's no surprise that a man who loves and believes in art should feel that our work is worthwhile. In learning to draw, our students work very freely from natural figures and objects using colors [watercolor?] to illustrate scenes they visualize from the term's reading. We don't teach drawing as a means of self- [pg 276] expression. Our students aren't expressing themselves, but what they can see and what they can think of.

I've shown (in chapter ten) how we teach foreign languages. Having a habit of paying close attention, and being prepared to narrate should be a great help for PUS students. I believe that the day is coming when we British will finally become competent linguists. At the House of Education, students narrate in French even more easily and more abundantly than they do in English. They narrate from courses of lectures about French history and French literature that are part of their term's work. In German and Italian, they can read a scene from a play and tell back the scene in character. Or they can tell back a short passage from a narrative. We like to focus on Italian because the language is so beautiful and there's so much good literature. I think other schools should emphasize Italian, too. We teach Latin and Greek the same way that other schools do, except that we also use narration in Latin.

I hope readers will look further into the reasons behind our choice of curriculum. We have a standard of coordinating all things that are essential, but not so meticulously that it becomes a bore. I'll make one more remark, a daring one, and I beg for your complete attention. Society's current theory and method of education are on trial. There's no point in 'developing the faculties' if there's no such thing as faculties to develop. What there is—is the mind. It's like the cloud in Wordsworth's poem—when it moves, the whole thing moves as a unit. So, those individual school subjects designed to develop this, that or the other 'faculty' [such as reasoning skills, judgment or imagination] don't even count. As an educational method, it must be rejected, and we need to look for another basis of teaching. Programs designed to develop those faculties become laughable when we realize that those faculties don't exist. Education needs to be in touch [pg 277] with real life. We need to learn the things that we want to know about. Nobody chats with his friend about stinks [*?*], or the subtle differences of German accents, or irrational numbers (unless they both happen to be mathematicians!) But when Jupiter is rising, that's interesting to know, and to talk about! A friend who can distinguish between bird calls is always good to have around! And we're always grateful to be with someone who's read history and can talk about parallels to events that happened in the great war [*WWI*]! We tend to throw all our effort into one thing in the hopes that we'll get another different thing. But that doesn't work. If we focus our efforts on SAT's, then the things we need to teach become very narrow and academic, and the result is a narrow, academic, sterile-minded graduate. We reap what we sow.

Our future depends on secondary schools. School officials need to plan a broad field of study. If we allow seeds to be sown from various kinds of knowledge, then the garden of the student's mind will yield surprisingly beautiful things. I boldly propose that school officials from all across the country should adopt the method I've been writing about, the one we use in our Parents Union Schools. They should do this for the good of the country.

Mr. Masefield said,

'There can't be great art without great stories. Great art can only exist where great men reflect intensely about the kinds of things that common men think about a little. Without a popular body of legends, no country can have any unselfish art. Shakespeare's art, for example, was selfish until he turned to the great tales in the four most popular books in his time—Raphael Holinshed, Thomas North's *Plutarch*, Geraldi Cinthio's *Hecatommithi* and Francois De Belleforest's *Histoires Tragiques*. Ever since newspapers became popular, topical events have replaced epics. Now inspiration comes to artists directly, without the life-giving cropping and enlightening of many previous minds.'

It's this life-giving vitality of many minds that we want. We beg educational workers and thinkers to join us in forming a collective body of thought that will be common to everyone. Then England will surely be great in both art and life. [pg 278]

This is the way to make great men. Petty attempts to form character in one direction or another won't work. Let's admit that great character only comes from great thoughts, and those great thoughts need to come from the minds of great thinkers. Only then will our purpose in education be clear. Character originates in *thought*, not behavior.

[pg 279]

Chapter 3 - The Scope of Continuation Schools

[*It was customary for students in Victorian England to graduate at age 14 and enter the job market. A recent law had just passed in England at the time of this writing (the preface says 1922), allowing youths who had graduated and started jobs to have seven or eight hours a week for compulsory education in 'Continuation Schools.' This is Charlotte's plea to use that time to give youths a real, life-enriching, character-building education, rather than using the time for more vocational training.*]

A hundred years ago, just after the wars with Napoleon were over, there was a similar re-awakening to the issue of education, like we're experiencing now. Just like today, everyone knew that the result of ignorance and wrong thinking was the war, and that education could be the only cure.

Prussia [*Poland/Lithuania*] took the first step. They didn't start with their little children, but with the youth. Following the philosophy of Johann Gottlieb Fichte, and under the leadership of Karl Stein, a league of noble youth was created, called the Tugendbund. Prussia was miserably impoverished, but instead of looking to the arts to inspire them to great thinking, they focused on philosophy to teach them principles, and history to learn lessons by examples. As a result, their country made some progress.

That kind of intellectual renaissance wasn't experienced only in Prussia, but in all of western Europe. But, either because the time wasn't ripe, or because the people weren't worthy, what began with high ideals evolved into more utilitarian concerns and financial gain.

When the interest in 'Continuation Schools' revived, there was some envy of England's commercial and manufacturing success. By 1829, a Bavarian politician was already encouraging his people to sow the seed if they wanted the fruit. In other words, in order to make money in manufacturing, education would need to focus on vocational training rather than broadening the mind. [pg 280]

We've all seen how good organization and quality teaching in Munich have improved manufacturing in German industries. But those with understanding in Germany are very much aware that 'an education motivated by money will become too narrowly utilitarian. It will lose the ideals that give education the ability to influence character.' Mr. Lecky said that 'the utilitarian theory is very immoral.'

One man rose above the rest. In 1900, Dr. Kirsehensteiner happened to see an announcement offering a prize for the best essay on training youth. He wrote an essay and won the prize. His essay was reprinted as a pamphlet, and went on to influence opinion and motivate change throughout the west. In the US, John Dewey and Stanley Hall are its biggest proponents. Dr. Armstrong and Sir Philip Magnus lead the way here in England.

And what was the message of that pamphlet? The same thing that had been said a hundred years earlier in England, France and Switzerland—that a utilitarian education should be compulsory for everyone. Children and teens should be 'immersed with the concept of service, and given the skill to serve effectively.' Imagine the paradise if every person was skilled, body, mind and soul, to work for society. But what about the child himself? What about *his* needs and *his* development? Apparently it isn't important, the person doesn't matter.

It isn't that the leading educational philosophers I've mentioned would deliberately sacrifice their young people for the economic gain of their country. They believe that giving each person a role and the capability to be of use will provide him with opportunity and give him a place to belong in the world. But that's a faulty view of what education should do. We've been led to believe that we can only know [pg 281] what we experience through our senses. Only what we see with our eyes and handle will provide the food that our souls need. And it's true that when a child builds an elaborate model, his mind is involved, but it's a mistake to think that, since we can see the mind participating during work, knowledge and work are the same thing. It may be true that work provides food for the body because a job provides a paycheck. But there is no such parallel for the mind—physical work doesn't feed the mind. A mind always working at the same drudgery, never learning anything new, is like a menial laborer who's only allowed just enough food to keep his body working. England's great politicians, such as Gladstone, and Lord Salisbury, understood this. They made sure to read about lots of other things besides just politics.

WWI has forced us to realize certain things. such as the readiness of the adult mind to learn new things. We were surprised to read that 1500 soldiers applied for a class with room for twenty students! We begin to see that the minds of all people in varying circumstances and conditions, need regular servings of nutritious mind food. As it is, we'll need to make sure that everyone is provided with the mind food they need. But in the future, we hope to bring up people to be self-sustaining so they can feed themselves, not just their bodies, but their minds, too. This will be done with carefully planned education. We hope to awaken and direct every person's intellectual appetite [*curiosity and desire to know*] so that each person will be able to take care of his own mind.

We've already discussed what kind of intellectual food the mind needs. First of all, a good education should make children rich towards God, and not like the fool Jesus talked about in Luke 12 who was not rich towards God. A good education should also make children rich towards society, and rich towards themselves. I won't belabor the point by observing that moral bankruptcy has co-existed [pg 282] along with utilitarian education, if not been the outright result of it. The catastrophe has been accelerated by the kind of immoral madness that we've experienced in the past, the kind that are like scenes in the books Barnaby Rudge and Peveril of the Peak. Yes, we've been swept off our feet by a bad idea once again, but each instance of our national lapse in sanity has so far been short-lived because, up until now, our education has taught us not to believe lies.

We're no worse than anyone else. If we think well of ourselves as a nation, it's okay, because national pride and national modesty usually accompany each other. For instance, during times of peace, we're hyper-critical of the British working man, but we still prefer him to the hostile Austrian, or the sullen German that we fought in the war. We're only critical of our own people because we want them to be better. We know that a better man will do better work. We've heard a lot about German efficiency. Maybe the Germans do a better job at making doors that shut, blinds that draw, springs that give, and other domestic items whose components make more difference because of their extreme climate. But those are minor concerns. Perhaps our failure is that we don't give 100 percent until there's a major occasion. Give us a big job or a big war, and then we'll show what we can do.

But we probably excel in all our various industries. German women admire the fabric that we make our dresses out of. Well-dressed men wear English clothes sewn by English tailors. We might buy things 'made in Germany' because they're cheaper, but the most expensive and desired goods in Germany are advertised as 'Englisch.'

We need to remember one thing when it comes to educating adolescents. We tend to put ourselves down and deprecate each other, but, the fact is, we have nothing to be ashamed of. In manufacturing and industry, we can compete with anyone. We don't have to look to anyone else [pg 283] to teach us how to do things.

Before I get to the point I wanted to make, let's consider whether the concept of Continuation Schools has been put down more successfully anywhere than in Middle Europe. Some of those countries, especially Germany, have done everything in their power to urge efficiency with its high wages and profits. But ever since the Continuation School movement began in around 1806, the four northwest countries have done things differently. In Denmark they call their Continuation Schools a more pleasant name: People's High Schools. Perhaps the schools themselves are more pleasant, too.

Denmark wasjust as devastated as Germany after the wars with Napoleon. But they had experienced some new spirit after freeing their serfs in 1788, and that spirit prepared the ground for Nicolai Grundtvig, the poet/historian who became the 'Father of the People's High Schools.'

He said, 'Wherever there's the most life, that's where the victory will be.' And he saw a way to increase life by making 'Danish High Schools accessible to young people all over the country.' These schools would inspire 'admiration for what is great, love for what is beautiful, faithfulness, affection, peace, unity, innocent cheerfulness, pleasure and happiness.' Notice that nowhere does his vision even mention 'efficiency.' Yet he assured King Charles VIII that such a school would provide 'a wellspring of healing in the land' so that he would never need to fear whether the newspapers chose to praise or blame. The king listened to him. In fact, he urged an even broader implementation than the original pamphlet advised. By 1845, the dreamed-of schools began to be a reality.

We won't trace the complete history of those schools, but by 1903-4, their schools had over 3000 men and even more women. Wise men embraced the hope that 'the new Danish [pg 284] school for youth will be fortunate enough to blend all social classes into one people.'

All of the Danish High Schools bear the influence of their 'Father,' and their students sometimes sum up his teaching with the three statements, 'Spirit is might; Spirit reveals itself in spirit; Spirit works only in freedom.' We can easily trace where these statements came from. In fact, the entire movement seems to have been very Christian from its very beginning. And I don't mean Christian in a narrow, exclusive sense, but in the broad sense illustrated by Simone Memmi's fresco in Florence's chapel in Santa Maria Novella. Some of the teachers pictured there as being divinely gifted by God's spirit were actually notable pagans. Yet they were still under Divine inspiration. This seems to me to be an educational concept worth reviving, especially in these days of utilitarian vocational emphasis. Grundtvig seems to have understood this concept, although he probably came up with it on his own. His great hope is that 'above all, some knowledge of literature, especially the poetry and history of one's own country, will create a new breed of readers all over the land.'

I can't go into the question of Agricultural Schools. They say that 'the Danish Agricultural School belongs to the Danish people, and must be just as much based on Christian faith and national life as the people are.' In the carefree days before WWI, we all admired the quality of Danish butter. But did we ever think about the resolve and efficiency with which the Danish peasants went from making poor butter in their individual little farms, to manufacture butter of uniform quality in national dairy co-ops? One leading Swedish professor attributes this to the High Schools. He said, 'Enriching the soil provides the best ground [pg 285] for seeds to grow. In the same way, training the people's fertile minds in classic literature is the best way to make them productive. And this is even true for farmers. [Thanks to Continuation Schools, ed. by Sir Michael Sadler, and published by the Manchester University, 1908.] These are serious words. They deserve our consideration at this moment when we're also at the brink of a new venture.

The three countries around Denmark watched the experimental schools with keen interest, and it wasn't long before People's High Schools sprang up in their countries, too.

The northern High Schools can only operate in the winter [*when farming can't be done*], so they weren't open when I was visiting. But I did notice a couple of things that I can trace to their influence. For one thing, Copenhagen impressed me as a city with a soul, unlike Munich. At the Hague, I saw a craftsman in his work clothes showing paintings in a gallery to his seven year old son. The little boy listened carefully and looked eagerly. In the great Delft porcelain factories, young workers manifested evidence of culture and gentleness in their faces and manner. But the thing that struck me most was what I saw in a general store in some remote market in Sweden. The villagers were peasants. One shop sold cabbages, herrings, cheese and calico cloth. But in its small-paned window was a shelf tightly packed with paperback books that hadn't been left alone long enough to get dusty. I couldn't make out all of the titles, but I noticed that they included books in French, German and English. I saw thin volumes of Scott, Dickens, Thackeray, Ruskin, Carlyle and the latest popular literature. It made a person feel like the village was a slice of heaven. One could imagine a long winter evening in any home, with one person reading aloud as the rest of the family did the evening's chores. When friends meet, or when lovers stroll, they must have lots to talk about. How sad for us when we hear that a youth we [pg 286] know and like is quick at making friends, but the friendships never progress because they never have anything to talk about. Imagine the little plays acted out, or public readings given by the villagers. I wish such things would happen in our own country. Then the excitement of city life wouldn't be such a draw to our young people. A village with a happy community life sustained by the villagers themselves will satisfy its people so that they're content to stay.

Our upper and middle classes, whether professionals or not, are also content—not because of their money, but because of their intellectual well-being. It's their mental stimulation that makes them 'haves' as opposed to 'have nots.' You don't have to look far to find the reason why. Some people make it their business to sow seeds of discontent in the gaping minds of the masses. A full, satisfied mind passes by, but an empty mind will grasp at *any* new notion eagerly. And who can blame it? A hungry mind will take whatever it can get, and even a bakeshop owner tends to be lenient with a starving man who steals a loaf of bread. I'm not hesitant to say that the Labor Unrest that plagues our times isn't so much the fault of the working man, but of the society that hasn't considered that its citizens have hungry minds and they need the right kind of intellectual nourishment.

I've tried to explain that:

1. The kind of 'education' offered by Germany's Continuation Schools doesn't positively influence morals or behavior. To be honest, I haven't noticed that it's improved the quality of the goods they produce, either. [*ouch!*]

2. We are under no obligation to follow their example. The fact is, our manufactured goods are the better ones, as evidenced by the fact that Germans will pay higher prices for British goods.

3. But Denmark and its surrounding countries excel in the very areas we need improvement.

4. Therefore, the People's High Schools of Denmark are [pg 287] more worthy to be our model than the Continuation Schools of Germany.

5. They are more worthy because a broad education that makes knowledge of God its first priority results in worthy character, right actions, higher intelligence and more initiative.

But we can't take someone else's medical prescription. Grundtvig's Schools are for students aged 18-25, but we're dealing with students in the more challenging age bracket of 14-18. Also, the Denmark Schools are boarding schools. Since they're so dependent on agriculture, it works for most of their young people to live five months of the year every winter at one of the schools. But that's not the case here. Our country is mostly manufacturing.

But we're blessed to have been given 7 or 8 hours a week for the purpose of educating our youth. How shall we adapt Denmark's model to our situation? How can we make the most of those hours to make the best use of the student's time? If we take the easiest way, we'll just use that time to let the student do what he does all week—work 7-8 more hours for his employer, either directly by showing up at his job and producing more output, or indirectly by increasing his skill with more training. But that would be betrayal. No ethical employer really wants to take away with one hand what it gives with the other. Besides, employers trust their own staff to train their workers sufficiently. As I said earlier, it doesn't usually take much training to learn the skill to do a particular job. It's how the skill is done that matters, and that takes practice—which means more hours working on the job. Continuation Schools shouldn't exist to give technical job training. They should be for the kind of education that doesn't come from vocational classes. After all, evenings after work will still be as free as ever for technical classes, or working out at the gym, or other recreation. [pg 288]

If we truly believe that the mind needs its nourishment, and that *using* the mind isn't the same thing as *feeding* it, then we'll see that this gift of 7-8 hours a week must be dedicated to things of the mind.

If we resolve to give youths some mental meat to chew on, some real mind food to digest and assimilate, then we'll find that the flood gates will be opened. An ocean of possible things to learn will overwhelm us—and we only have eight hours a week. We'll need to compromise in one of two ways if we want to make good citizens in such a limited amount of time. Good citizens need to have rational, solid opinions about things like law, duty, work, and wages. So one way is to pour opinions into them by way of lectures from the teacher, so that they'll adopt his opinions as their own. With so much to learn and such a limited time frame, the information will need to be selective. The youths are 'poured into like a bucket,' and, as Carlyle says, 'that's not exhilarating to any soul.' In that way, some knowledge is taught, and teachers and education authorities are satisfied. But the students leave school at the end of their time not fully satisfied. They're bored at work, bored in their free time, and they spend their weekends doing trivial, empty things. They become people who are excited, instead of cautious, about the prospect of a strike. If that's the outcome of our Continuation Schools, then we will have failed our youth.

That's really the challenge of education for *all* ages. There's so much to cover in so many fields of knowledge in order to live intelligently and with moral insight. The method of learning just one thing, but learning it so well that you can handle any kind of knowledge may work on an academic level, but it won't work if our vision is to 'Enlighten the Masses.' That method [pg 289] assumes that the mind, like the physical body, can develop in various areas with the right exercise. But recent educational thought shows us that the mind is more than that. It's independently active, it exists in everyone, and it only asks for one thing: nourishment. Feed the mind what it needs, and it will take care of all the things it needs by itself. As a well-fed worker is capable of doing his job, a well-nourished mind can do its job—it can know, think, feel, and make wise judgments in most cases. The good, noble-minded person is the one who has been fed with the mental food that's appropriate for him.

This kind of view of education naturally includes religion. It isn't just because 'his God instructs him and teaches him,' but because all knowledge falls under three types. First is knowledge of God, which is gotten first-hand from the Bible.

Second is knowledge of mankind, which comes from history, poetry, stories; the customs of cities and nations, civics, the laws of self-government and morality. Third is knowledge of the wonderful world around us. Every youth should know something about the flowers in the field, the birds in the air, the stars in the heavens, the many fascinating wonders that happen every day. Every student should have some knowledge of physics, although chemistry can be reserved for the few students who are inclined that way or are headed for a career that needs it.

Here we stand on the verge of that new life for our country that we all want. We're faced with infinite possibilities on either hand—both the vast amount of knowledge in the universe, and the incalculable ability of the mind to learn. One thing we're sure of: we don't have time for short cuts. Training muscles and experiencing through the five senses may be necessary, but that's not the way the mind grows. And lectures from a teacher are rarely assimilated. The only true education is self-education—it's only when the student applies his own mind to learn that the mind is affected.

But we aren't without hope. A promising new field [pg 290] lays before us. Thousands of children even now are showing what incredible things they can do, and they do those things happily, without being coerced. They've taken charge of their own education, and they're hungry to learn simply for the sake of knowing. They want to know about things in all three categories that I listed earlier.

The fact is, a wonderful discovery has been entrusted to us. This discovery is the greatest thing to happen to education since the invention of the alphabet. Listen again to what Coleridge said, on page 106 of this book, about where great discoveries come from. He makes no distinctions about what kinds of minds receive divine great ideas. In fact, he doesn't even describe them as particularly great minds. They were just 'prepared beforehand to receive' the great ideas. If you'll forgive me for saying so, I believe that my mind has been prepared for a great idea. On the one hand, I've been hindered when it comes to academic achievement, yet, on the other hand I've had some degree of academic success. I've gradually come to realize that this capacity and incapacity aren't uncommon. Maybe that's one of the keys to education. More preparation came to me because of the unusual position I was in to test and learn to understand the minds of children. I'm anxious to tell you what my great discovery is because our methods are so simple and so obvious that people tend to grab them randomly and say, for instance, that lots of reading 'is a good idea that we've all used, more or less.' Or narration 'is a good idea, but not very original.' Yes, it's true—we've all read, and we know that narration is as natural as breathing. The value of narration varies in proportion to what's being narrated. But what we've failed to see until now is that a craving for knowledge (curiosity) exists in everyone. All people have the ability to focus their attention without measure. Everyone prefers knowledge in a literary form. People should learn lots of different things about all the different [pg 291] thoughts that humans reflect on. But learning can only happen if the person's mind participates in an active 'act of knowing.' Narration encourages this kind of actively involved self-learning, and it also assesses it. Later tests can record what was learned. You might say, 'that's nothing new.' And you're right, I don't think that any natural law seems very original or innovative. We already think of flying as pretty routine. Yet, although there may be no astonishing surprises when we look at natural laws, the results of following them can be very astonishing. We willingly submit these methods to the test of results.

'Everything isn't for everyone,' was the sad conclusion that Grundtvig, the Danish patriot and prophet, came to. He was probably thinking about the impossible obstacles that uneducated people would face with a limited vocabulary and lack of literary background. So he said 'everything isn't for everyone' in the same way that one of our own prophets says that higher education is only for the elite. Grundtvig came to the conclusion that books weren't meant for the masses. So instead, the youth of his country listened to lectures delivered by enthusiastic men who had their country's literature and history at their fingertips and could articulate it with their own personal flair. A lot of good resulted, but minds spoon-fed from a teacher's lecture will never be as stable as those who cut and chew their own mind food.

But what if it *were* for everyone? What if Comenius's great hope of 'all knowledge for all people' was in the process of coming true? This is exactly what we've seen happen in thousands of cases. Even in cases where the children were mentally handicapped, we've seen that any person can understand the appropriate book (one that's suited for his age) but the book has to be in literary (story) form. Students don't need anyone to explain what the story means to them and their attention doesn't wander when they're occupied this way. They can master a number of pages so well after just one reading that they can tell it back immediately, or even months later, [pg 292] whether it's *Pilgrim's Progress*, one of Bacon's essays, or a Shakespeare play. They add their own individual touches so that no two students tell it back in quite the same way. A natural side effect of this is that students learn to write and speak with confidence and flair, and they can usually spell well, too. This art of telling back is *real* education, and it's very enriching. We all do it naturally. We go over the points of a conversation or sermon or article in our mind. We're made so that only those points and arguments that we go over in our mind are the ones we retain. Haphazard listening and reading might be refreshing and entertaining, but it's only educational here and there, the random times that our attention is strongly engaged. When we go over information in our mind, we don't just retain it, we also come to understand it better. Every incident stands out, every phrase takes on new meaning, each link in an argument seems more firmly linked to the next one. What's happened is that we've taken an active part in the 'act of knowing' and what we read or heard has become a part of us. We assimilate it by rejecting what our mind doesn't need. Like the famous men of ancient times, we've discovered 'the knowledge best suited for people,' and we're surprised to find that people need the very best knowledge, conveyed in the very best form. Are we like the teachers in the Bible who were reprimanded because they took away the key of knowledge? They didn't enter themselves, and they kept those who wanted to enter from coming in.

Are we doing that today? We understand that people have to participate in the act of knowing. Nobody can learn without involving his own mind in the process. Each person has to do his own learning for himself, but it's as pleasurable and as natural as a bird singing its song. In fact, the act of knowing is a natural function.

Yet we hear of apathy that prevails in most schools, while right in front us, we see youth consumed with curiosity, if we can only figure out what they want to know and how it needs to be taught to them. [pg 293]

Humanistic education (learning about mankind and what affects him) whether lessons are in English or Latin, affects behavior in a powerful way. Students like knowing these things. They can cover a lot of ground because they only have to read things once. This method has been used successfully. If our Continuation Schools are going to do any good [*with the limited time they'll have*], they'll have to use this method in some way.

The Parents Union School [*PUS, originated 1891*] was started for the benefit of children taught at home. It works like a correspondence school, with program schedules sent out every term, and exams sent out at the end of the term. When the same plan was implemented in the Council Schools in 1913, the advantages became obvious because it offered the same curriculum to children of all socio-economic classes. With this single curriculum, we saw that children from the inner cities in economically disadvantaged schools did as well as children of privileged, educated parents who were concerned and involved with their children's education.

Right now, one of our national concerns is that we have no unifying shared bond of thought, nothing in common to reflect on. Undoubtedly, with a lot of reading, some links of common interest could be created. Thus, the classroom could do as much for our national spirit as the beginning of baseball season. Our plan works smoothly in Council Schools. Here's a sample of the work being done successfully and enjoyably by the highest classes: They read English, French and History from three or four books; two or three books dealing with citizenship and morals from various points of view; several works of literature that parallel the time period being studied in history; three or four books in nature, physical geography and science; and Scripture (using mostly the Bible). Every term they have a new schedule of work, often [pg 294] continuing books from the previous term. Students in Secondary Schools, or learning at home via our correspondence school, stay in Form IV [*about 9th grade*] for one year, and the work at that level seems like it would work for the first year or two of the Continuation Schools, with a bit of adapting. After that, the more advanced work of Forms V and VI [*about grades 10-12*] could be adapted in the same way. The work isn't like the regular grind of most school work, so it would be appealing to the students. It would also provide opportunities for them in public speaking and writing essays.

Probably the best test of a broad-minded education is the number of names and proper nouns that a person can use correctly and naturally when various topics come up. We all remember a character in one of Jane Austen's novels who didn't know whether the Bermudas were in the West Indies or not because she had never called them anything in her whole life!

As an example, here's an uncorrected, alphabetical list taken from a 13-year-old's exam paper. It contains 213 proper names, and all of them were used accurately, easily and with interest.

Granted, this is the work of a Secondary student, but imagine if young people in a Continuation School who couldn't read all the books in the schedule, were able to become familiar with perhaps 100 of these kinds of names in a term. I think we'd be able to satisfy ourselves that they were receiving a liberal education then. This is just the kind of work we'd like to see being done by students in Continuation Schools between the ages of 14-16. Youths aged 16-18 should be ready to handle the kind of work done by our PUS students in Forms V and VI [*grades 10-12*].

I'd like to point out that it isn't just the best students who answer exam questions. Usually, every student answers every question. And I've only mentioned the more humanities-related subjects, since I figure that the Head of the Continuation Schools will undoubtedly arrange for things like Math. In fact, most students have learned enough math already because of the excellent math training they got in elementary school, that I think it would be enough for students at Continuation Schools to practice the skills they already have by keeping pretend account books.

There won't be any additional cost incurred to adopt and continue the plan I propose in Elementary and Continuation Schools, beyond the cost of the books themselves. And students could pay for those themselves so that they would gradually be building up their own little library of good books that they've read, understood and gotten familiar with. I'd like to quote Rudolf Christoph Eucken, Professor at Jena, Germany:

'When we talk about education of the people, we don't mean a special kind of education. We're not talking about a condensed collection of our own spiritual and academic knowledge, watered down to be suitable for the specific urgent concerns of the masses. We're not talking about a diluted version of real knowledge that we would then condescend to dispense to the public, like patronizing benefactors. No! Only one education exists that's common to all of us.' 'We can all unite and work together to create a spiritual world that transcends the petty routine of daily life. So then, there could be a real human education, a true education of the people.' [pg 297]

Eucken gives an accurate assessment of the task before us, but he doesn't offer any way to accomplish it. The only possible way to accomplish it is with the methods I've described to provide a liberal, broad-minded education. The method has already been discovered, and doesn't need to be worked out again. After all, the electric telegraph didn't need to be discovered twice.

In spite of all our protests about utilitarian education, our method actually does serve some utilitarian purpose after all. No other education pays off such dividends as the humanities. Consider this point. Instability, labor unrest, and discontent among wage-earners is a serious threat to our social life. They say that you have to act where you are. And the class of people who are involved where they are, whether it's in some diplomatic outpost of the British Empire, or an estate within England, or in Parliament, is the class that received their education from the Public Schools—the students who received an education in the humanities. No doubt there will be strong protests about the deadwood and decadence of these men, although no one can deny that they're the ones doing our national work. Their faults are many and obvious, but, still, the public work that's done for our benefit is mostly done by these men, and they can hardly be called progressive. Could there be some mistaken ideas about our fixation on progress? Are we confusing progress with motion, assuming that wherever we see activity, there must also be improvement? Yet much of the activity we see is like the waves of the ocean, always churning, but never going anywhere. What we really need is the still progress of *growth* that comes when a tree sends strong, solid roots downward, and results in abundant fruit growing upward. This is what progress in character and conduct is like. It doesn't come from environmental manipulation, or pressure to conform. It can only come from the inner growth of ideas received by the mind with deliberate, active involvement.

It's possible that the limited time provided will only allow a little bit of these mind-growing ideas to be offered in Continuation Schools. But a little goes a long way, as our Public School graduates prove. A final analysis concludes that it isn't [pg 298] Latin or Greek, or competitive sports programs or athletics, or an enhanced environment that bring the stability and efficiency we want to see in all classes of people. It's the humanities, taught and read in our own language.

I said before that we have a great gift with which to make some changes: we have seven or eight hours a week. In that time, we might get in, page for page, or book for book, as much education in the four years between ages 14-18 as our educated public officials got in their schools. This education would encompass all of the humanities—poetry, history, essays, plays and philosophy. I admit, classically educated students learn it in classic languages while we propose teaching it in plain English. Yet, no matter how much we may revere Greek literature, we have to admit that English literature is second to none. We can give our youth the thoughts and ideas of the best minds, and we can ensure that students do their part in applying their attention so that their own effort bears fruit, resulting in skilled ability, noble character and proper behavior. With the time we have, we can't make Rhodes scholars of the students, but those who earnestly desire that will find a way to continue their education. If there's any benefit in toiling over grammar, well, they'll have to forego that. But the inspiration and joy that come from entering into an intellectual world that has all kinds of pleasant things to relate to is something that every student should have. It's like a wellspring of healing, and a fountain of joy.

The value of a cohesive thought bonding the people can't be calculated. What we want is to give the whole nation a common background of thought, similar to what students at exclusive Public Schools get. Those students have read the same books, so they're all familiar with Pitt, Fox, 'Dick Swiviller,' 'Mrs. Quickly,' the daffodils, clouds and nightingales that poets have seen, and a thousand other various and trivial-seeming scenes and sayings that somehow combine [pg 299] to create a backdrop that puts today's current opinions and events into perspective. Therefore, like the Public Schools, we have our students reading the same books. They read them just once, but so intensively, that they never forget them. For the rest of their lives, phrases and inferences they come across will dawn on them with the kind of 'light that never touched sea or land.' We hope that the Public Schools will soon begin teaching some classics in English. Then during elections, candidates will have a better reason for getting elected than their own self-interests. During government assemblies, there's a lack of any literary or historical quotes *in English*. Is that due to the fact that the public can't be counted on to recognize any reference outside of their old schoolbooks? If that's the case, we can change it once and for all. Whatever the masses read, the upper educated classes will have to read, too. Then there will be national peace and unity created by a common bond of intellectual life.

Goethe said, 'The most dreadful sight in the world is ignorance in action.' And isn't this the dismaying sight that we see every day? The common masses rule today, and who can dispute their right? But let's give them the chance to also be wise in philosophy, so that they can be fit to rule. It's a hopeful sign that the people themselves are seeing their lack and demanding the education in humanities that they see as their salvation.

[pg 300]

Chapter 4 - The Basis of National Strength
A Liberal Education from a National Perspective

I - Knowledge

From time to time, there's some discussion about our failure to educate the average child. This issue, and some others, seems to me to be based on a couple of fundamental principles. It might be useful to take a look at them. Because if our conception of education is confused and disconnected, it's only natural that we'll end up with a tangle of tests to assess what wasn't planned very well to begin with.

Educationally speaking, we're not doing too well. A while ago in *Across the Bridges*, we read about how bright, sensitive schoolboys who had graduated with honors were rapidly going downhill. Why? Tough times sometimes reveal a streak of goodness, or even a trace of heroism, in the average man. But there's also a tragic lack of education. He seems to have no insight, no imagination, no power of reflection. Among the working class, there's a 'dangerous tendency that we all need to try our hardest to resist,' as a Mr. Burns said at a public meeting a few years ago. He said that 'the spirit of mob rule is being encouraged. In [pg 301] exhibitions, sporting events, laws, the individual person is becoming less significant, and the mob is becoming more important.' 'In all our modern events, the tendency is to bring huge crowds together to see other people play. And I don't just mean at sports, but other things, too. Is there any more accurate diagnosis of today's industrial movement? And we ask again, Why? Enough has been said about the young men from exclusive Public Schools who fail in England's territories overseas. But even the ones who have some success overseas because of the spark of virtue in them, still fail just as often because they don't have the insight, imagination, and intelligence that's supposed to come from education. What about the 'educated' young people who stay in this country? I'm an old woman who remembers how people used to talk about 'countenance' a lot, back in the 1860's and 70's. People commonly remarked that a person had 'a fine countenance' or 'a noble countenance.' The phrase has dropped out of use now. Is it because good countenance doesn't exist anymore? Countenance reflects thought, feeling and intelligence. We don't see any of those things in people's faces these days, just flat indifference, even though the person is apparently in fine physical health.

If this is our complaint, then we have education to blame, even though our teachers are more dedicated and devoted than ever. They benefit because the giver always receives a blessing, but the children are suffering, poor things. They receive generously, poured into as if they were buckets, but little comes of it. Teachers are enthusiastic enough, but there's a tendency among us to devalue knowledge and underestimate our students. Education is made of knowledge in the same way that bread is made of flour. There are substitutes for knowledge [pg 302] just like there are substitutes for flour. Before there was such a thing as the free lunch program, I heard of a little girl in East London whose mother gave her a penny to buy lunch for her and her little sister. The little girl confided to her teacher that a penny's worth of licorice candy 'fills your stomach' more than a penny's worth of bread [*but is hardly a nutritious lunch*!] Yet our schools use a method very much like filling the stomach with licorice candy. We use grades, rewards, scholarships, and first place standings, which are all ways of temporarily satisfying the child without really giving him the knowledge he needs. And that's the point. He needs knowledge as much as he needs bread and milk. He's as hungry for knowledge as he is for lunch. An abundant regular diet at frequent intervals providing lots of variety is the necessary right of every child—not just for his growing body, but for his curious mind, too. Yet we try to satisfy him with licorice candy.

Or we do even worse than that! We say, 'What practical value does education have? Give a boy the vocational skills he needs, whether it be in accounting or masonry. Get rid of Greek and geography and whatever else has no utilitarian value. Teach him the tools of his profession and the tricks of the trade, and you'll have done the best you can for him.' And this is the most tragic fallacy, thinking that a child should be brought up only for the best use he can be to society, with no thought for what's in his own best interests and what's best for him. A recent survey of the condition of education seemed to feel like vocational training was the answer for our educational concerns. We start children on a life journey that's too dry and confined. One of the main purposes of education is supposed to be personal pleasure and joy in living. Socrates understood that knowledge is for enjoyment. He thought that knowledge was, not *one* of life's pleasures, but *the* source of pleasure.

Children should get educated for their own sakes. The ability to think the best of people, to give other people's motives the benefit of the doubt, to find the greatness in a person's character, to change one's perspective and [pg 303] judgment of current events based on illustrations gained by reading history and literature that parallels modern situation, to be able to view things comprehensively before forming a judgment—these things are available to everyone depending on the measure of his mind. But that's not all knowledge does. A person who can live contentedly on his own intellect and can entertain himself during dull hours (although worries and sad times will affect even the most resourceful person) is to be envied, especially in these days of intellectual drought when most people have to rely on spectator amusements to pass the time [*and Charlotte was saying this **before** TV was around!*]

Now that we've gone on and on about the importance of knowledge, you might be wondering, 'What is knowledge?' And we can only tell you what it's not. It's not instruction or information. It's not becoming scholarly or having a lot stored up in a person's memory. Knowledge is something that passes from mind to mind, like the light from a torch. But the torch can only be lit by the mind that generates the original idea. [*Which makes teachers merely torch-bearers, not the fountain of all knowledge that they sometimes fancy they are!*] We know that thought brings forth more thought: it's only when an idea sparks our own mind that our own mind is vitalized to bring life to ideas of its own. And it's these ideas of ours that direct what we do and how we act. We hardly need to convince anyone that reform is badly needed. But now we actually begin to see what could make reform work. To educate a child, you need the direct, first-hand impact of great minds to interact with his own mind. We may not know lots of great minds in our circle of friends, but most of us can get in touch with great minds by reading books. If we want to know whether a school is truly providing an intellectual diet that really feeds its students, all we have to do is look at their booklist for the current term. If the booklist is short, we know that students aren't getting enough mind food. If the books aren't varied enough, we know they won't be well-rounded. If the books are second-hand compilations [*which textbooks are*] rather than original works, then they won't have any real food in them to nourish the mind [*much like vitamins that may have some chemical value, but no real food.*] If the books are too easy [not just reading level, but if they don't make him question], if they're too direct and tell him what to think [*rather than challenging him to form his own opinion*], then students will read them, but they won't chew on them and assimilate them so that the books become a part of them. A person needs a good meal to stimulate his body to secrete digestive juices. In the same way, the mental [pg 304] energy need to be stimulated so that the mind will digest and extract what it needs. And it needs a large variety and generous amount from which to select the nourishment it needs. And it needs it to be disguised as something appetizing and appealing. As our example, we have the highest authority [*Scripture*] demonstrating that the indirect method is the best way to dispense literature, and especially the indirect form of poetry. It's true that the Parables of Jesus are mysterious—but is there any knowledge in the world more precious than what they contain?

So our tendency to undervalue children is damaging. We water down their books and drain them of their literary flavor because, in our ignorance, we think that they can't understand what we understand ourselves. And, even worse, we explain and then ask questions. A few educational catch-phrases might do us some good: 'Don't explain.' 'Don't question.' 'One single reading of a passage is enough.' 'Make the student tell back the passage he's read.' The student has to read in such a way that he knows, and the teacher's job is to see that he knows. The activities of generalizing, analyzing, comparing, judging, and so on, are things that the mind does for itself. That's part of the process the mind goes through when it's actively learning. Do you doubt it? Try it yourself. Before you go to bed, read a chapter of something like Jane Austen, or the Bible. Then put yourself to sleep by retelling it back to yourself in your mind. You'll be surprised at the degree of insight and visualization you gain from this kind of mental exercise.

As I've already said, a seven-year-old can retell *Pilgrim's Progress* chapter by chapter, even though he can't read it himself, and a half dozen other of the best books we can find for him. At age eight or nine, he'll work contentedly with a dozen books at a time—history, adventure, travels, poems. Between the ages of 10-12, he reads a good number of seriously written books about British and French history, Shakespeare's historical plays, Plutarch's *Lives* translated by Thomas North, and a dozen other worthy books. As he progresses in school, his reading becomes wider and more difficult. But everyone already knows what kind of books are appropriate [pg 305] for high school students. The problem isn't the kind of books given in high school, but the amount—not enough are used. The reading list is too meager to make a full, well-balanced man. Lots of first-rate books should be scheduled in *every* term. The one point I must make is that, from the time a child starts school at age six, he should be distinguished as being 'an educated child' as compared to other children his age. He should love his school books, and he should enjoy his end-of-term exams based on those books. Children brought up mostly on books compare favorably to children educated with more lectures and less books. They're enthusiastic about a lot of things, keenly sympathetic, have a wider focus, and make sound judgments. And all because they were treated from the beginning as human beings capable of serious conversation and able to remember and think ahead to the future. They're people who enjoy leisure time, too, and have time for hobbies, since their school work is easily completed in the mornings.

It isn't necessary for me to talk about modern foreign language, math, nature study, handiwork, etc., since schools are pretty much agreed about how to teach those subjects. As far as Latin and Greek, the question of teaching them and having time to cover any work in them is crucial. But I think teachers at the boarding schools would discover that students who have learned to read and think, and have kept the habit of almost perfect attention that all children are born with, will be able to complete more work in the Classics in their original languages in less time. Students' minds are more alert because they've gotten used to being busy with lots of different subjects.

Maybe some enlightened teacher will perceive the difference between scholarly book-learning and real knowledge. That's a distinction that practical men like Napoleon have always understood. Maybe there's never been any one life that was more influenced by 'humanities' than Napoleon's. Has there ever been a better example of the power of an informed mind to conquer [pg 306] the world? Napoleon is proof against the criticism that knowledge of books has no practical value. There wasn't any single episode in his career that wasn't suggested or inspired by some historical precedent or literary illustration that he had read about. We all know he was no great scholar, but he did read diligently, even while other absorbing affairs were going on. He read books like Homer, the Bible, the Koran, poetry, history and Plutarch's *Lives*.

Nations become great when inspired by books, just like people do. We've all heard how heroic young Queen Louisa of Prussia came to see that her country's downfall wasn't just due to Napoleon, but also to her people's ignorance. She knew that if her country was going to rise, it would have to be through the study of history. So, while she was living in Memel, as poor as a peasant, she studied the history of modern Europe. Some followers of Kant formed a league to arouse Prussian students to the duty of patriotism. Fichte effectively issued the trumpet call, and Prussia became a nation of students. The result was that Queen Louisa's son established the German Empire. Unfortunately, the day has come when Germany has condemned the teaching of humanities, and as a result, humanity has followed Germany into exile. A noble ideal of education exalts a nation as much as righteousness. But, sadly, we all know the universal chaos and disaster that comes from a corrupt materialistic theory of education, the kind promoted in Munich.

The Danes, who were mentioned before, were inspired to rise from illiteracy because of the threat of Napoleon. After England seized their battleships to help slow down Napoleon, the Danes decided to become the best farmers in Europe. They were successful in doing that because of their schools and continuing education, where they don't teach technical skills, but a wide course of history and literature. And the Japanese revolution about fifty years ago [*possibly the Boshin War of 1868, which led to the reforms of the Meiji Restoration?*] was also [pg 307] carried out by a literary people. History tells of few finer revolutions than that one.

If we don't want to be left behind by the East and the West, we need to do what other countries have done. We need to 'add knowledge to our virtue.' It is still within our power to climb up that Apostolic educational ladder, even though we're starting on the bottom rung. Even that much is no longer possible for every nation. It's up to us to add virtue to our faith, and knowledge to our virtue. It's unbelievable that the youth of such a great nation as ours should grow up without those inspiring ideals. These ideals mature slowly enough even when they're introduced at an early age. They come mostly from wide reading that's been wisely planned.

II - Books, Knowledge and Virtue

Here's part of an enlightening letter. It will help explain the concern I'll detail in this chapter.

'One thing I want to bring up is my disappointment in that last paragraph, the one about classical education. I wish it had been explained more. I'm convinced that your general perspective is all true. In fact, my own experience proves that early education done with reading and enjoying great books in our own language scheduled each year so that they suit the age of the child, is the best foundation for all later education. Here's my story: My three daughters grew up hearing Walter Scott and Shakespeare. Later, when they were between 10-12, they decided to read Plutarch's Lives, John Bunyan, Defoe—but in that time, they also refused to do math and geography. They said math was too monotonous, and geography, which they loved, should be learned by going to places instead of learning about it in school lessons. I knew better than to try and force the issue. So I meekly suggested that they find something else to study instead. And they

had a response already prepared for me. 'That's just it, what we want to learn is Latin and harmony.' And this is where your point comes in, which you wrote about in that paragraph that was way too short: [pg 308]

'If children have read and thought, and have maintained the habit of paying almost perfect attention that they were born with, then the work they need to do in the classics can be done in a lot less time. The student's mind will be more alert because it's busy with different subjects.'

*Six months later, my daughters knew more Latin than I learned in six years of studying under famous, respected teachers! They could rattle off quotes from Horace correctly, they knew the first two Eclogues and half of the Aeneid by heart, they thought of Cicero's letters to Atticus as a 'penny post' affair, and were a little too familiar with the private life of Seneca. None of this interfered with their painting, or horse-riding, and they maintained their expertise at baseball and horse-racing. That's my story. In my mind, it proves that early education from great books with broad-minded ideas and noble virtues is the **only TRUE** foundation of knowledge. It's the only knowledge worth having.'*

This is an interesting letter, and it brings us back to the question that I thought I had answered thoroughly. I'm a little hesitant to tackle it because an outsider might see aspects that even an expert could overlook. The main criticism against exclusive boarding schools is that they spend so much time on Classics that there's no time left for any other character-building literature. It's easy for us to say, 'Give up teaching Greek to gain more time.' But those schools in conjunction with the universities they lead to, are our crowning educational achievement. There may be other experimental efforts going on in the field of education, but those schools are tried and true. The men they turn out have more quality, culture and ability than any others. Even a student who gets only a B.A. in one of those schools does better than B.A. students from other schools. And an art degree is pretty common at most other schools.

To get back to my original concern—is book-learning pretty much all there is to knowledge? Wellington attributed the winning of Waterloo, not to the battle-field, but to the classrooms at Eton. Caesar, Thucydides and *Prometheus Bound* [pg 309] have won more battles off the military fields than on them. Just a little bit of meat goes a long way, so even the average boy at one of the boarding schools becomes a capable man from the bit of literature he gets there. Unfortunately, as capable as he is, he's also ignorant. He doesn't know the literature and history of his own country, much less any other. He thinks of knowledge as something to be filed in storage rather than a state that a person is in, or isn't in. Once he earns his degree, he closes his books and packs them away. He might read the headlines in the newspaper every morning, or maybe even a magazine or two, but otherwise, he fills his time with sports, games, TV, or his own projects. We wonder vaguely how we might get some knowledge into such a person, and impart a taste for knowledge in him. We consider dropping Greek to make room for other things, but, on reflection, this doesn't seem like such a good idea. Culture begins with the knowledge that everything has always been known, and everything has already been said as well as it can be said two thousand years ago. If we can only drum this knowledge into a student slowly over twelve years, then we can prevent him from thinking too much of himself, or joining the mobs crying for power and revolution. There's no better way to know what people are like inside than to know something about what they said in their own words and language.

Let's not forget that we, as a nation, have to make up for something we've already lost. Not so long ago, the entire population, whether rich or poor, were intimately familiar with one of the three great classical literatures—the Bible. Men's thoughts were influenced by it, their speech was molded by it, their conduct pretty much governed by it. The rustic adventure of Genesis, the passionate poetry of Isaiah, the divine philosophy of John, Paul's rhetoric, and the rest of the Bible are written in what Matthew Arnold calls 'the grand style.' This is the undefiled wellspring from which Englishmen have gotten the best of their literature, philosophy of life, ideas about history, and the most [pg 310] vital knowledge there is, although we're now trying to do without it. I'm talking about the knowledge of God. Yet we wonder why our politicians have forgotten that they're supposed to be public servants, and why the general population, who were brought up on Dick and Jane instead of great, noble literature, behave with obstinate recklessness, like ignorant people.

Let's get back to the main point. How can we educate the ignorance of the average people and still retain an elite classical culture in exclusively schooled students? I'd like to suggest again, with humility, that exclusively schooled students are ground through a mill that should turn them out as scholars. Scholarship is an excellent distinction, and we as a nation need some of our students to be scholars. But if an Army gives all of its soldiers a badge of honor, who among them would value it? Some things are more esteemed simply because they're a rare distinction. To ask all schools to make Rhodes scholars of all their students is as ridiculous as the little boy who wanted to be a Red Cross Knight when he grew up. It can't be done. Some men are born to be scholars and it seems natural for them. The rest of us respect them, but we don't envy them, because being a scholar isn't the highest calling there is. Being a scholar doesn't necessarily mean that a person is in touch with living ideas. Making scholars out of our entire population isn't one of our goals. And we aren't concerned with the one out of a thousand who's a genius. He doesn't care what we add to our curriculum, whether it's classics, or foreign languages. A silly story, a puppet show, a dandelion blowing in the wind is enough for him; he'll learn on his own. Let's focus on the average child.

He does need to learn Greek and Latin, but there's an easier way to do it. The little girls in the letter I quoted had the right idea. Vittorino's favorite pupil was a girl who spoke and wrote Greek 'with remarkable purity' at [pg 311] the age of twelve, after learning Latin at an even earlier age. I can assure you that she never went through the regular grind of a grammar school. Neither did the educated ladies during the Renaissance whose accomplishments dazzle us. We all know how early they got married while they were still practically children themselves. Yet, by that time, they had an amazing knowledge of the classics, although not many wholesome ones, they spoke two or three languages, they could mend wounds, nurse the sick, make herbal medicines, manage large households with servants, join in the hunt on horseback, and even make a kill, and do beautifully exquisite embroidery. British ladies from the Tudor age were also well informed and enjoyed learning more. Maria Theresa was never considered a great scholar, but she was able to make speeches, and talk to Magyar nobles in Latin. They couldn't speak her language, yet they were able to communicate. If this is how well the women were educated, how well-educated must the men have been!

Do we have less intelligence than they did? No. Then how did they do it? Every prep school already knows how! It's possible that the exclusive schools only admit students who are bright and prepared enough to pass their entrance exam. One Dean said,

'A boy learns as much Latin as he'll need to pass any exam by the time he's twelve. He spends the next eight years repeating and going over and over the same work. A clever twelve-year-old could easily pass a university entrance exam.'

A Dean in Newfoundland mentions in his 1905 report a boy who 'started learning Greek in October, and passed his Oxford exams three months later, in January.'

That means there's wasted time somewhere, and too much overlapping. Both are the result of the exams that determine who gets a scholarship. Something has to be done. Exclusive boarding schools, in spite of their great track record, aren't [pg 312] effective. They take average boys and turn them into decent all-around men. Whether that's for better or worse is anyone's guess. The mob is clamoring for change, and our old foundations will be tossed aside unless we hurry to strengthen their weak places. Perhaps a commission should be formed, made up of a couple of deans, a few prep school teachers, University heads, and alumni who have gone on to public service and sent their own sons to these same schools. This commission could look into the question and come up with an exam that would keep ancient and modern scholasticism exclusive, yet not make it impossible to get in.

Once all the teachers agreed and were on the same page, they'd be sure to come up with a way for the average student to get enough exposure to the classics to make a life-long learner of him. He'd be like the 'Baron of Bradwardine,' going around with a compact copy of 'Livy' (Titus Livius) in his pocket to be read for enjoyment, not to be labored over a few lines at a time. *The Seven Against Thebes*, *Iphigenia in Aults* and other great tragedies left by the great dramatists would form a familiar background in his mind. He'd know a bit of the best books ever written in Greek and Latin, but with English translations. At the same time, he could be doing his share of the regular grind of grammar and interpreting two or three works that he's only skimmed before. But, as an average student, he wouldn't be expected to write poetry in Latin or Greek.

Meanwhile, his teacher would require him to read and know a hundred worthy books besides great novels. He could read them in class, after school, and over vacations. To test his comprehension, he'd do a single narration, either oral or written in prose or verse. 'He did his grind of grammar' is the experience of every [pg 313] boy who succeeds at school, in the same way that the ancient 'grammarians' did. But 10-12 years of school should do more for him than that.

I won't say anything right now about science. Most schools do fine teaching that. Our generation seems to me to need science for intellectual advancement. But our topic here is scholarship, learning about the humanities. Humanities includes men and their motives, the sequence of historical events, guiding principles to teach how to live. In fact, practical philosophy is required in these times with so much happening in the world. And it's important to be able to communicate well. You don't get that with any short-cut methods teaching economics, or selective breeding to advance the race, or anything like that. You get it from many years and seasons of sowing the seeds of poetry, literature and history. Our country is in desperate need of wise men, and we'll have to get them by educating our youth.

III Knowledge, Reason and Rebellion

For sixty years we've been working as hard as a gardener in the field of education, weeding, pruning and watering. But our tree of knowledge isn't thriving like we expected. Its fruit, both good and bad, is hard and tiny. And there's so little of it that intelligent people who are trying to choose between them can't tell which are any good. To thoroughly inspect each piece of fruit would take a long time. But I'll just pick one at random. How about the sense of irresponsibility that seems to characterize our generation?

If this is the case, and if people tend to think the way they've gotten used to thinking, then education is to blame. It's education's fault if private property is damaged in broad daylight, or if men are so focused on doing something to help their own little group that they're oblivious to the way their actions [*probably referring to labor strikes*] are harming the country itself. And there are those who are happy with it [*like news reporters?*] as long as [pg 314] it doesn't affect them. The sad truth is that all those people who are destroying private property, damaging what's in the public interest and bringing down public opinion, which is itself a fragile value to a nation—have all received an education. They can all express themselves clearly, think logically even though their reasoning may be selfishly motivated, and they all have some kind of marketable skill. WWI has changed a lot of things and made people less selfish. But if we don't try to take the opportunity to make the changes last by improving education, then things will become even worse than they were before.

We are no worse than our ancestors. In fact, we are as good as they were—but we are ignorant. The worse crime that ever happened [*the Crucifixion*] was responded to with the words, 'You did it because you were ignorant and didn't know better.' And that crime was committed only because men who are well-read but not wise tend to follow 'specious' arguments with logical precision. There's an Eastern myth where Lady Lugard tells how 'the Copts have a saying that, when God created all things, He gave a mate to everything. So, when Reason went to Syria, Rebellion went with him.' We won't pursue how the others paired off, but it does seem evident that when stern Reason sets out in search of a logical issue, it's usually accompanied by Rebellion.

It's a grave mistake to think that reason can replace knowledge, that reason is infallible, or that a reasonable conclusion is always a right conclusion. Reason is a man's servant, not his master. It acts like a good and faithful servant, as a sort of Caleb Balderstone (from The Bride of Lammermoor by Sir Walter Scott) who is even willing to tell a lie out of loyalty to his master. Reason will attempt to logically prove any argument that a man's will decides to entertain. The will is the spirit of man. It's the will that makes choices. The man has to have knowledge in order for his will to make fair, wise decisions. Shakespeare was as great a philosopher as he was a poet. That's what he set out to teach us in every line. His characters [pg 315] 'Leontes,' 'Othello,' 'Lear,' 'Prospero,' 'Brutus,' demonstrate the same thing: that a man's reason will try to bring infallible proofs to any notion that a person decides to take up. There's no shortcut and no way around it, the art of life takes a long time to learn.

It used to be that a working man only spoke for his own family. He picked up enough knowledge to get by from his church, by watching his neighbors, village politics, and gossip at the tavern or from the local paper. But things have changed. Groups of working men have discovered that they can unite together in unions to act with enough momentum to paralyze or pressure their company to act, even when the men don't really know what's going on. Without knowledge, Reason can carry a man off into a wilderness, and Rebellion will join it. It's not the man's fault. It's exhilarating to sense your own mind's reasoning power acting as if it had a life of its own, coming up with point after point to support any notion. When a man is stirred to this tremendous power within himself and experiences his mind reasoning all by itself, how can he be convinced that his conclusions might not be correct, and that reasoning without knowledge is like a child playing with power tools? The man follows his reason and perceives this or that freedom that he fancies he should have. But it's written,

'But (write this upon your heart!)
even if spiritual things
Are lost because of apathy, or contempt, or fear,
You shall uphold inferior privileges
That may have been won through bitter struggle, and costly sacrifice.'
    [Wordsworth, from Obligations of Civil to Religious Liberty]

If the conduct and destinies of men are decided by knowledge, then it's worth our while to learn something about the nature of knowledge, even though it's vague. Matthew Arnold helps us by offering three classifications of knowledge that make common sense: knowledge of God, knowledge of mankind, [pg 316] and knowledge of the natural world. Another way to say it might be The Divine, the Humanities, and the Sciences. But I think we can go a step further. I think that Letters (a scholarly education), if they don't make up the main content of knowledge, are at least the container that knowledge comes in. Letters are the silver bowl, the exquisite vase, even the alabaster box that holds the ointment.

If man can't think without words, and if the person who thinks with words is sure to express his thoughts, then what about that habit of speaking in single syllables that's becoming common among all classes? The trivial, silly chatter that many women and a few men like to engage in doesn't count. That isn't meant to express real, intelligent thought. The Greeks thought that the main purpose of education was to teach a person how powerful words could be, and train him to use words well. They understood that, if words come from thoughts, then thoughts also come from words. The Greeks didn't bother with learning and studying any other languages, modern or ancient, they just focused on their own. Thus, they became experts in their own language. With their well-developed language came great thoughts expressed in just the right form needed for the occasion—in wise laws, victorious battles, glorious temples, beautiful statues, and classic drama. Great thoughts promise great deeds. And great deeds only come to a people who are familiar with the great thoughts that have been written and said before. How did the youngest of our great Premiers bring about the 'revival of England'? He was strengthened with vast reading that made him believe that impossible things could be accomplished because he'd read of such feats before. He'd read about a thousand things spoken about so wisely that the only result could be a wise action. When we say that our nation is suffering from a contempt for knowledge, we mean that men are ridiculing Letters, which is the container for all knowledge.

Let's take a look at the three classifications of knowledge to find out which one we're most misusing. Some people think that they have all the divine knowledge they need by listening to a sermon every week in [pg 317] church. But, even though our preachers may have a degree, they still don't lift us as much as they should into that gentle realm where words fitly spoken bring about thoughts of peace and divine purpose. It's a worthy ideal to make worship the main purpose of our church services. But people need to hear about 'the Way that enables us to go, the Truth that enables us to know, and the Life that enables us to live.' And we need to hear it in 'words that burn' and ignite our spirits. We wish for the kind of preachers from the old days, who shook the pulpit and 'shook the nation's soul.'

Maybe it's true that the church doesn't feed us enough of the knowledge that gives life, but we aren't starved, either. We also get a small share of literature, poetry, and history—a phrase here, a line there, just enough to light up our day once in a while. Charles Fox said, 'Poetry is everything,' and the black conqueror of the Sudan said, 'Without learning, life wouldn't have any pleasure or flavor.' Knowledge is good for us, although we aren't sure why that's true.

But our intellectual life has a whole region that's sterile. Science refuses to mingle with literature, and insists on being the focus of our age. Whatever we study ends up stripped to the bone, and the principle of *life* goes out the window with the meat. History dies in the process, poetry lies buried, religion never wakes up. We sit down to study the dry bones of science and we think, This is knowledge, this is all there is to know!' One little girl answered an exam question asking what makes a leaf green, 'I think it's so wonderful.' She had found the principle of wonder and admiration that makes science come to life. Without that wonder, the value of science is strictly utilitarian, not spiritual. A person might as well collect matchbooks like the charming people in Anatole France's novels, instead of diatoms, if there's [pg 318] no wonder of the world in his soul. In the 1700's, science was alive, exciting, and it therefore was written about in literary language. We're still fascinated and emotional about people like Lister and Louis

Pasteur. We feel like the scientists in one field are still passionate about humanity (scholars at the top of the field?) and are doing great work.

But, for the most part, science seems dull. The practical value of scientific discoveries doesn't excite the highest good in us, although it might make a strong appeal to our more sensory interests. But that's not science's fault. Science might be considered the vehicle God uses in our age to present revelation. It's the way we present it that's the problem. We use facts and figures and technical demonstrations that mean nothing to the general public. The wonder and the awe of the scientific law that it manifests is never shown. The Hebrew poet was glorifying life when he wrote, 'The grain is ground to make bread. People do not ruin it by crushing it forever. The farmer separates the wheat from the chaff with his cart, but he does not let his horses grind it. This lesson comes from the Lord All-Powerful, who gives wonderful advice' [*Isaiah 28: 28, 29, NCV*] Coleridge has revealed the deepest secret of both science and literature when he says, 'The concept of Nature is presented to selected minds by a Power that's higher than even Nature itself.' If a person would write about the true principle of wireless technology by saying what a discovery it was to find something that had been there all along, then we might be inspired and excited within our hearts. Yes, there are some scientists who are also humanities scholars, and there are some science books that are as inspiring as beautiful poems. But, for the most part, science is still waiting for its literature. In the meantime, we can't live in ignorance while we wait for it to be written. We have to use what's available. It's a shame that science is all too often taught in a way that leaves us sketchy about scientific thought, and narrow-minded.

We hear that in times of crisis, it does [pg 319] no good to blame this or that segment of society. We're all to blame, even for the offenses of each individual. We partly believe it because our fathers told us it was true. In the same way, the prophets humbled themselves before God and repented of their own great sin when speaking of the sin of the people. We're also humble enough to confess our sin when we're being punished, but we're also vague enough to be insincere.

Maybe our duty is to give serious consideration to the problems of our society. Maybe then we'll finally realize that man truly can't live by bread alone. Maybe we'll understand that intellectual 'bread' (or even cake) is all we ever offer to people in all socioeconomic classes. We are losing our sense of every kind of values, except financial. Our young men no longer see visions. Instead, they're attracted to a career only if 'there's money in it.' Nothing comes from nothing. If we bring up our children on corrupt dreams and selfish ambitions, should we be surprised if every man looks out for number one?

Every now and then, when we notice some social discontent, we see that the nation is ready to revolt. But do we bother to find the underlying cause of labor unrest, and then try to correct the public's attitude towards it? As I see it, the revolution we're experiencing might develop along two possible lines. The people may win the petty rights they want so badly, but it will cost them the loss of spiritual things like integrity that ensures fairness, honest exchange, and loyalty to a contract. We pride ourselves in thinking that those things are a distinctive of British character. But what about the fear that men's minor rights will be lost?

Trade unions are nothing new. As we all know, for centuries and centuries England and Europe were under the governing authority of Trade Guilds. From our perspective, we can afford to admire them for the spiritual principles that they maintained, for their religious organization, for the thorough training they gave their apprentices, and for [pg 320] the obligation of each and every member to use honest weights and measures and produce work of the highest quality they could. But even with these ethical safeguards, they became too powerful and disappeared, as everything does when it's not useful any more. Or, could Socialism have a more perfect place to do good than the villages of Russia? But even that turned into a tyranny that was even more oppressive than the serfdom it was supposed to relieve. The Russian *mir* [*village community living and governing communally; Marx based his visions of communism on their model*] has disappeared, lost forever in the same black hole that swallowed up the guilds.

We should learn something from Wordsworth's prophetic lines. Whatever 'bitter struggle, and costly sacrifice' are paid to purchase inferior privileges by those tens of thousands of men who are boldly standing together in solidarity out of devotion to a cause that their Reason has justified, they won't be able to maintain those privileges if the true, spiritual things of life are sacrificed in order to get them. So we can predict that the present movement will bring in even worse things. It won't usher in the triumph of trade unions, or mob rule.

This should be our opportunity. We blame the working men [*miners, in this case*] for being irresponsible. They seem to be causing more hardships for the poor, and they force workers to stop being industrious. But those of us on the outside who are neither employees or owners can't afford to think or speak irresponsibly. We can contribute to finding a peaceable agreement. Everybody has a circle of friends and family whose opinions they can influence, even if it's only one or two people. We can raise the discussion to a higher level and bring the focus to spiritual things, like duty, responsibility, brotherly love towards all mankind that can make people think beyond the short term. We aren't able to stop the revolution that we vaguely sense is going on, nor should we try to. But we should try to influence it so that it will bring us [pg 321] out of the darkness of a narrow tunnel into enlightenment that's as bright as if coming out into an open, green field. When we consider the demands of the miners, we see that what they're asking for isn't much, and they aren't fighting for things that really matter. Even the shock of a revolution is worth it, if it convinces us that the strength of our nation lies in knowledge, and in the education of its people.

IV- New and Old Concepts of Knowledge

So far I've stated that 'knowledge' hasn't been defined, and is probably undefinable. It's not something a person piles up in storage to access later, it's more like a state of being that people often leave, but they can re-enter. The hunger for knowledge is as universal as hunger for food. The best way we know how to pass on knowledge works well with an elite few, but not so well with everyone else. Those whose educations fill them with a collection of facts and statistics instead of enriching them with real knowledge will base their reasoning on those facts [*in place of experienced, discerning judgment.*] In England's current crisis [*presumably the miner strikes*], England has found that her people lack intellectual spirit. For various economical reasons, England has had a failure in her food supply—the supply of the proper mental diet for minds. I've explained how knowledge can be divided into three categories, as suggested by Coleridge, who has some authority. I've tried to point out how, even though knowledge can be divided into categories, the vehicle that carries it is one and can't be divided: It's generally impossible for the mind to receive knowledge in any way other than letters [*books*].

We know that medieval people had a better concept of knowledge than we've come up with. We think of knowledge as something compiled of shreds and bits and pieces— [pg 322] we have sketchy knowledge of this or that, with huge gaps in between.

Medieval people, with their scholarly minds, worked out a magnificent 'Philosophy of the Catholic Religion.' They were probably basing that on the scattered hints in Scripture. Their concept is pictured in the great fresco painted by [supposedly] Simone Memmi and Taddeo Gaddi that John Ruskin taught us about. It's also implied in the Van Eycks' 'Adoration of the Lamb.' In the first fresco, we see the Holy Spirit descending, first upon the four cardinal virtues [prudence, justice, temperance, and fortitude] and the Christian graces [faith, hope and charity], then upon the prophets and apostles, and, under these, upon the seven Liberal Arts [grammar, rhetoric, dialectic, arithmetic, geometry, astronomy, and music]. Each of these Seven is represented by its leading figure—Cicero, Aristotle, Zoroaster, etc.—and not one of them is a Christian or a Hebrew. This presents the idea that all knowledge (in its original, untainted form) comes directly from heaven and is planted in minds that are prepared to receive it, as Coleridge says. It's planted in whichever mind is prepared, without regard to whether it's the mind of a pagan or a Christian. This seems to me to be a truly enlightened, broad-minded idea that corresponds perfectly with the way the world operates. Another idea that's just as wonderful and even more specific is the Greek myth of Promethius. This makes us suddenly aware of how haphazard and useless our own notions of knowledge are. We're tempted to cry out with Wordsworth,

'God, I'd rather be
A pagan who was brought up believing an outdated creed!'

and yet know that God, at great sacrifice, brought gifts of knowledge to all mankind. That seems much better than to sit serenely with some vague misconception that knowledge arrives as confused odds and ends, and nobody knows how or from where it comes from, or that knowledge is created by itself in the thoughts of a few men here and there who find in their own minds new insights about the ways of the mind and heart, or new perceptions about the ways of life. or an idea about improving the species. [pg 323]

Our confused theories of education stem from our jumbled concepts of knowledge. Let's quote a passage from Ruskin's description of the fresco in the Church of Santa Maria Novella that I mentioned above:

'On either side of the chapel, Simon Memmi has represented the power of God to teach, and the power of Christ to save. That's how the Florentines understood the world at that time...

'...Let's look at the intellect first. Under the descending Holy Spirit, we see the point of the arch, with the Three Evangelical Virtues (faith, hope, love) under it. Florentines believed that, without these, there could be no science or intelligence. Under those are the four Cardinal Virtues: Temperance, Prudence, Justice, Fortitude. Under those are the great Prophets and Apostles. Under the Prophets, pictured as if the Prophets were summoning them, are the allegorical figures of the seven theological sciences, and the seven natural sciences. Under the feet of each of these is the figure of the man who taught it to the world.' (from Ruskin's book Mornings in Florence.)

In other words, the Florentines living in the Middle Ages believed that 'the Spirit of God had the power to teach.' They believed that not only the seven Liberal Arts were completely under the direct outpouring of God's Spirit, but every fruitful idea or original concept, whether geometry, grammar or music, was directly derived from a Divine source.

Whether we accept it or not, we can't fail to see that this is a harmonious and uplifting blueprint of education and philosophy. The Scriptures abundantly support this kind of theory about how knowledge comes to us. It's too bad that the demands of Ruskin's immediate work prevented him from researching further into the ultimate origin of knowledge. But that doesn't mean we can't do some research ourselves. In the phrase, 'the power [pg 324] of God to teach,' we have an inspiring idea that's full of possibilities. If we entertained this medieval philosophy right now in our current crisis, what good might come of it?

First, there would be a great sense of relief when we had some unity of purpose and real progress in the way we educate the race. There's great ease of mind in knowing that knowledge is dealt out to us according to how prepared we are and what our needs are, and that God whispers knowledge into the ear of the person who's ready. God does that for the purpose of delivering that knowledge to the rest of us. The poem *Abt Vogler* [by Robert Browning] says, 'God has a few of us that He whispers in the ear.' Another poet [Rudyard Kipling, *The Explorer*] says,

'God chose me for His whisper, and I've found it, and it's yours!'

The next benefit is that knowledge would no longer be divided between sacred and secular, great and trivial, practical and theoretical. All knowledge is sacred, and is dealt out to us in proportion to how ready we are for it. Knowledge isn't a scrappy collection of shreds and bits, but a beautiful whole, a great unity that embraces God and man and the universe. It's one unit, but it has many parts and none is superior or less important than any other. All are necessary because each has a specific function. The third benefit is our understanding that knowledge and man's mind go together like air and lungs. The mind can only live on knowledge. Without knowledge, the mind goes stagnant, gets weak and dies.

Next, it isn't up to man to decide, 'I'll learn this or that, but the rest of it isn't my concern.' It's even worse for a parent or teacher to limit a child to less than he can get of the whole field of knowledge. The domain of the mind is every bit as much under a Divine Master as morality or religion. A child has to know just as urgently as he has to eat.

Next, life doesn't have just one segment of time [pg 325] singled out for regular intellectual meals. We have to eat food daily for our entire lives. And our minds also need mental food every day for our whole lives.

Next, we shouldn't confuse knowledge with the kind of 'learning' that happens in school. A person can 'learn' by amassing a pile full of facts, but it's only true knowledge that enriches personal growth and makes a child a better person. That is its own reward [*i.e., it shouldn't be necessary to 'prove' the validity of a person's character growth with economic productivity charts.*] We're sometimes amazed when a person who's known for their intelligence is well-grounded and modest. They're not trying to hide their talent. It's just that they truly don't feel that they have any unusual giftedness. They're just being themselves, yet we can feel the force of their personalities. People with confidence and integrity, with forceful personalities, who can make decisions and have sound judgment are just what this country needs most. If we want to train up this kind of person to lead in our country, then surely knowledge should be one criteria we want to instill.

There are various trendy 'new' educational systems that seem fun, but that feature only the tiniest grain of knowledge diluted in a gallon of warm, weak water. One theory says that it doesn't matter what a child learns, what matters is how he learns it. That makes about as much sense as saying that it doesn't matter what a child eats, what matters is how he eats it—so let's just feed him sawdust! Another theory is Rousseau's primitive man theory. It says that a child can only learn what he experiences first-hand through his five senses and from his own wits. One would think that there wasn't such thing as knowledge waiting to be passed on by a torch-bearer. Then there's the frivolous theory that originated in the Church of England and shows up in some of Scott's Waverley novels—in the games that Lady Margaret Belleden had her tenants play, for example. Those young men and women had been trained from childhood to be 'flexible, active, healthy, alert, prepared to dance and sing, and with eyes and ears ready for whatever was beautiful, intelligent, happy and able. (I'm quoting from a useful letter in The Times). Between our [pg 326] morris dances (folk dancing), pageants, living pictures, miracles plays and things like that, we're reviving the ideals of education in the Stuart days. It's not a bad thing to have a goal of bringing more joy to life. But we live in complex times and more is required of us. Real knowledge plays no part in the sort of self-activity and self-expression of this kind of educational theory, or a half dozen other educational theories I could bring up. Whatever we determine to cultivate will eventually be manifested in perfect displays of active fun, alert minds and enjoyment of performances.

The message we really need is, 'With all that is in you, get understanding.' In one sense, understanding is an active thing that the conscious mind does to assimilate knowledge. And that's relative—the mind can't do that if it hasn't already acted on the intellectual food that was presented to it. The Gospels keep repeating the poignant question, 'Why won't you understand?'

This is what's wrong with our nation—we don't understand. I'm not just talking about ignorant people. Even educated men and women use erroneous arguments, rely on prejudices instead of principles, and mistake cliches for ideas. Perhaps these failures aren't ignorance so much as insincerity. But insincerity is a result of ignorance. Darkened intelligence can't see clearly. 'It's as bright as day for those who know,' but knowing doesn't come easily for those who 'cram to pass tests instead of to really learn,' as Ruskin says.

I don't mean to cast criticism on the vast excellent educational work that almost all teachers are doing. No matter which elementary school you go into, you're impressed with the competence of the teachers and how intelligent the children seem. I've already mentioned how well the public boarding schools do, and I'd like to give warm, hearty applause to High School girls, too. They're thoughtful and well-educated. They don't deserve the stings and arrows of criticism that are often thrown [pg 327] their way. As for our Universities, they remove the stigma that many of us have experienced. We sometimes feel that stigma when we're in the middle of one of the places where intellectual people gather. Those places add dignity and grace to metropolitan cities. Our new Universities are promising for our future.

We've undoubtedly come to a good place to start, but the journey is far from over. I don't need to repeat all the weaknesses that arise from ignorance, but I'll take a closer look at the field of education as it relates to knowledge and the inborn desires of the mind for the knowledge suited to it. For now, we need practical people to understand that what the nation really needs is abstract knowledge. The general weakness of the population to understand the science of relations [*everything relates to everything else*] should prove that, as well as the failure to understand the science of the proportions of things.

V - Education and the Fullness of Life

'I must live my life!' said the notorious bandit who terrorized Paris before the war. We've heard the same sort of thing a lot [*'I gotta be me!'*], even before The Doll's House made self-expression seem so trendy that it's practically a cult. Yet it hasn't done society any favors. A bad theory expressed brilliantly is more dangerous than a bad example.

We're all disgusted at a person who claims to live at everyone else's expense, or a youth who lives life to annoy and worry his parents. But we have a perfect opportunity to consider what kind of life a person should live, and what will best provide individuals with the opportunity to live their own lives.

We are trying to do something. We're trying to unlock the [pg 328] nature of children by using the right key. That key is knowledge—familiarity enough with birds and flowers and trees to know them by name, if not more. And the magic of poetry makes knowledge come to life. Adults and children should be able to quote a verse that will make the bud of an ash tree seem blacker, or add sweetness and wonder to a 'flower in the crannied wall,' or make a lark's song sound more thrilling. All of the field clubs around the northern towns have members who are accomplished botanists, bird experts and geologists. Their Saturday nature rambles don't just add zest to their week. They're also just plain fun. We hope that schools will offer opportunities so that women will be more prepared to participate in these excursions. Right now, the field work is so thorough that it requires more endurance than they're used to, and more than has ever been expected of them.

In one sense, we're doing well. Our bodies are made so that any physical movement that involves contact with the earth is a source of joy for us, whether it's a game of leap frog or flying kites. We've noticed this, so we're encouraging things like swimming, dancing, and hockey. All of these give immediate enjoyment and permanent health. We also know that the human hand is a wonderful and precise tool that can be used in a hundred different ways that require intricacy, accuracy and strength. Using the hand in this way brings pleasure in the process itself that's separate from the end result. We understand this, so we make an effort to train young students to accurately handle tools and do handicrafts. Maybe someday we'll see a revival of apprenticeship in various trades, and we'll start to see quality work again as people take pride in the work of their hands. Our goal should be to make sure that each person 'lives his life' with pleasure, but not at the expense of someone else. The world is such that, when a person truly lives his life [*rather than just survives day to day*], it benefits those around him as much as it benefits himself. Everyone thrives on the well-being of others. We also understand that the human ear is attuned to [pg 329] harmony and melody. Each person has a voice that can express musical notes and hands that are capable of delicate motion to draw out musical tones on instruments. The ancient Greeks were the first ones to realize that music is a necessary part of education. Art is also necessary. We are finally realizing that anyone can draw, and everyone enjoys it. Therefore, everyone should learn how to do it. Everyone enjoys looking at pictures, so education should train people to appreciate pictures of quality.

People can sing, dance, enjoy music, appreciate the beauty of nature, sketch what they see, be satisfied in their skill at crafting things, produce honest work with their hands, understand that work is better than wages, and live out their individual lives in any of a number of ways. In fact, the more interests a person has, the more enjoyable his life will be. When he's doing all of these things, his mind is agreeably occupied and challenged. He thinks about what he's doing, often with excitement and enthusiasm. He feels like he must 'live his life,' and he does. He lives it in as many ways as there are open to him, and he takes nothing away from anyone else to fulfill his abundance. In fact, the collective joy of well-being increases all around him through shared feeling, and others following his example.

This is the kind of ideal that's beginning to be awakened in our schools and in public opinion. It will provide the next generation with lots of ways to live their own lives—and in ways that don't encroach on anyone else. This worthy gift is what our generation can contribute towards the science of relations. Now we understand that a person should be raised and educated for his own benefit and what's best for his own personal growth, not primarily for the uses of society. Yet he *will* benefit society, because it's the person who 'lives his own life' most fully who is the greatest blessing to others. He'll be the one with the most skills because he wants to be able to do many different things in order to fully enjoy life. And, with the skills to live on his own resources, he won't be a drain on society. [pg 330]

But a person is more than eyes that enjoy beauty, a heart that finds satisfaction, limbs that delight in moving, hands that find joy in creating something that's done right. Anyone can have these things, except those who are totally depraved. But what about man's eager, yearning, restless, insatiable mind? It's true that we teach him the mechanics of phonetic reading in school—but we don't teach him to read. He can't focus his attention for very long, he has a poor vocabulary, and he's not in the habit of thinking of anyone besides himself. His best concept of fun is buying tickets to a football game.

We neglect the vast region that belongs to every human, and is, therefore, his birthright: his mind. I'm not talking about the physical tissue of the brain. If the mind is well-fed and exercised, it will take care of maintaining the physical tissue. But what we fail to do is to feed our children's minds enough mental nourishment. Picture the mind like a spiritual octopus, reaching out in lots of different directions, trying to pull in lots of raw material that the mind will turn into knowledge. Nothing in the world's infinite variety bores it. The heavens, the earth, the past, present, and future, giant things and miniscule things, nations and men, the universe—the mind is fascinated by all those things. But there seems to be an unwritten law we never suspected about what kind of raw material is assimilated and converted to real knowledge. It wasn't a coincidence that the Greeks made up the word *logos*. Logos, translated The Word, isn't just some meaningless title applied to the Son of God. And it's no accident that every time Jesus spoke, His words had the distinction of having exquisite literary quality. In fact, one girl remarked after hearing the lyrics to a hymn, 'That's not poetry. Jesus would have [pg 331] said it much better.' When Jesus prayed about His final days and work, He said, 'I have given them the words You gave to me.' One disciple spoke for the others when he said, 'You have the words of eternal life.' The Greeks understood better than we do that words aren't just things or events. With all primitive societies, rhetoric seems to have been an important skill. The wonderful old sayings that we discarded as outdated inventions are becoming popular again because we're finding that no modern mind can come up with sayings as good as the old ones. Men may change the world, but it's words that inspire them and motivate them to action. A person is limited by how many things he knows by their proper names and can qualify by using the correct terms. This isn't just some nitpicky rule. It has to do with the mystery we call human nature. Our newfangled method of education that emphasizes 'things not words' is inherently demoralizing. The human mind needs 'letters,' or literature, and desires them more urgently than the body craves bread. It was recent enough that some people still remember how newly-freed slaves in America devoured books with the appetite of the famished Israelites who fell upon food in Sennacherib's deserted camp.

A man is only able to 'live his life' in the proportion to how much his mind has been nourished on books. A lot of menial factory labor is done alone. Miners and farmers can't focus on the block being hewed or the furrow being plowed forever. How fortunate it would be if a worker could be going over in his mind the trial scene in *Heart of Midlothian*, or the antics in *Guy Mannering*. How beneficial if his imagination is busy thinking about 'Ann Page' or 'Mrs. Quickie.' His work will go faster if, within the deepest parts of his soul, a holy tune is playing. Yes, regular working people do these things. Many of them are able to say, 'My mind is like an entire kingdom within me!' And many can cry out with Browning's *Paracelsus*, 'God, you are mine! The human mind must seem [pg 332] precious to the greatest Mind. Spare my mind.' Many of us have seen the words, 'Have mynde' on the tiles that pave the choir loft at the church of St. Cross. But do we remember that the 'mynde' needs its meat as much as the body does?

Faith is growing weaker these days. Hope languishes in the seriousness of our times. But love and charity are as strong as ever. If it were within our power, we'd make everybody rich, or, at least, we'd take some of the money that billionaires have and share it with the multitudes who really need it. There will undoubtedly be some good, bold hero who will rise up like Robin Hood and do that sort of thing. Maybe he's already risen. Yet, after all the charity has been done, we'll find that we still haven't enabled the people to fully 'live their lives' until we provide them with a literary education so successfully that they'll want to continue learning on their own for the rest of the their lives. Someone might object, 'That all sounds good, but look at the masses. Are they capable of learning about literature? When they talk, they use the kind of language you find in newspapers. The only way they can understand books is if they're condensed and abridged to make them easier to read.' But, don't working men speak in journalese because their newspapers are willing to meet them halfway and present news in the language they understand? Neither their schools nor society has exposed them to real books. The fact that they adopt the language of the only source who will write for them proves my point: people have a natural aptitude to understand literature. I'm going to go straight to the top and appeal to the highest authority by citing Christ, who didn't shrink from presenting the most profound philosophical truth to the multitudes. Even Socrates didn't think the multitudes were worthy to receive such knowledge, but Jesus did.

I'd like to quote a letter from 'a working man' who responded to a letter of mine that *The Times Weekly Edition* did me the honor of reprinting. My apologies to the author. (By the way, I think it's wonderful that this kind of newspaper is being read by working men.) The man who wrote this letter says that he's 'Thankful there are still [pg 333] people left in England who think of education as something other than a way to earn a living.' And we should all be thankful that there are a few working class people who value education for its own sake, and don't want it offered to them simply as a means to increase their income.

The truth is, literature has a universal appeal. Books satisfy a certain desire in all of us. People like young Tennysons and De Quinceys will read profusely no matter what. They'll find their own books on their own. It's the average youth, or the slow ones that I urge us to provide with a literary education. Minds like theirs will respond to literature even when they won't respond to anything else, and turns them into intelligent young people who are open to learning more about lots of different things. For working class people who have more intelligence than the limits of the education they received, books are an accessible method for them to learn more. They've already learned to read, spell and do arithmetic, so it isn't necessary to make them take remedial classes in those things. They have intelligent, mature minds and can deal with finding answers to their literature questions when they need them. To help in this regard, every working men's club should have an encyclopedia. Some people naturally take to learning, and they'll tackle Latin grammar, Cicero, Euclid and trigonometry on their own. They're fortunate! But, in general, for most people of all ages and classes and frames of mind, literary books are a necessity. They need them every day to satisfy the intellectual craving that everyone has. Neglecting that need causes emotional disturbances that lead to evils that distress all of us.

VI - Knowledge in Literary Form

So far, I've been trying to impress on readers the idea that knowledge is a necessity for people, and that, in the beginning, at least, it has to come from [pg 334] a literary [*interesting story*] source. It doesn't matter whether the knowledge is physics or literature. There seems to be some inborn quality in the mind that will only respond to a literary form and nothing else. I said 'in the beginning' because I think it's possible that once the mind is familiar with a certain type of knowledge, it unconsciously converts even the driest formula into living dialog. Maybe that has something to do with the reason why math seems to be the exception to the rule about knowledge being in literary form. Math, like music, is a language in itself. Its speech is logical without fail, and always clear. It meets the mind's requirements.

Viewing literature as the essence of education is nothing new. Neither is the belief that education means turning a youth into a library of facts. But now we know that the mind needs information presented in a methodical, orderly way. It needs that just as surely as it demands knowledge. Maybe our educational failures are the result of us adopting any haphazard educational scheme if the person suggesting it is persistent enough.

But no one can live without a philosophy that makes some sense of things by bringing out order, pointing out an end goal, and showing a way to work towards that end. That's true of any effort, whether it's education, or life in general. If we aren't able to come up with a way to make sense of things, we fall into depression—or even into full-on madness. So, we go through our lives picking up an adage here, a motto there, an idea somewhere else. Then we make a patchwork of the whole thing and call it our 'principles.' Yet it's no more than a collection of shreds and threadbare fragments that we cover our vulnerabilities with. All the quips and catch phrases we hear any day of the week betray lives built on nothing more than shabby dogma. It's undoubtedly true that people are better than their words, or even their own thoughts. We call ourselves 'finite beings,' but almost every person has an unlimited amount of generosity and nobility [*or, at least, the potential for it*]. When the Titanic sank, one lady remarked that men who gave up their seats on lifeboats for women and children were only doing their duty; 'it's the rule at sea.' But the men's deed shows us such heroic kindness [pg 335] in the sacrifice of their very lives! Human nature hasn't failed, it's still there. What has failed is philosophy, and the applied philosophy that we call education. All of the philosophies, old and new, leave us with a dilemma: do we do what's best for number one and work to improve our own nature and comfort, or do we seek to improve the lot of others through our own sacrifice? If a happy medium exists, philosophy doesn't tell us what it is.

There are some things we need desperately. We need a new set of values. Before WWI, we all read about how a few millionaires died in the Titanic. At that fateful moment, all their money meant nothing. It didn't matter to them. In fact, it's possible that they felt relieved of a weary burden. We don't need more money. What we crave is more *life*. We need more abundance in our lives, we don't have enough compelling interests. We rush from one meeting to another, glancing anxiously at the clock to see how we're doing with time. We're glad to have made it through another week—who can say that perhaps, at the final end, we might not just be glad it's over? We need hope. We keep ourselves so busy and excited about some new purchase, not realizing that the satisfaction we get is in the process of attaining and the effort, not the thing itself. Before the war, we read about Continental school boys committing suicide. [*This could be referring to a sensory-based/existential Continental philosophy that made boys too introspective and encouraged them to question the ethical value of life.*] What is there to live for? We want to be under some kind of authority. Servants like to know what's expected of them, soldiers and students enjoy discipline, there's satisfaction in the rigid rules of court etiquette, and we feel more dignified when we're acting under orders. Revolt is only a transferring of our allegiance. When we're tired of ourselves and knowing what we're supposed to believe and how we're supposed to feel, we want a fresh start. The change we half-consciously crave is a change of direction, and a different way of looking at things. We feel confined [pg 336] and wonder if a new situation would give us more room, we don't know. At any rate, we're uneasy. These are some of the private concerns that oppress us. What we need is a philosophy that deals with these spiritual needs. We believe that, if we had such a philosophy, we'd rise to it, however challenging. It isn't in us to fail. It's not human nature that causes our failure, it's our limited knowledge of the way things are.

We hear that people are getting more immoral. Is that true? The beautiful heirloom gowns that some families cherish aren't long enough to fit our tall, lovely daughters. We've become sincere, truthful and kind. Our conscience and charity sometimes makes us obsessive worriers—we lose sleep because we're anxious about the well-being of everybody else. We even go beyond the Scripture quote that says, for a good man, someone might die. In our day, we see almost any man risking his life to save someone else without even considering whether the person is good or bad. And we expect no less from firemen, doctors, coast guard personnel, pastors, and the general public. And WWI gave us lots of examples of the heroic potential within our men!

One ridiculous case concerning risks at sea almost resulted in a law that nobody could allow himself to be saved if others were in danger. It's preposterous, yet that's what human nature expects of itself. No, we aren't getting more immoral as a whole. Our uneasiness might be a sign of growing pains. We may be pathetic beings, but we're ready to break into songs of praise if we could ever find a full life of passionate devotion. If we only knew it, all of our heartfelt needs and burning desires can be met by the words in the Bible, and by the manifestation of Christ. What the world is waiting for is a Christianity unlike any it's seen before. Up till now, Jesus has existed for our own convenience. But what if the day came when we too tasted the 'orientall fragrancie" of our Lord? We'll cry, 'My Master!' [pg 337] when the King is among us, and we already have premonitions of His coming. But it takes more than prayer and fasting, good works and self-denial. There's something under all of this that our Master insists on urgently: 'Why won't you know? Why won't you understand?'

My reason for bringing up the intimate needs of our heart is that even this relates to studying literature. If we want to seek knowledge, we have to do it in an orderly way, remembering what the most important knowledge is. I can write and touch the sympathies of my readers because we're all moved by the same concerns of our age. These are our secret preoccupations. We've just come out of a long period of alienation. We're tired of trivial things. We're ready and anxious for a new age. We know how to get there and we know where to find our travel instructions, but we need fresh enthusiasm and a new method for our studies. It's no longer enough to glance at a page, or read an assigned chapter hoping to find some word of help or comfort. We're actively engaged in studying and watching the development of a complete philosophy that meets every occasion of our lives—all the needs of our mind, and the worries of our soul.

It's arrogant to denounce the Bible when all you've read is enough to fill a page or two of Jesus' greatest sayings. That limits Divine teaching to the Sermon on the Mount, which we can rattle off in a few sentences. That's ridiculous and unacceptable. We should be working as hard at understanding the teachings of Jesus as Plato's disciples did at comprehending his words of wisdom. Let's take up our notebooks and study the orderly and progressive sequence, the penetrating quality, the irresistible appeal, and the uniqueness of the Divine teaching. For this kind of study, it might be good [pg 338] to use a chronological arrangement of the Gospels. Let's not just read for our own benefit, although we will benefit. Let's read for the love of the knowledge that's better than silver or gold. Soon we'll understand that this knowledge is the most important thing in life. We'll see what Jesus meant when He said, 'Look, I make all things new.' We'll get new concepts about the relative worth of things. New strength, new joy, new hope will be ours.

If we believe that knowledge is the main thing, that there are three kinds of knowledge, and that the foundation for all knowledge is the knowledge of God, then we'll bring up our children as students of Christianity. And we'll learn right along with them, continuing that study for our entire lives. We'll be prepared for Sunday sermons and find them as satisfying as bread to a hungry man. We might even realize what an enormous demand we make on our pastors to provide us with living, original thought. It's only when we familiarize ourselves with knowledge that science and nature help us understand more. As we learn more, they proclaim God in a way that we can hear. But if we're ignorant about the most important knowledge, we'll miss what they're telling us. Literature and history always have important things to say or suggest, because they deal with phases of moral government and moral anarchy. They indicate what the only key is to this confusing world. Literature doesn't just reveal the deepest things of the human spirit, it also profits us by giving us 'examples of life and lessons about how to act.'

We're at a fork in the road. Our most recent educational expert, someone who knows and loves children [*Maria Montessori?*], is recommending that we discard stories and history tales that appeal to the imagination. She charges us to let children learn through use of things, and her charm and tenderness in telling us may blind us to the desolation of her message. We recognize traces of Rousseau and his book *Emile* in her teaching. Emile [pg 339] was a self-sufficient person who wasn't supposed to know anything about the past. He would see no visions, and be constrained under no authority. But the human nature of real children is stronger than some eighteenth century philosopher's theories that continue to be spread. Anyone who has ever told a child a fairy tale has seen the natural appetite for literature, and it's our job to provide that literature for them. Is it so hard to believe that words are more than food? And if we believe that, shouldn't we rise up and insist that children not be deprived of the abundant spiritual diet of words that they need? In spite of his false analogies and erroneous arguments, Rousseau was able to summon fashionable mothers and fathers all over the world to the work of education. His eloquence convinced them that it was their duty, and that the task was do-able. From our perspective of hindsight, we should value his legacy of persuading the past generation that education is the responsibility of every age.

Yet, even as we're just now emerging ourselves from the trap of materialism, we're all too willing to plunge our children into its heavy ways via 'practical' and 'useful' education. But children have rights. One of their rights is the right to be free within the world of their minds. Yes, let them use things, know things, learn by handling things, by all means. But the more they know of literature, the better they'll be at handling things, with proper instruction. I don't hesitate to say that all of a child's education should be provided through the best literary book available. His history books should be written clearly, focused, with personal conviction, direct, and appealingly simple. That's what characterizes works of literary value. The same is true of his geography books. The current trend to teach geography using the scientific method is designed to give a child a stuffy, prudish relationship with Mother earth. The human mind is unable to [pg 340] assimilate the sentences in most books written for children. Yet they're retained by the memory, so the child gets a false sense of having information, but it's only psuedo-knowledge. Most geography books need to be written in literary terms before they can be taken in. We put a lot of confidence in diagrams and pictures. It's true that children enjoy diagrams and understand them as much as they do puzzles. But they often miss the connection between the diagram and what it's supposed to be illustrating. We rely too much on pictures, slides, and films. But without work there's no profit. Probably the pictures that stay with us are the ones we imagined in our own minds from words we've heard or read. Pictures can help to correct our false notions, but the imagination doesn't work with visual displays. When we process the phrases of a description on the palette of our mind, we create our own pictures. (I'm not talking about great works of art; works of art are in another category.) Dr. Arnold was always uneasy with new places until he had enough details to form a mental picture of it in his mind. It's the same with children, and with all people who have original minds. We like to have a map to figure out where a place is, but, after that, it's details about the place that we want.

Readings in literature, whether prose or poetry, should generally illustrate the historical period being studied. But books containing selected portions of works should be avoided. Children should read the whole work they're introduced to. And here we have a serious difficulty. Plato wanted poets in his republic to be watched over lest they write poems that would corrupt the morals of the youth. When the floodgates of knowledge were thrown open in Europe, Erasmus was worried for the same reason. Even Rossetti had the same thought. I hope that [pg 341] publishers will help us in this regard. Ever since German bookseller Friedrich Perthes discovered the mission of publishers to further education, publishers have done a lot for the world. Might they help us now? They could remove the smallest bit of offensive material, under the guidance of an exacting expert. What peace of mind it would be for teachers to be able to throw open the world of books to their students with no fear of moral smudges left on students' minds from an offensive passage! And many people who don't feel comfortable in the world of literature would be happy to keep complete libraries of these editions on their shelves to be used daily with no worries.

Even the Old Testament itself, with a little guarded editing, would be more available for children to read. And not many people would object to removing a few obscenities here and there from Shakespeare. In this regard, we have a bit too much superstitious piety. In another matter, let's listen to the advice of that great 'remedial thinker,' Dr. Arnold: 'Let your reading time be adjusted to your personal schedule and inclination. But, whether you decide to spend a lot of time or just a little, let your reading be varied in the kind of books you read—widely varied. If there's one thing I'm confident of regarding the improvement of the human mind, it's this.' This gives us support for a varied, broad-minded curriculum. In fact, we find that the student who studies lots of different subjects knows them as well as the student who studies just a few subjects.

Children should read books—not *about* books and authors. Reading books about books can be done in the child's spare time. School reading should be carefully planned so that most of it is in historical sequence. Children should read with the goal of knowing, whether the book is *Robinson Crusoe* or Huxley's *Physiography*. Their comprehension should be tested with oral (or occasional [pg 342] written) reproduction of the passage, not with comprehension questions. And they should do this after only one single reading. Everything else that the mind does to process the information, the mind does on its own, in spite of our concerns about how to teach it. And, last of all, this kind of reading should be the main business of the class room [*i.e., reading and narrating should be done during school time, not as after-school homework.*] We're standing at a crucial moment in the history of English education. John Bull [*England's version of Uncle Sam*] is contemplating. He says, 'I've labored to get higher education for women. But now, let them get back in the kitchen to learn the science (?) of domestic economy. For forty years I've tried to educate the nation's children. And look at the result—labor strikes and swelled heads! Let's give them apprentice schools instead so they'll learn the work they'll be doing for the rest of their lives!' But John Bull is wrong. Our failing has been that we've offered the pretense of education, the mere wordiness of knowledge, instead of knowledge itself. It's time for all those people who don't undervalue knowledge to roll up their sleeves and get to work. There's still time to save England and make her an even greater nation, worthy of her blessings and opportunities. But our beloved country won't stand still. If we let our people sink into the mire of a utilitarian, materialistic education, our doom will be sealed. This generation will see us take third place in the world. It's knowledge that exalts a nation, because righteousness comes from carefully planned knowledge, and prosperity is the result.

Our familiar counselor, Matthew Arnold, said, 'Think clear, feel deep, bear fruit well.' His caution fits our needs and is exactly what we need to hear.

[pg 343]

Too Wide a Mesh

The whole world, with visions in its mind of a wonderful future, is pinning its hopes on a promising kind of education. This education isn't clear yet, we can just make out a hint of it. It will change the world by giving all people more possibilities, new thoughts and goals. But, sadly, on closer inspection, this new education appears to do nothing more than to provide the same opportunity as always. Those with the talent are benefited, but everyone else is left behind.

Education, like a fishing net, is cast out over a wide area, but its mesh is so big that it can only hold the biggest fish. This has been the history of education since the world began.

The medieval Abbey schools, Renaissance schools, even the schools of China, are designed this way. Education is available for the few who want it and are intelligent enough to get in, but it doesn't affect and benefit everyone like the air around us, or the sunshine that warms everyone.

We regret that this limits the number of children from the lower classes who get into the better schools. Very few of them are able to pass the entrance exams, even though the entrance exams try to be fair for everyone. A few are able to do well and work towards careers in government and other important posts, but most of them are illiterate, for all practical purposes. The extent of their reading is the sports page, or the church bulletin.

Does this disadvantage only apply to the children of the lower classes? No, the truth is, most schools [pg 344] focus their teaching on the few students who are likely to distinguish themselves. Meanwhile, teaching goes on with the rest of the students, and they can take it or leave it, as the mood strikes them.

Recently we were all fascinated by the story of a charming pair of 'Twins.' They had the usual prep school education, then they went on to an exclusive boarding school where they were educated until age nineteen. They had 10-12 years of excellent educational opportunities. They were pleasing enough boys, so we can assume that their teachers were perfectly willing to teach them. They should have had a successful story. Although it's trendy to make fun of boarding schools, we know that they have turned out the best and most intellectual men in the nation, and still do. So what happened with these 'Twins' doesn't reflect on the boarding schools. It just shows the weakness of the Big Mesh system. Here are some excerpts from that delightful biography:

'While he was recovering in the hospital from a polo accident, R—— wrote to F——, 'I enjoyed it immensely! We're so lucky to be interested in so many things!"

Surely these boys would have been ideal students for any teacher! Again, we read,

'The boys never grew tired of the wonder at the magnificence of the world. They had a divine innocence that stayed with them through the military, traveling, sports, business, and, finally, even the darkness of WWI.'

And this 'wonder' of theirs set them apart at school. Again, what great pupils they would have been for any teacher!

But then we read, 'at X—— they didn't show much interest in books. Later, they complained to each other that they had left school totally uneducated.' [pg 345]

The kindly biographer, a friend of theirs, goes on:

'But they learned other things—the gift of leadership, for instance, and the ability of getting along with different kinds of people.'

But wasn't this more a trait they were born with rather than a skill they learned in school? Those characteristics seem to have been a family inheritance. They were born in 1880 and left school in 1899, and then one of the brothers goes on to a life of success and adventure, but,

'R—— was soon swept up by the excitement of city life. He began to regret his lack of education.' 'While F—— was in Egypt, he was greatly impressed by Lord Cramer and wrote to his brother, He is the biggest man we have! To hear him talk is something worth hearing!'

The two brothers write back and forth constantly. R—— becomes a sort of mentor to his brother. He advises him to memorize articles in The Times by heart to improve his writing style because the writers 'are very good at English.' And,

'I'll mail you a really good book next week, *Science and Education* by Professor Huxley. I've underlined the book in several places. It's the kind of book you can read over again.' R—— 'had discovered that he was badly educated and he was determined to correct that. 'I don't think it matters that I didn't learn at X——. What matters is that I learn now.'

See what a fine character he had? He didn't even blame his lack of education on his school!

If the schools pride themselves on one thing, it's that they teach their students how to learn. Did they teach R—— how to learn? We read that he set to work on an odd assortment of books. He writes to his brother,

'Anyone can improve his memory. The best way is to memorize something, it doesn't matter what. Then, when you think you know it, say it or write it. After two or three days, you'll probably forget it. Instead of looking it up, strain your mind and try to remember it. The most important thing is to keep your mind always busy. One great man, I forget who, used to play a game with himself where he'd see a number, maybe the number 69 on a door, and he would make himself try to remember all the things that had happened in years ending with 69. [pg 346] Or, if you see a horse, try to remember how many you've seen that day. Aquith always learns things by heart. He doesn't waste a second—as soon as he has nothing to do, he picks up a book. He reads until late at night. Then, during his drive to Temple the next morning, he thinks over everything he read the night before. The result is that he has a marvelous memory and seems to know everything.'

Think about the insurmountable work that poor guy set up for both himself and his brother! They were running an intellectual race through a plowed field after a heavy rain. It's a wonder they made any progress at all! Yet these two brothers had enough intellectual enthusiasm that they could have worked hard enough to have been great ambassadors. governors, senators, or whatever. But instead, they spent their days in a hopeless struggle, looking for any clue that might help them make intellectual progress. And all because, according to their own confession, they 'had learned nothing at school.' Here are more words about R——'s work to get knowledge.

'I'm reading Rosebery's Napoleon; I'll send it to you. What a wonder he was! He never spent a moment of his life without learning something. I'm including an essay from a book of Bacon's essays. Memorize it if you can. I have, and I think it's really good. I also finished Life of Macauley. I've always wondered how our great politicians and authors live. I'm also sending you a copy of Shakespeare. I learned Antony's tirade to the Romans after Caesar's death. I'm also trying to learn a little about electricity and railroad organization, so my time is filled up. I'm also sending you Pickwick Papers. I've always avoided that sort of book, but Dickens' books are much funnier than the rotten novels we usually see. I've learned one thing from all my reading and from talking with Professors. You and I are going at subjects all wrong.'

These letters are pathetic. Thank goodness they're also reassuring. They prove that the desire for knowledge can't be extinguished, no matter what schools do, or leave undone. But schools are to blame when a pursuit that should result [pg 347] in perpetual refreshing becomes as hard as laboring under a heavy burden, and there's no pleasure in the process.

Here's another area where a total lack of education results in failure. A cultivated sense of humor goes a long way in adding joy to life, but these young men had no sense of humor. Often young people who are addicted to sports can't appreciate delicate nonsensical humor and airy, playful fun. Read on:

'R—— heard Mr. Balfour and Lord Reny talking about how much they enjoyed *Alice in Wonderland*. He was very much impressed. As soon as he got back to London, he bought a copy and read it eagerly. But, to his dismay, it made no sense. Then it struck him that perhaps it was supposed to be nonsense, so he read the book again. He decided that it was pretty funny, but he was still disappointed.'

We don't need to follow the experiences of these interesting young men any further. Their fine qualities and personal fascination stayed with them all their lives. Unfortunately, so did their ignorance. They kept working tirelessly, but, as R—— had remarked, 'We're going at subjects all wrong.'

The schools need to explain why these men who had mediocre success and popularity due to their charming manners and sweet natures, were yet somewhat depressed and disappointed because of their ignorance. They made blind, futile efforts to learn, but they never got far enough to figure out that the value of knowledge is *that it's enjoyable*. No attempt at self-education can have any success until you find out how delightful knowledge is.

We should note that this great school's failure to serve its purpose of educating happened twenty years ago. Headmasters of these boarding schools have made careful and enlightened improvements since then. It's likely that [pg 348] those delightful Eton schoolboys in *Coningsby* were typical—there's a certain noble character in the way the Head Boys carry themselves and speak that indicates that their minds are intelligent. But the question is, can more be accomplished with average students?

Schools should feed their students knowledge until they've created a healthy appetite in them. Then the students will go on satisfying their hunger for knowledge every day for the rest of their lives. We need to give up the farce of teaching students how to learn. That's just as ridiculous as teaching a child how to lift a fork to his mouth and chew without giving him any real food! They already *know* how to learn. Lessons given for the sole purpose of improving the mind shouldn't be a priority in the future.

The multitude of things that all people want to know about should be made accessible at school. Students shouldn't learn with diagrams, condensed summaries, or abstract principles. Like 'Kit's little brother,' children should learn 'what oysters is' by eating oysters! The only way to knowledge is with knowledge itself. Schools must not begin by getting the mind ready to deal with knowledge. They need to begin by reading all the best books about all the sorts of things that these 'Twins,' like anybody else, wanted to know about. We have to correct two fallacies. We don't believe that children are intellectual beings, and we don't believe that knowledge is necessary and required for intellectual life. It's a pity that education is conducted in such a way that the focus is on exams that showcase only the few top students. Teachers are very conscientious, and prone to putting more attention into teaching the few who will do well on exams to enter exclusive schools. Thus, an entire school of four or five hundred students is sacrificed for a dozen of the top students.

The End

47302751R00128